Economics and Finance Readings

Evan Lau • Jaime Moll de Alba • Lee Ming Tan
Editors

Economics and Finance Readings

Selected Papers from Asia-Pacific Conference on Economics & Finance, 2024

Springer

Editors
Evan Lau
Faculty of Economics and Business
Universiti Malaysia Sarawak UNIMAS
Kota Samarahan, Malaysia

Jaime Moll de Alba
Division of Regional Bureaus
United Nations Industrial Development
Organization
Vienna, Austria

Lee Ming Tan
East Asia Research
Singapore, Singapore

ISBN 978-981-96-6997-4 ISBN 978-981-96-6998-1 (eBook)
https://doi.org/10.1007/978-981-96-6998-1

This Springer imprint is published by the registered company Springer Nature Singapore Pte Ltd.
The registered company address is: 152 Beach Road, #21-01/04 Gateway East, Singapore 189721, Singapore

Preface

The Asia Pacific Conference on Economics and Finance (APEF 2024) was successfully held on December 12–13, 2024, at the Holiday Inn Singapore Atrium. The conference brought together researchers from diverse countries, including Australia, Cambodia, Canada, China, Croatia, India, Indonesia, Italy, Japan, Kazakhstan, Korea, Kuwait, Macao, Malaysia, Morocco, Philippines, Poland, Singapore, Slovakia, South Africa, UAE, UK, and the USA, to present a total of 41 research papers covering a wide range of pressing topics in economics and finance.

The conference featured keynote presentations from Heron Lim, Assistant Director at APAC Economist, Moody's Analytics, Singapore, who provided insights into *'Détente, Deglobalisation, Disaster—A Preview of 2025 Topics'*, and Dr. Kai-Hong Tee from Loughborough University, UK, who explored *'Liquidity and Trading in the Mutual Fund Market'*.

Beyond serving as a research platform, APEF plays a vital role in sustaining the development of economics and finance research in the Asia Pacific. By fostering collaboration across institutions, disciplines, and geographical boundaries, APEF provides an avenue for knowledge exchange that supports policy innovation, financial resilience, and economic sustainability. The conference not only highlights emerging challenges and opportunities in the region but also nurtures a continuous research ecosystem that informs decision-making at both institutional and governmental levels.

This book presents a curated selection of 11 outstanding papers from APEF 2024, offering readers profound insights into the evolving economic and financial landscape of the Asia Pacific. The collective contributions within these papers serve as a valuable resource for scholars, policymakers, and industry professionals committed to shaping a more resilient and sustainable economic future.

Looking ahead, APEF 2025 will be held in person on December 11–12, 2025, at the Holiday Inn Singapore Atrium. As the conference continues to drive the sustainability of finance and economics research in the region, we warmly invite you to participate in this dynamic knowledge-sharing platform. For more details, please visit APEF.ear.com.sg. We eagerly anticipate your engagement in advancing research and policy discourse in the Asia Pacific.

Kota Samarahan, Malaysia — Evan Lau

East Asia Research (EAR)

East Asia Research (EAR), based in Singapore, fosters intellectual exchange through inclusive and representative academic conferences and books. Guided by Confucian principles, we promote respect, integrity, and community, advancing research worldwide.

APEF Advisory Board

Conference Chair

Prof. Dr. Evan Lau, Professor, UNIMAS

Committee Members

Dr, Kai-Hong Tee, Loughborough University, UK
Prof. Dr. Didi Achjari, Department of Accounting, Universitas Gadjah Mada, Indonesia, Fakultas Ekonomika Dan Bisnis
Dr. Arika Artiningsih, Faculty of Economics and Business, Universitas Gadjah Mada, Indonesia
Dr. Widya Paramita, Faculty of Economics and Business, Universitas Gadjah Mada, Indonesia
Associate Professor Dr. Chor Foon TANG, Centre for Policy Research and International Studies (CenPRIS), Universiti Sains Malaysia
Professor Dr Erginbay Uğurlu, Istanbul Aydın University FEAS, Department of Economics and Finance
Dr. Rayenda Khresna Brahmana, School of Economics, Finance and Accounting, Coventry University
Dr. Mohd Norfian Alifiah, Department of Accounting and Finance, Faculty of Management, Universiti Teknologi Malaysia
Professor Dr. Mansor H Ibrahim, Deputy President Academic INCEIF (International Centre for Education in Islamic Finance)
Professor Dr. Biagio Simonetti, University of Sannio, Benevento, Italy; WSB University in Gdansk, Poland; National Institute of Geophysics and Volcanology (INGV), Naples, Italy
Dr. Pedro A. Mart in-Cervantes, Department of Finance and Accounting, University of Valladolid

Conference Organizer

(East Asia Research)

(Universiti Malaysia Sarawak)

(Loughborough University)

Supporting Journals

Journal of Indonesian Economy and Business

Contents

Disclaimer

About the Editors

Evan Lau currently serving as Deputy Dean of Research and Commercialization at Universiti Malaysia Sarawak (UNIMAS), is a distinguished academic with a rich background in economics, finance, and business. Throughout his career at UNIMAS, he has held various pivotal roles including Deputy Dean for Research and Postgraduate, Director of the Centre for Business, Economics and Finance Forecasting (BEFfore), and Head of Strategy. Internationally recognized for his scholarly work, Evan has held visiting positions at prestigious institutions such as the University of Cambridge and several universities in Indonesia. Notably, he was twice selected for the World Class Professor (WCP) programme by the Ministry of Education and Culture in Indonesia (2020 and 2021) and appointed as a Visiting Research Fellow for the Central Bank of Malaysia in May 2021. Evan's research prowess is evidenced by his extensive publication record, which includes 108 journal articles and 91 research papers across various mediums. He has received numerous accolades for his research excellence, including the Young Researcher Award at UNIMAS, research medals from Research Expos, and the Highest-Impact Journal Paper Award. As an active researcher, Evan has secured 35 research grants and has supervised a significant number of postgraduate and undergraduate research projects. His contributions to academia extend beyond UNIMAS, with his participation as a speaker at international conferences in several countries including Indonesia, UAE, Sri Lanka, Italy, India, Philippines, China, and Malaysia. Evan's impact on the field of economics is recognized internationally, with his inclusion among the Top 9% of economists in Malaysia and ASEAN, as well as the Top 10% in Asia by the Research Papers in Economics (RePEc) network. Additionally, he is among the highly cited authors at UNIMAS. Outside of academia, Evan maintains a passion for running and travelling. His multifaceted achievements and dedication to research excellence and academic leadership underscore his significant contributions to the field, bringing sustainable impact to academia and beyond.

Jaime Moll de Alba leads the identification of programmatic priorities for UNIDO's services and the Organization's responses to the needs of Member States and development partners at the regional and country levels. He also leads the development and monitoring of regional strategies and country programmes. He manages UNIDO's 48 field offices and its 5 regional bureaus covering Africa, the Arab Region, Asia and the Pacific, Europe and Central Asia, and Latin America and the Caribbean. Prior to joining UNIDO, Dr. Moll de Alba gained international experience in economic development and innovation strategies. He worked for the European Commission in Luxembourg for a decade supporting regional economic development, enterprise competitiveness, small and medium-sized enterprise development, and innovation and technology transfer. Jaime Moll de Alba holds a PhD in Economic Development, and a Diploma of Advanced Studies and Research Sufficiency from the Universitat Politècnica de Catalunya in Spain, where he started his professional career as Visiting Lecturer. He graduated from the same university as an Industrial Engineer specialized in Industrial Organization. Dr. Moll de Alba's research on sustainable economic development has been published in various international peer-reviewed journals.

Lee Ming Tan is the founder of East Asia Research and he obtained his Master of Applied Finance from the University of Adelaide. He is deeply interested in how humans function and react with each other. An insight into how people's minds think and how they work together is invaluable in just about every field. Outside of work, Anthony Tan enjoys outdoor activities and occasional computer games.

Quantitative Analysis of Japanese Integrated Reports by Using Word Embedding

Ryohsuke Tanaka and Kazuhiko Tsuda

Abstract Currently, institutional ESG investors in Japan qualitatively evaluate the integrated reports of potential investment universe. They evaluate the completeness of descriptions regarding elements such as E (Environment), S (Social), and G (Governance). In fact, it is not easy to evaluate each integrated report, because there are differences in the descriptions among companies depending on their industries and businesses. Under such circumstances, this study proposes the method to calculate the volume of how much each description is mentioned in an integrated report. This method is applied to integrated reports issued by Japanese companies. As a result, by calculating the volume from the co-occurrence pairs using GPT-3.5, it is possible for ESG investors to quantitatively evaluate integrated reports.

Keywords Integrated report · Word embedding · Text mining

1 Introduction

Since the United Nations proposed the Principles for Responsible Investment (PRI) to institutional investors in 2006, ESG investing has expanded among institutional investors. ESG investing is an investment approach that evaluates companies based on their ESG performance. Institutional investors who have signed PRI are required to make such ESG investing.

R. Tanaka (✉)
Graduate School of Science and Technology, University of Tsukuba, Tokyo, Japan

Investment Research Department, Okasan Securities Group, Tokyo, Japan
e-mail: s2230142@u.tsukuba.ac.jp; ryou-tanaka@okasan.co.jp; https://www.tsukuba.ac.jp; https://www.okasan.co.jp/

K. Tsuda
Graduate School of Science and Technology, University of Tsukuba, Tokyo, Japan
e-mail: tsuda.kazuhiko.gn@u.tsukuba.ac.jp; https://www.tsukuba.ac.jp

E. Lau et al. (eds.), *Economics and Finance Readings*,
https://doi.org/10.1007/978-981-96-6998-1_1

In recent years, integrated reports have become increasingly important among institutional ESG investors. This is because integrated reports play a role in communicating corporate ESG information (Camilleri, 2018). Integrated report is a report that combines financial and non-financial information. Integrated reports are an important source of information for ESG investors because it contains non-financial information about a company's ESG initiatives. In fact, the amount of information available from integrated reports has in some cases led to investment in companies that are proactive in their ESG performance, while companies that are passive in their ESG performance have been excluded from the investment universe.

In Japan, ESG investing began to increase after the GPIF, the largest pension fund, signed the PRI in 2015. Since GPIF outsources its investment funds, ESG investing has spread in Japan and a growing number of pension funds and financial institutions have signed the PRI.

Currently, ESG institutional investors in Japan evaluate integrated reports qualitatively. Specifically, by reading the integrated reports, companies' initiatives on EGS are qualitatively evaluated in terms of E (Environment), S (Society), and G (Governance), respectively. However, from a practical standpoint, it is difficult for them to qualitatively evaluate the contents of each company's integrated report in a unified manner. One of the reasons for this is that there is no common format for integrated reports, which can be freely edited, and also that there are differences in the descriptions among companies depending on their industries and businesses. For these reasons, qualitatively evaluating the integrated reports can create a bias in its evaluation. In other words, even the same integrated report may be evaluated differently depending on the evaluator's practical experience. On the other hand, if the contents of the integrated report could be evaluated quantitatively, it would be possible to evaluate without bias and without depending on the evaluator's practical experience.

Text mining is a possible method for quantitatively evaluating integrated reports. This method includes word embedding that is to represent the meanings of words as vectors. For example, there are word2vec (Mikolov et al., 2014), BERT (Devlin et al., 2018), and GPT (Brown et al., 2020), for word embedding models. Since words can be represented as vectors by using these models, similarity between words can be calculated. In short, it is possible to define a set of words that are similar to defined topics. Therefore, by aggregating the words included in these set of words from integrated reports, it is possible to score how much each topic is mentioned in an integrated report.

This study proposes a method to score how much defined topics are mentioned in an integrated report, by using word embedding models. In this study, these topics are defined as E (Environment), S (Social), G (Governance), and VC (Value Creation). E, S, and G are selected as the defined topics because in practice ESG investors evaluate integrated reports based on these aspects. VC is also chosen as the defined topics. IIRC: International Integrated Reporting Council, an international organization that publishes guidelines for integrated reports, states that the purpose of an integrated report is to explain the process by which corporate value is created

(IIRC: International Integrated Reporting Council, 2013). Once these topics are scored, ESG investors can quantitatively evaluate each integrated report.

2 Analysis of Integrated Reports

2.1 Overview of Integrated Reports

IIRC provides internationally recognized frameworks for integrated report. In this framework, an integrated report is a report that aims to explain a company's long-term value creation process.[(5)] A research conducted in 2023 from KPMG Japan (KPMG Japan, 2024) shows that while it is only 22 Japanese companies that issue integrated reports in 2010, it expands to 1017 companies in 2023. Also, it indicates that the average number of pages is 101 pages, and the market capitalization of issuing companies shares 81% of the total market capitalization of the Tokyo Stock Exchange Prime Market.

2.2 Previous Studies

Dummy et al. (2016) collect the literature on integrated reports submitted to top journals in 2011–2015 and find no submissions from Asia including Japan, mostly from EU, Australia, and South Africa. There are previous studies on integrated reports focusing on several aspects such as the role and purpose of integrated reports (Beattie & Smith, 2013; Beck et al., 2017; Brown & Dillard, 2014; Lodhia, 2015; Stacchezzini et al., 2016), the relationship between integrated reports and CSR reports, sustainability reports, and other reports issued by companies (Adams et al., 2016; Mass et al., 2016; Martinez-Ferrero et al., 2015; Sierra-Gracia et al., 2015; Fasan, 2013), the determinants of companies issuing integrated reports (Frias-Aceituno et al., 2013; Jensen & Berg, 2011; Bommel, 2014), the methods to evaluate the quality of integrated reports (Pistoni et al., 2018; Marrone & Olivia, 2019; Barth et al., 2017; Pavalopoulo et al., 2019; Gerwanski et al., 2019; Fasan & Mio, 2017; Lee & Yeo, 2016; Songini et al., 2022; Andrikopoulos et al., 2014; du Toit, 2017). Pistoni et al. (2018) propose the method to score the quality of integrated reports. This score is qualitatively evaluated by experts, based on IIRC Framework. Other studies (Marrone & Olivia, 2019; Barth et al., 2017; Pavalopoulo et al., 2019; Gerwanski et al., 2019; Fasan & Mio, 2017; Lee & Yeo, 2016; Songini et al., 2022; Andrikopoulos et al., 2014; du Toit, 2017) propose different methods than Pistoni et al. (2018) to assess the quality of integrated reports. In summary, there are many studies focusing on integrated reports, but not many studies yet focusing on integrated reports issued by Japanese companies, and also not many studies yet proposing the method to score quantitatively how much defined topics are mentioned in an integrated report.

3 Scoring Method by Using Word Embeddings

3.1 Overview of the Proposed Method

This study aims to propose the method to score how much the defined topics are mentioned in an integrated report. The proposed method is calculated by defining a set of words or co-occurrence pairs associated with word embeddings. In this study, three word embedding models, including word2vec, BERT, and GPT, are used for comparison. In other words, this study compares the usefulness of six different patterns of the calculations, using words or co-occurrence pairs as well as three word embedding models.

3.2 Data

The data covered in this study are integrated reports issued by Japanese companies as follows. The first data is 46 integrated reports awarded as "Excellent Integrated Reports" by GPIF from 2018 to 2020. GPIF is a government pension fund in Japan, which stands for Government Pension Investment Fund. GPIF sponsors this award every January or February. The second data consists of 245 integrated reports issued from 2017 to 2019 by companies included in the TOPIX 100 constituents. The integrated reports are manually obtained from each company's website. The text of these reports is also extracted by optical character recognition.

The purpose of this study is to propose the method of scoring how much the defined topics are mentioned in an integrated report. In order to evaluate the proposed model, the two datasets above are defined. Therefore, if a score of the first dataset calculated by the proposed method is higher than the score of the second dataset, it shows the usefulness of the proposed method.

3.3 Overviews of Word Embedding

Word embedding is a technique in text mining to represent words as vectors. The proposed method is to score how much the defined topics are mentioned in the integrated reports, by using word embedding models. In this study these models include word2vec, BERT, and GPT-3.5. These models are chosen because these models are well-known models in the field of natural language processing. The number of dimensions gradually increases from word2vec to GPT. Even for the same word, the vectors assigned by each model are slightly different representations of the meaning.

There are three steps to get word embeddings for each word, there are three steps as follows. First, only nouns are extracted from each integrated report. Second, word embedding is assigned to each of the nous from each of the three models. For word2vec, this model (Gensim, 2024) is created beforehand using the dataset presented in Sect. 3.1. For BERT and GPT, pre-train models (Tanaka et al., 2021; OpenAI, 2024) are used, respectively.

3.4 *Procedure for Scoring with Words*

The objective of this study is to propose the method to score how much the defined topics are mentioned in an integrated report. These defined topics include E (Environment), S (Social), G (Governance), and VC (Value Creation). This method is defined as Eq. (1). The equation represents the volume of each topic k mentioned in the integrated report d, by using word embedding model m. N is the total number of words similar to topic k, using word embedding model m. D represents Euclidean distance between topic k and word i calculated by word embedding obtained from word embedding model m. R refers to ratio of the frequency of word i over the frequency of all occurrences of the word in the integrated report d.

$$\text{Volume}_{k,d,m} = \sum_{i=1}^{N} D_{k,m,i}^{-1} * R_{d,i} \tag{1}$$

To collect groups of words similar to each topic k, it is done by assigning word embedding to each word in topic k and each word in the dataset presented in Sect. 3.1, and then calculating the cosine similarity of the two vectors. For example, to find a group of words related to the topic of E (Environment), the cosine similarity cos is obtained from word embedding of the words i and "*Environment*" assigned by the vector representation model m, respectively, as in Eq. (2). In Eq. (2), x and y refer to word embedding given by word embedding model m, respectively. Finally, only words with a cosine similarity greater than 0.3 are defined as a group of words in terms of E obtained by word embedding model m.

$$\cos = \frac{\sum_{k=1}^{n} x_k y_k}{\sqrt{\sum_{k=1}^{n} x_k^2}\sqrt{\sum_{k=1}^{n} y_k^2}} \tag{2}$$

Euclidean distance D in Eq. (1) is obtained as in Eq. (3). In Eq. (3), x and y represent word embedding given by word embedding model m, respectively.

$$D = \sqrt{\sum_{k=1}^{n} \left(x_i - y_i\right)^2} \tag{3}$$

In short, in Eq. (1), the larger Euclidean distance D^{-1} is, the closer the word is to the topic k in meaning. In addition, R represents ratio of word occurrences. In other words, the method proposed in this study means that the volume of the integrated report containing relatively more words that are close in meaning to topic k have a higher value.

3.5 Procedure for Scoring with Co-Occurrence Pairs

Co-occurrence pairs are two words that occur on the same sentence. Since co-occurrence pairs consist of two words, they are more informative than words. Therefore, in this study, for each defined topic two volumes are calculated: one from the words, the other from the co-occurrence pairs.

In a case of calculating the volume from the co-occurrence pairs, word embedding for a co-occurrence pair is represented by the average of word embedding for each of the two words included. Then, the volume for each topic is calculated through Eq. (1), (2), and (3), by the average of word embedding.

4 Evaluation

4.1 Word Groups by Word Embedding Models

Tables 1, 2, 3, and 4 show the word groups of the topic for E (Environmental), S (Social), G (Governance), and VC (Value Creation) respectively, by word embedding models. Each table lists the top 10 words with the largest reciprocal Euclidean distance D^{-1}. In other words, these 10 words are the most similar words to each topic, based on the three word embedding models. In fact, these words are literal translation into English.

Table 1 Words in E (Environment)

Word2vec
Global environment, biodiversity, environmental protection, working environment, ecosystem, environmental impact reduction, sustainability, natural environment, water resources, global warming
BERT
Forecast, eco, therapy, treatment, future, validation, holdings, analysis, strength, domestic
GPT
Social environment, global environment, natural environment, business environment, environmental issues, external environment, environmental protection, environmental consideration, environmental improvement, environmental activities

Table 2 Words in S (Social)

Word2vec
Society, society building, social, society as A whole, community, social problem solving, problem solving, international society, living, age
BERT
Rational, life, public interest, City, home, correction, works, film, daily life, series
GPT
Social, international society, society as A whole, companies, local communities, social environment, social Mission, social development, social value, social structure

Table 3 Words in G (Governance)

Word2vec
Corporate governance, governance structure, management structure, strengthen governance, management foundation, group management, group governance, corporate management, corporate governance, improve effectiveness
BERT
Group governance, corporate governance, governance structure, governance enhancement, full revaluation, off-balance sheet, commitment, work-life balance, originator, due diligence
GPT
Governance structure, governance enhancement, group governance, corporate governance, finance, guidance, consumer finance, BANDAI NAMCO group, financial services, coverage

As Tables 1 and 2 show that, in the topic of E and S, comparing these extracted words by the models, words from word2vec and GPT are quite similar to each other. Also, only the words from BERT tend to be different from those from the other two models.

On the other hand, as Table 3 shows that, in the topic of G, the words extracted from the three models are relatively similar to each other, compared to the topic of E and S. For Table 4, in the topic of VC, the words extracted from the three models are not similar to each other.

4.2 Co-Occurrence Pair Groups by Word Embedding Models

Tables 5, 6, 7, and 8 show the co-occurrence pair groups of the topic for E (Environmental), S (Social), G (Governance), and VC (Value Creation), respectively, by word embedding models. As Sect. 4.1, each table lists the 10 co-occurrence pairs which are the most similar words to each topic, based on the three word embedding models. As a result, there is relatively no significant difference in the co-occurrence pair groups obtained compared to the results for the word groups shown in Sect. 4.1.

Table 4 Words in VC (Value Creation)

Word2vec
Value creation, sustainable growth, story, business growth, Mission, embodiment, raison D'etre, value delivery, important, conviction
BERT
Value creation, business growth, value enhancement, action plan, asset building, revenue growth, value, social value, added value, growth strategy
GPT
Value creation, value co-creation, value, value delivery, corporate value, economic value, value enhancement, creation, present value, values

Table 5 Co-occurrence pairs in E (Environment)

Word2vec
(Environment, environment) (global environment, environment) (environment, biodiversity) (environment, environmental safety) (work environment, environment) (environment, ecosystems) (environment, Environment & Society) (environment, environmental impact reduction) (sustainability, environment) (environment, natural environment)
BERT
(Environment, environment) (forecast, environment) (plan, environment) (eco, environment) (future, environment) (verification, environment) (holdings, environment) (environment, analysis) (strength, environment) (domestic, environment)
GPT
(Environment, environment) (environment, social environment) (global environment, environment) (environment, natural environment) (business environment, environment) (environment, environmental issues) (external environment, environment) (environment, environmental protection) (environment, environmental considerations) (environment, environmental improvement)

4.3 Comparison of the Volumes from Words and Co-Occurrence Pairs

In this section, the proposed method is applied to the dataset to calculate the volume of each topic. This calculation is conducted in the following steps.

First, each integrated report in the dataset is classified into two groups. That is, the first group consists of the awarded integrated reports by GPIF's "Excellent Integrated Reports." The second group includes integrated reports that are not awarded. Second, the proposed method is applied to each integrated report of the two groups. Thus, a total of the 12 volumes are calculated for a single integrated report, since there are three word embedding models and four defined topics. Third, for each volume, the mean of the two groups is calculated, in order to compare the averaged volumes between the two groups. Then, the mean difference is obtained by deducting the mean of the non-awarded group from the awarded group. Therefore, if the mean difference is positive, the volume of the awarded group is higher than the other group.

Table 6 Co-occurrence pairs in S (Social)

Word2vec
(Society, society) (the world, society) (society, social development) (society, social) (society, society as a whole) (community, society) (society, social problem solving) (society, problem solving) (international society, society) (living, society)
BERT
(Society, society) (rationality, society) (life, society) (public interest, society) (society, cities) (family, society) (correction, society) (film, society) (everyday, society) (series, society)
GPT
(Society, social) (society, social) (international society, social) (society, society as a whole) (each company, social) (local society, social) (society, social environment) (society, social Mission) (society, building society) (society, social value)

Table 7 Co-occurrence pairs in G (Governance)

Word2vec
(Governance, governance) (governance, corporate governance) (governance, governance structure) (Governance, management structure) (governance, strengthening governance) (governance, management structure) (governance, group management) (governance, group governance) (governance, corporate management) (governance, corporate governance)
BERT
(Governance, governance) (governance, governance structure) (governance, governance enhancement) (governance, group governance) (governance, corporate governance) (governance structure, group governance) (governance structure, governance enhancement) (guidance, governance) (governance, financial services) (strengthening governance, corporate governance)
GPT
(Governance, governance) (governance, group governance) (governance, corporate governance) (governance, governance structure) (engagement, governance) (governance, cyber security) (CSR Committee, governance) (governance, matching) (governance, insider) (governance, alliances)

Figure 1 indicates the bar chart for the mean difference of each topic from each model. In this chart, the mean difference is calculated by using words. Figure 2 is the same chart as Fig. 1, but the mean difference is calculated by co-occurrence pairs.

Figure 1 shows that the mean differences for word2vec are all positive. In other words, it can be interpreted that the selected integrated reports have higher volume than the non-selected integrated reports. That is, the selected integrated reports have more descriptions on each topic. On the other hand, the mean differences for BERT and GPT are all negative. Therefore, when using words to calculate the volume, inconsistent results are obtained among the models. In Fig. 2, the mean differences for all three models are all in positive. That is, the selected integrated reports have more descriptions on each topic, when using co-occurrence to calculate the volume.

In addition, comparing the mean differences in each topic by the three models, the use of GPT results in the highest mean difference for all topics. In short, the use of GPT shows the largest difference in the volume between the selected and non-selected integrated reports compared to other models.

Table 8 Co-occurrence pairs in VC (Value Creation)

Word2vec
(Value creation, value creation) (value creation, value creation) (stories, value creation) (value creation, sustainable growth) (value creation, embodiment) (Mission, value creation) (business growth, value creation) (value creation, root) (value creation, driving force) (value creation, cornerstone)
BERT
(Value creation, value creation) (value creation, value creation) (business growth, value creation) (value creation, action plan) (value creation, asset formation) (value creation, value) (value creation, social value) (value added, value creation) (value creation, growth strategy) (value creation, value provision)
GPT
(Value creation, value creation) (value creation, value creation) (value creation, value co-creation) (value creation, value creation) (value creation, value provision) (value creation, corporate value) (value creation, economic value) (value creation, creation) (value creation, values) (value creation, creativity)

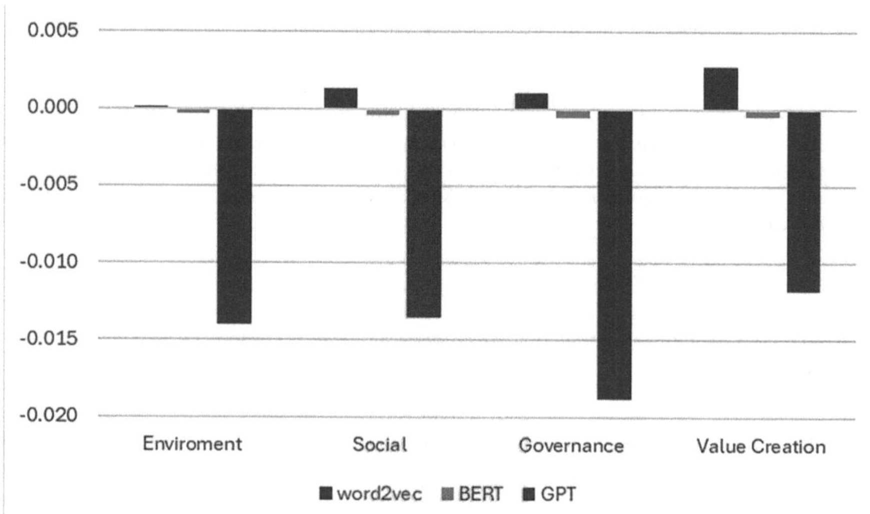

Fig. 1 The bar chart shows the mean difference of each topic by the models. This difference is calculated by using words

5 Conclusion

In this study, Chap. 4 proposes the method to calculate the volume of how much each defined topic is mentioned in an integrated report. In Chap. 5, this method is applied to both the awarded and non-awarded integrated repots to get the volume. As shown in Fig. 1, when using the words to calculate the volume, inconsistent results are obtained among the models. On the other hand, Fig. 2 indicates that, when using the co-occurrence pairs to calculate the volume, all the volumes of the

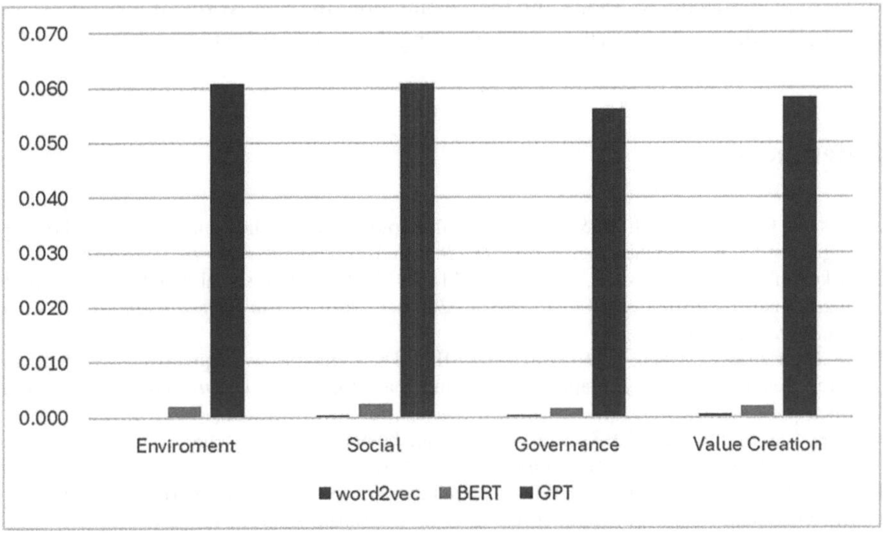

Fig. 2 The bar chart shows the mean difference of each topic by the models. This difference is calculated by using co-occurrence pairs

awarded integrated reports are higher than the non-awarded integrated reports, that is, a consistent result. In addition, using the co-occurrence pairs from GPT results in the highest mean difference for all topics.

A series of results suggest the usefulness of calculating the volume using co-occurrence pairs from GPT. Co-occurrence pairs show better results than words because occurrence pairs include more information. That is, co-occurrence pairs consist of two words. GPT shows better results than the other two models. That is because, since word embedding from GPT has the largest dimension of vector among the three models, this vector could be a better representation of the meaning of the word, compared with the other two models.

There are many studies focusing on integrated reports, but not many studies yet focusing on integrated reports issued by Japanese companies, and also not many studies yet proposing the method to score quantitatively how much defined topics are mentioned in an integrated report. Also, currently, ESG investors in Japan qualitatively evaluate the integrated reports of potential investment candidates. In such circumstances, this study proposes the quantitative method of scoring how much the defined topics are mentioned in an integrated report. As a result, the co-occurrence pair and GPT can be used in the proposed method to evaluate integrated reporting. The proposed method could be useful for ESG investors who currently evaluate integrated reports qualitatively in Japan.

In addition, one of the purposes of preparing an integrated report is to be evaluated as an investment target by ESG investors. While it is not easy to prepare an integrated report that is evaluated by ESG investors, the model proposed in this study may contribute to improving their evaluation. In other words, it is conceivable that this model could contribute to improving the company's stock price.

References

Adams, C., Potter, B., Singh, P., & York, J. (2016). Exploring the implications of integrated reporting for social investment (disclosures). *The British Accounting Review, 48*(3), 283–296.

Andrikopoulos, A., Samitas, A., & Bekiaris, M. (2014). Corporate social responsibility reporting in financial institutions: Evidence from Euronext. *Research in International Business and Finance, 32*, 27–35.

Barth, M., Cahan, S., Chen, L., & Venter, E. (2017). The economic consequences associated with integrated report quality: Capital market and real effects. *Accounting, Organizations and Society, 62*, 43–64.

Beattie, V., & Smith, J. D. (2013). Value creation and business models: Refocusing the intellectual capital debate. *The British Accounting Review, 45*(4), 243–254.

Beck, C., Dummay, J., & Frost, G. (2017). In pursuit of a 'Single Source of Truth': From threatened legitimacy to integrated reporting. *Journal of Business Ethics, 141*(1), 191–205.

Bommel, K. (2014). Towards a legitimate compromise? An exploration of integrated reporting in The Netherlands. *Accounting, Auditing & Accountability Journal, 27*(7), 1157–1189.

Brown, J., & Dillard, J. (2014). Integrated reporting: On the need for broadening out and opening up. *Accounting, Auditing & Accountability Journal, 27*(7), 1120–1156.

Brown, T. B., Mann, B., Ryder, N., Subbiah, M., Kaplan, J. (2020) Language models are few-shot leaners. In Advances in neural information processing systems (NeurIPS).

Camilleri, M. K. (2018). Theoretical insights on integrated reporting: The inclusion of non-financial capitals in corporate disclosures. *Corporate Communications: An International Journal, 23*(4), 567–581.

Devlin, J., Chang, M. W., Lee, K., & Toutanova, K. (2018). BERT: Pre-training of deep bidirectional transformers for language understanding. *arXiv preprint arXiv:1810.04805.*

du Toit, E. (2017). The readability of integrated reports. *Meditari Accountancy Research, 25*(4), 629–653.

Dumay, J., Bernardi, C., Guthrie, J., & Demartini, P. (2016). Integrated reporting: A structured literature review. *Accounting Review, 40*(3), 166–185.

Fasan, M. (2013). Annual reports, sustainability reports and integrated reports: Trends in corporate disclosure. *Integrated Reporting, 127*(3), 41–57.

Fasan, M., & Mio, C. (2017). Fostering stakeholder engagement: The role of materiality disclosure in integrated reporting. *Business Strategy and the Environment, 26*(3), 288–305.

Frias-Aceituno, J. V., Rodriguez-Ariza, L., & Gracia-Sanchez, I. M. (2013). Is integrated reporting determined by a country's legal system? An exploratory study. *Journal of Cleaner Production, 44*, 45–55.

Gensim. https://radimrehurek.com/gensim/. Accessed September 12, 2024.

Gerwanski, J., Kordsachia, O., & Velte, P. (2019). Determinants of materiality disclosure quality in integrated reporting: Empirical evidence from an international setting. *Business Strategy and the Environment, 28*(5), 750–770.

IIRC: International Integrated Reporting Council. (2013). International Integrated Reporting Framework.

Jensen, J. C., & Berg, N. (2011). Determinants of traditional sustainability reporting versus integrated reporting. An institutionalist approach. *Business Strategy and the Environment, 21*(5), 299–316.

KPMG Japan. (2024). Survey of corporate reports in Japan 2023.

Lee, K. W., & Yeo, G. (2016). The association between integrated reporting and firm valuation. *Review of Quantitative Finance and Accounting, 47*, 1221–1250.

Lodhia, S. (2015). Exploring the transition to integrated reporting through a practice lens: An Australian customer owned bank perspective. *Journal of Business Ethics, 129*(3), 585–598.

Marrone, A., & Olivia, L. (2019). Measuring the level of integrated reporting alignment with the framework. *International Journal of Business and Management, 14*(12), 110–120.

Martinez-Ferrero, J., Gracia-Sanchez, I. M., & Cuadrado-Ballesteros, B. (2015). Effect of financial reporting quality on sustainability information disclosure. *Corporate Social Responsibility and Environmental Management, 22*(1), 45–64.

Mass, K., Schaltegger, S., & Crutzene, N. (2016). Advancing the integration of corporate sustainability measurement, management and reporting. *Journal of Cleaner Production, 133*(1), 859–862.

Mikolov, T., Sutskever, I., Chen, K., Corrado, G., & Dean, J. (2014). Distributed representations of words and phrases and their compositionality. *In NIPS*.

OpenAI. https://openai.com/. Accessed September 12, 2024.

Pavalopoulo, A., Magnis, C., & Iatridis, G. E. (2019). Integrated reporting: An accounting disclosure tool for high quality financial reporting. *Research in International Business and Finance, 49*, 13–40.

Pistoni, A., Songini, L., & Bavagnoli, F. (2018). Integrated reporting quality: An empirical analysis. *Corporate Social Responsibility and Environmental Management, 25*(4), 489–507.

Sierra-Gracia, L., Zorio-Grima, A., & Gracia-Benau, M. A. (2015). Stakeholder engagement, corporate social responsibility and integrated reporting: An exploratory study. *Corporate Social Responsibility and Environmental Management, 22*(5), 286–304.

Songini, L., Pistoni, A., Tettamanzi, P., Fratini, F., & Minutiello, V. (2022). Integrated reporting quality and BoD characteristics: An empirical analysis. *Journal of Management and Governance, 26*, 579–620.

Stacchezzini, R., Melloni, G., & Lai, A. (2016). Sustainability management and reporting: The role of integrated reporting for communicating corporate sustainability management. *Journal of Cleaner Production, 136*(A), 102–110.

Tanaka, Y., Murakawa, Y., Kawahara, D., & Kurohashi, S. (2021). Building a Japanese typo dataset and typo correction system based on Wikipedia's revision history. *Journal of Natural Language Processing, 28*(4), 995–1033.

Empirical Evidence of Behavioral Biases in Investment: Should We Be Looking for Financial Variables to Moderate Them?

Parinaaz Mehta and Nishta Nahata

Abstract Behavioral finance integrates cognitive psychology into financial decision-making, challenging the rational assumptions of traditional finance. This study investigates the presence and intensity of cognitive and emotional biases among Indian investors, focusing on variations across age, gender, and education levels. Using a descriptive research design, data was collected through a structured questionnaire targeting 151 respondents from urban areas in India who actively engage in investment activities. The survey included hypothetical scenarios to identify eight key biases, such as loss aversion, overconfidence, and conservatism. Descriptive, graphical, and cross-sectional analyses were employed to evaluate the findings. Results reveal that cognitive biases are more prevalent than emotional biases, significantly influencing investment decisions. This research provides insights for financial intermediaries to address these biases effectively, emphasizing the importance of moderating variables to enhance rational decision-making and mitigate the impact of behavioral biases.

Keywords Behavioral finance · Heuristics · Bias · Decision-making · Moderating variables

1 Introduction

Behavioral Finance is an innovative and promising field in financial markets that has the potential to provide a more accurate representation of investor behavior in Financial Markets. The field makes an attempt to address anomalies in investment

P. Mehta (✉)
Kirit P Mehta School of Law, Narsee Monjee Institute of Management Studies, Mumbai, Maharashtra, India
e-mail: parinaaz.mehta@gmail.com; https://www.nmims.edu

N. Nahata
Deutsche Bank, Mumbai, Maharashtra, India
e-mail: nishtanahata6601@gmail.com; https://www.db.com

E. Lau et al. (eds.), *Economics and Finance Readings*,
https://doi.org/10.1007/978-981-96-6998-1_2

behavior thereby driving the investment sentiments. The assumption of rationality is a basic premise of the standard financial models. These assumptions of rationality are being challenged by investment anomalies. These anomalies drive the market prices thereby affecting individual to consistently earn abnormal returns. Behavioral finance has challenged the theory of market efficiency by showing that markets might be inefficient due to human irrationality (M. Sewell, 2007). Behavioral finance recognizes the integral role of human emotions in financial decision-making. As an emerging discipline within modern finance, it asserts that emotions, alongside motivation and cognitive processes, are fundamental to all decision-making frameworks. Mitroi and Oproiu (2014) emphasize that emotions are not merely incidental but essential components influencing financial choices, challenging the purely rational assumptions of traditional finance theories.

Traditional finance theories, such as Modern Portfolio Theory (MPT), the Efficient Market Hypothesis (EMH), and the Capital Asset Pricing Model (CAPM), are predicated on the assumption that investors act rationally and that financial markets are inherently efficient. However, the validity of market efficiency remains a subject of current debate. If financial markets were truly efficient, arbitrage opportunities would be systematically eliminated. However, empirical evidence suggests otherwise, as various market anomalies such as speculative bubbles, crashes, and volatility clusters persist, challenging the assumptions of these traditional models.

The inability of classical finance theories to account for these anomalies underscores a fundamental gap in their explanatory power. The recurrence of bubbles and market crashes suggests that factors beyond rational decision-making influence financial markets. Behavioral finance, which integrates insights from psychology (W. Forbes, 2009) and cognitive biases, provides a more comprehensive framework for understanding such deviations. Consequently, a growing body of literature argues that financial market inefficiencies arise due to investor sentiment, heuristics, and bounded rationality (Kumar & Goyal 2015) necessitating a paradigm shift beyond the conventional rational actor model (Trversky & Kahneman, 1992). Behavioral biases in investment decisions can be categorized into cognitive biases and emotional biases. Cognitive biases arise due to systematic errors in reasoning and processing information, while emotional biases stem from feelings and emotions that impact decision-making. These biases influence investors' ability to assess risk and return, leading to suboptimal investment choices.

The aim of this research paper is to explore the role of cognitive biases and emotional biases in financial decision-making among Indian retail investors. A survey-based methodology along with descriptive analysis was employed to investigate unobservable psychological factors influencing financial behavior, to quantify the prevalence of identified biases.

The paper is divided into five sections, Section One is the introduction, followed by Section Two Review of literature, Section Three introduces the data and research methodology, Section Four discusses analysis and findings, Section Five discusses the limitation, and Section Six concludes the paper.

2 Literature Review

Fama (1970) posited that capital markets efficiently allocate resources when prices fully reflect all available information. In an efficient market, investors cannot consistently outperform or exploit mispriced stocks, as assets always trade at their fair value. Consequently, achieving high returns would primarily depend on taking higher risks. Kahneman and Tversky (1979) introduced Prospect Theory, which explains how investors make decisions under uncertainty. The Prospect Theory incorporates a probability weighting function, which suggests that investors overweigh low probabilities and underweigh high probabilities, affecting their investment behavior. This theory provides crucial insights into behavioral biases such as loss aversion, framing effects, and probability distortions, which significantly impact financial decision-making. Shefrin and Statman (1985) expanded on this by introducing the disposition effect, showing that investors tend to sell winning stocks too early and hold onto losing stocks for too long, hoping for a reversal. Thaler (1980, 1985, 1999) introduced mental accounting, explaining how investors categorize their wealth into separate accounts based on subjective criteria rather than an objective financial assessment. This bias leads to irrational decision-making, such as investing differently based on whether money was received as a windfall or earned through labor.

During the 1990s, researchers began systematically identifying cognitive biases that impact investment decisions. Tversky and Kahneman (1974, 1992) expanded their earlier work, emphasizing how heuristics—mental shortcuts—lead to anchoring bias and representativeness bias in financial decision-making. Nickerson (1998) investigated confirmation bias, showing that investors tend to seek information that supports their prior beliefs while ignoring contradictory evidence, leading to suboptimal investment choices. Barber and Odean (1999, 2000) explored overconfidence bias, demonstrating that overconfident investors trade excessively, leading to higher transaction costs and lower returns. Their research provided empirical evidence that male investors, in particular, exhibited greater overconfidence, trading 45% more frequently than female investors, reducing net returns. Barber and Odean (2001) found that overconfident investors trade more frequently than their less confident counterparts, leading to higher transaction costs and lower net returns. Their study reinforced the view that male investors tend to be more overconfident than female investors. Gervais and Odean (2001) demonstrated that overconfidence increases with past investment success, leading investors to attribute luck-based returns to their skill. Barberis and Huang (2001) argued that mental accounting leads to suboptimal portfolio diversification, as investors categorize investments into separate accounts rather than viewing them as a holistic portfolio. Benartzi and Thaler (2001) studied myopic loss aversion, showing that investors checking their portfolios frequently tend to take fewer risks, negatively affecting long-term gains. Baumeister (2002) studied self-control bias, showing that investors often make impulsive financial decisions that do not align with long-term goals. Grinblatt and Keloharju (2001) examined sentiment-driven trading, revealing that investors tend to trade reactively based on market sentiment rather than strategic financial analysis. Nofsinger (2002) explored investor psychology, highlighting heuristic simplification, where the brain uses shortcuts to process complex financial data. This leads to biases such as overconfidence (Barber & Odean, 2000; Daniel et al., 1998; Abhijeet & Ravinder, 2012) in decision-making and the tendency to overvalue personal choices while neglecting opposing arguments. Biais et al. (2005) analyzed how investors systematically overestimate their predictive abilities post hoc, reinforcing their false confidence in future decision-making. Kaustia et al. (2008) found that investors anchor on past stock prices when making investment decisions, often failing to adjust their expectations when new information is available. Statman et al. (2008) examined how framing effects influence investment preferences, revealing that investors tend to choose investments differently when returns are framed in absolute terms vs. percentage terms.

The Rise of Emotional Biases and Market Anomalies (2000–2010) began with the dot-com bubble and financial crises occurring in this period, research began focusing on emotional biases and their impact on investor behavior. Kahneman et al. (1991) demonstrated the endowment effect, where investors overvalue assets they own, leading to reluctance to sell even when better investment opportunities exist. Bikhchandani et al. (1992) provided evidence of herding bias, explaining how investors follow market trends rather than conducting independent analyses. This phenomenon played a role in speculative bubbles and crashes, including the 2000 dot-com bubble. Prospect theory and heuristics can explain psychological factors affecting investment decision-making, which can help avoid future speculative bubbles and enhance global financial markets efficiency (Johnsson et al., 2002). Choi et al. (2004) found that employees participating in retirement savings plans exhibited status quo bias, avoiding changing default investment allocations even when better options were available. Coval and Shumway (2005) demonstrated that day traders who incurred morning losses were more likely to engage in high-risk trading in the afternoon, suggesting an emotional response to losses rather than a rational recalibration of strategy. Shiller (2005) examined irrational exuberance and found that emotional factors, such as optimism and social contagion, drive stock market bubbles. Malmendier and Tate (2008) found that overconfident CEOs were more likely to undertake excessive mergers and acquisitions, leading to financial distress and value destruction. Akerlof and Shiller (2009) linked investor herding behavior to market cycles, arguing that confidence fluctuations drive boom-and-bust cycles. Weber et al. (2010) found that investors overvalue assets they own due to the endowment effect, making them reluctant to sell underperforming stocks.

Latif, Arshad et al. (2011) also examine behavioral perspectives, distinguishing investors as Loyalists/Rationalists or Heretics/Behaviorists based on their beliefs in market efficiency and sentiment-driven biases. Nair and Antony (2013) introduced behavioral finance as a new approach to capital markets, highlighting the 2007–2008 financial crisis because of psychological distortions in judgment, such as excessive optimism and confirmation bias. This led to irrational behavior, deviations from the Efficient Market Hypothesis, and investors' conformity to status quo behavior. Charles and Kasilingam (2015) examined the impact of emotional swing variables on investment decisions in India. They identified five emotional states: Indecisive, Confused, Paranoid, Enthusiastic, and Dogmatic. Emotionally stable investors exhibit high dogmatism and moderate paranoia, making them long-term, deliberate decision-makers. Moderately affected investors exhibit a mix of rational and irrational behavior, while short-term investors approach markets with emotional instability. The study concluded that correct emotional identification and use can lead to success or failure in the stock market.

Kumar and Goyal (2015) conducted a systematic literature review of behavioral biases in investment decision-making, analyzing 117 peer-reviewed studies published between 1980 and 2013. Their study categorizes key biases; confirmation bias; Overconfidence Bias (Barber & Odean, 2000; Daniel et al., 1998); Disposition Effect (Shefrin & Statman, 1985; Odean, 1998); Herding Bias (Grinblatt et al., 1995; Lakonishok et al., 1992); Home Bias (French & Poterba, 1991; Coval & Moskowitz, 1999) affecting investor behavior and highlights critical gaps in existing research. De (2016) investigated role of loss aversion, endowment bias, and confirmation bias and their impact on investment decisions using used primary data from Tamil Nadu. Raheja and Dhiman's (2017) research explores personality traits, behavioral biases, and investment decisions of 500 Punjab-based investors. The study observed the presence of overconfidence, herding, and regret. Khan, Azeem et al. (2017) studied the impact of overconfidence and loss aversion bias on equity investors' decision-making processes. They used a survey and Prospect Theory to analyze data from 160 investors from the Islamabad and Lahore stock exchanges. The study found a 70% significant impact of both biases on investors' decisions, with overconfidence leading to increased investment and loss aversion reducing investment.

Joo and Durri (2018) investigated factors influencing investors' rational conduct in stock market judgments. They used a questionnaire and deductive research to identify psychological qualities affecting decision-making. Five psychological qualities, including faith, significantly impacted investor rationality. These qualities, along with faith, heuristics, confirmation, pessimism, overconfidence, optimism, and herd behavior, accounted for 35% of variation in investor rational behavior. The study suggests a unified theory of behavioral finance and standard finance to improve efficiency. Madaan and Singh (2019) investigated overconfidence, herding, anchoring, and the disposition effect to assess their impact on investment decision-making. Their study, based on 243 investors from the National Stock Exchange (NSE), utilized survey questionnaires and statistical analysis through SPSS. The findings confirm that psychological biases and cognitive limitations hinder rational decision-making, supporting behavioral finance's assertion that investor decisions are influenced by psychology and sociology rather than pure rationality, as suggested by the Efficient Market Hypothesis. Jyoti (2019) makes use of social and psychological theories in order to interpret a trader's behaviors using secondary data that was gathered from a variety of websites, scholarly publications, and topic-based books. This paper explains the following biases: Anchoring, Mental Accounting, Loss Aversion, Endowment Effect, and Hindsight Bias. In addition, an emphasis on comprehending the prejudices of Indian investors is placed, taking into account their traits, degree of awareness, investment preferences, and patterns. It also examines how Indian investors, both urban and rural, differ in their investment styles. Novianggie and Asandimitra (2019) found that herding bias, risk perception, and overconfidence significantly impact investment decisions among college students, with financial literacy playing a lesser role. Ahmad (2020) explored the link between personality traits and biases like overconfidence, herding, and disposition effect. Results showed that extraverted investors exhibited all three biases, conscientious investors displayed overconfidence and disposition effect, while neurotic investors were more prone to herding. Sattaf et al. (2020) analyzed behavioral biases during uncertain times, revealing that heuristic biases have a stronger influence than personality traits and prospect theory factors in investment decision-making. Mohapatra and Samal (2021) identified overconfidence, herding, cognitive dissonance, regret aversion, and loss aversion as dominant biases among Indian risk-seeking investors, with overconfidence being the most prevalent. Athota and Pereira (2023) investigated AI's impact on financial planners' cognitive biases, emphasizing that AI, combined with human intelligence, can help mitigate biases in financial decision-making (Athota et al., 2023).

A review of the existing literature on behavioral finance and investment decisions reveals that psychological biases significantly obstruct rational decision-making. While numerous studies have identified key biases affecting investors, several research gaps remain. First, there is insufficient research on the extent to which broad theoretical biases impact individuals across different demographics, particularly in a diverse and economically stratified country like India. Second, although some studies have attempted to identify financial variables that moderate irrational decision-making, their findings remain inconclusive. Moreover, limited research has examined whether such variables should be explored at all, considering that emotional biases may be inherently resistant to moderation. Addressing these gaps presents an opportunity for further investigation into investor behavior and decision-making frameworks. Expanding research in this area could lead to new methodologies that enhance financial decision-making by minimizing cognitive distortions. Behavioral finance remains an evolving discipline, and with continued empirical exploration, it has the potential to equip investors with strategies to mitigate biases and make more informed investment decisions.

3 Data and Research Methodology

The study was based on an initial survey, which served as the foundation for the research. The questionnaire included eight behavioral biases under investigation. The selection of the eight behavioral biases was guided by an extensive review of existing literature on investor decision-making. These biases—overconfidence, herding, anchoring, disposition effect, loss aversion, mental accounting, regret aversion, and familiarity bias—were chosen due to their prominence in previous empirical studies (Kahneman & Tversky, 1979; Barber & Odean, 2001). Each bias has been linked to systematic deviations from rational investment behavior, making them relevant for this study.

The questionnaire was developed based on a synthesis of established scales and prior empirical studies. While certain items were directly drawn from existing research (e.g., Barberis & Thaler, 2003; Ricciardi & Simon, 2000), others were refined to align with the specific cultural and economic context of Indian investors. The adaptation process included expert validation and a pilot study with a small sample of respondents to assess clarity and reliability. This process represents a methodological contribution, ensuring that the questionnaire captures investor biases effectively within an emerging market setting. The questionnaire was designed to measure these biases using validated constructs from prior research (Shefrin & Statman, 1985; Odean, 1998), ensuring alignment with established behavioral finance models. The items included in the questionnaire were adapted from widely accepted behavioral finance scales while incorporating modifications to suit the context of Indian investors.

Responses were collected from residents of major cities across India, with a total of 151 participants completing the survey. The data was analyzed using graphical methods to identify patterns and insights into investor behavior. Only participants who engage in investment activities are of interest to the study. Convenience and snowball sampling are used to include respondents from India's urban areas in the survey. Those who actively participate in financial decision-making and possess a suitable comprehension of stock market investments comprised 151 replies that were taken into consideration. The survey sample included a mix of students and retail investors. While students are a common sample in behavioral finance research due to their accessibility, they were not the sole focus. The inclusion of retail investors allowed for comparison and increased the external validity of findings. Furthermore, previous research (Tversky & Kahneman, 1981) has shown that cognitive biases affect individuals across all demographics, making students a relevant sample group for foundational insights. The respondents were selected from major metropolitan cities across India, ensuring diversity in age, gender, education level, and investment experience. While not exhaustive, this approach allows insights into key investor groups that actively participate in financial markets.

A key challenge in behavioral finance surveys is the introduction of hypothetical bias, where respondents might provide socially desirable or unrealistic responses. To mitigate this risk, the questionnaire was designed to include real-world financial decision scenarios rather than abstract, self-reported assessments of behavior. Additionally, behavioral priming techniques were incorporated to encourage respondents to recall past investment decisions rather than speculate about hypothetical situations.

Microsoft Excel's built-in features were used to assess the gathered data and created hypotheses. To further check for biases, a Google form was utilized to create the standard questionnaire, which included multiple-choice questions. The data was assessed using cross-sectional analysis, descriptive statistics, and graphical representation to show the bias's presence.

4 Analysis and Findings

This section's aims to examine 8 Behavioral Biases and how the occurrence of each differs among the selected demographics. The sample size of 151 respondents may appear limited given India's vast and diverse population; however, in behavioral finance research, such sample sizes are commonly used in exploratory studies to identify trends and establish preliminary findings (Barberis & Thaler, 2003). The purpose of this study is not to generalize findings to the entire Indian population but to highlight behavioral tendencies among investors, which can serve as a foundation for future large-scale studies. The survey was not designed to be representative of the general Indian population but rather of individuals engaged in investment activities. Since only a fraction of the population actively participates in financial markets, the sample captures relevant investor behaviors rather than attempting full demographic coverage.

4.1 Primary Survey, Results, and Interpretation

The distributed survey was split into two sections: the first part asked hypothetical questions to investigate financial decision-making and the effects of biases on these decisions, while the second part mostly recorded the investors' demographic data for classification purposes. To ascertain if investors' decision-making is biased, the relationship between demographic characteristics and investor behavior with regard to different market-based information is examined using cross-sectional tabulation and graphical analysis.

4.1.1 Demographic Factors: Age Distribution

According to the results, people from all over India who are interested in financial ventures and have a rudimentary understanding of how the market functions comprised the sample size that the paper defined for this study. Descriptive statistics were used to analyze the data, and it was discovered that the skewness for age was positive, indicating that the bulk of the observations was on the left side of the mean and that the distribution's tail extended to the right. The figure below illustrates this visually (Fig. 1).

4.1.2 Demographic Factors: Gender Distribution

The gender distribution of the respondents as shown in Fig. 2 below is as follows: Female—54% and Male—45%. Thus, there is not any significant bias toward a certain gender.

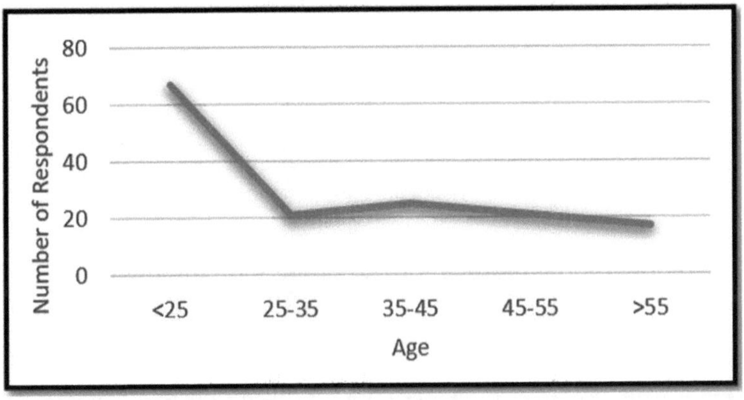

Fig. 1 Variation of respondents' ages

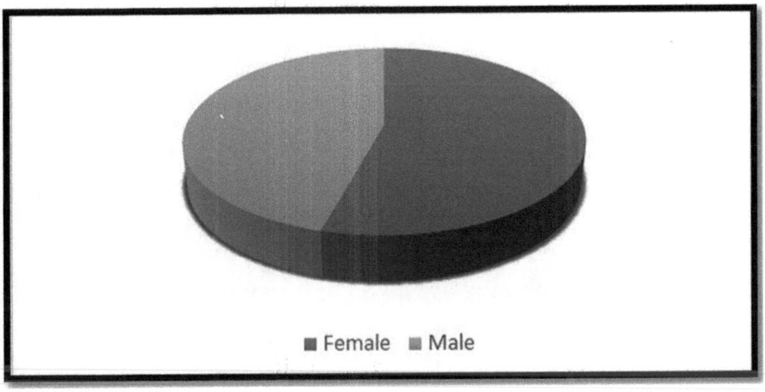

Fig. 2 Variation of respondents' gender

4.1.3 Demographic Factors Education Level

The variation across education level can be observed by the graph below. The number of graduates is much higher than the number of postgraduates and those who have completed their schooling (Fig. 3).

4.2 Investor Decision-Making and Choices

4.2.1 Emotional Biases: Loss Aversion

Participants were asked what they would do if a stock in their portfolio lost so much value that they could not stomach the thought of selling it. 66% of the respondents said they would hold the stock till the price increases again instead of selling it off

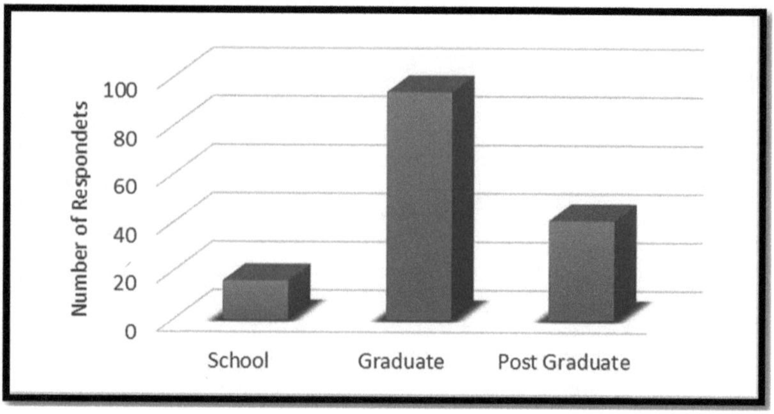

Fig. 3 Variation of respondents' education level

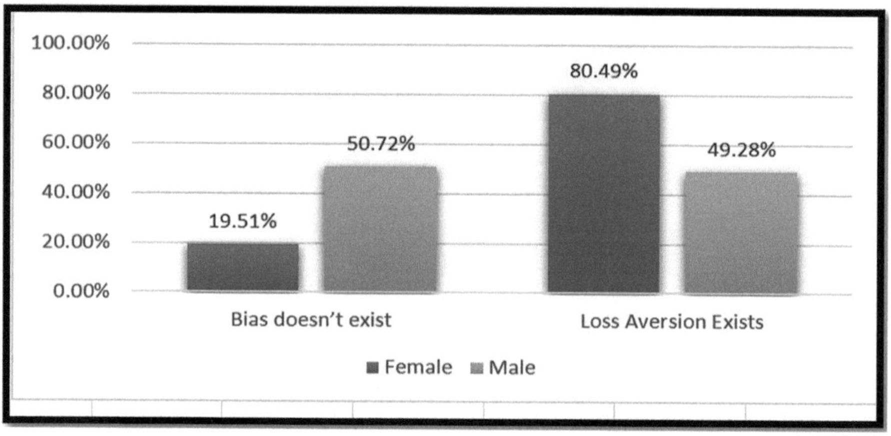

Fig. 4 Incidence of loss aversion across gender

immediately, showing evidence of the existence of the bias. The intensity was much higher in females (80%) as compared to males (49%) as is evident from Fig. 4. This is consistent with the literature reviewed. On further analysis, across the age groups considered, 60–68% of people exhibited the bias. The presence of the bias was high despite an increase in education levels, occurring in 71% graduates (Table 1).

4.2.2 Overconfidence

To check for Overconfidence, respondents were asked whether they thought they could correctly identify stocks that will profit in the markets in the future. Overconfidence was found in 54% of respondents as they agreed to be able to correctly predict which stocks would do well. Again, as consistent with literature,

Table 1 Incidence of loss aversion across gender

	Bias does not exist	Loss aversion	Total
Female	16	66	82
Male	35	34	69
Total	51	100	151

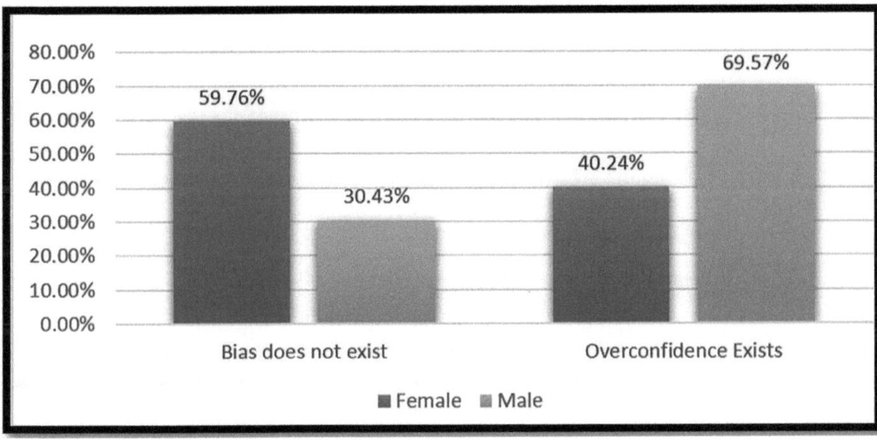

Fig. 5 Incidence of overconfidence across gender

Table 2 Incidence of overconfidence across gender

	Bias does not exist	Overconfidence	Total
Female	49	33	82
Male	21	48	69
Total	70	81	151

males tended to exhibit Overconfidence more than females. Almost 70% males exhibited the bias while 40% females did so. Again, a positive relation was observed between the existence of the bias and the level of education, with only 37.5% of those who have completed school exhibiting Overconfidence probably owing to lesser knowledge about the markets while more than 60% graduates and 53% post-graduates did so. Across the age demographic, it was widely found among those between 35 and 45 (86%) (Fig. 5 and Table 2).

4.2.3 Endowment Bias

Respondents were asked if they were trying to sell the house they had lived in for 15 years and they were attached to this property emotionally, would they be willing to sell it at the market price of 80 lakhs despite valuing the property personally at 1 crore (Figs. 6 and 7). A rejection of this offer would point to the Endowment Bias as people were not interested in the fair or market value. Their sentimental value was greater, and they expected the same from others. Overall, 56% respondents rejected the offer, and the intensity was higher in males. Figure 8 shows that older people, especially those above 55 have shown this bias the most, probably due to greater attachment to the property (Table 3).

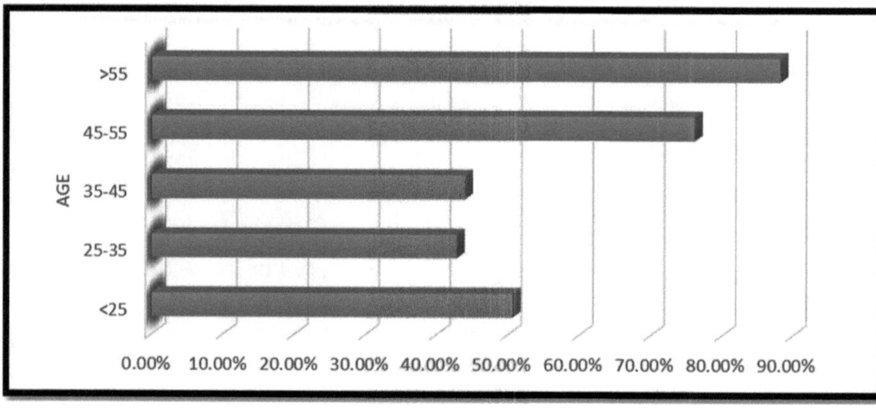

Fig. 6 Incidence of endowment bias across age

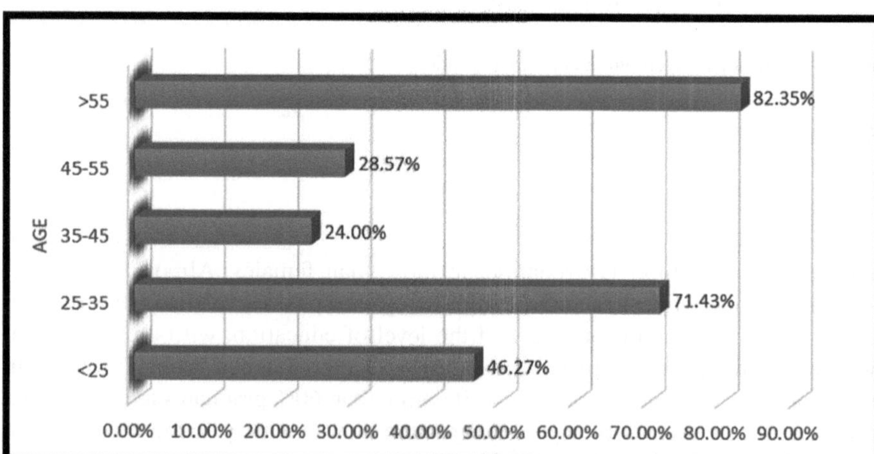

Fig. 7 Incidence of herding across age

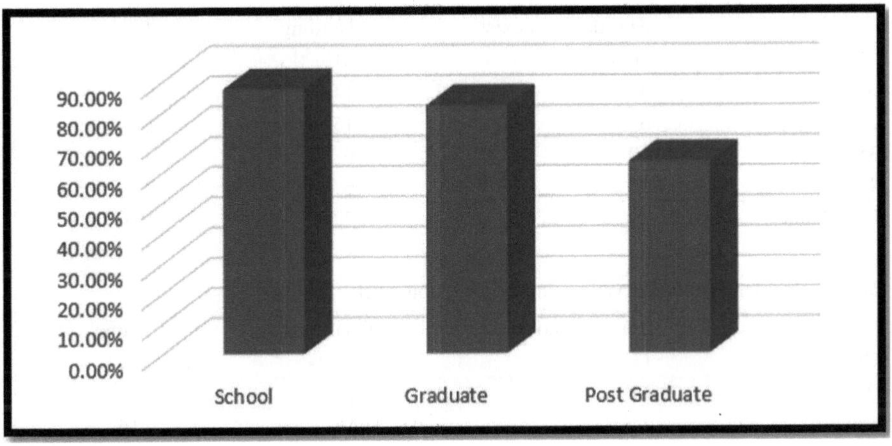

Fig. 8 Incidence of conservatism across education level

Table 3 Incidence of endowment bias across age

	Bias does not exist	Endowment bias	Total
<25	33	34	67
25–35	12	9	21
35–45	14	11	25
45–55	5	16	21
>55	2	15	17
Total	66	85	151

4.2.4 Herding

Herding may exist due to regret aversion. To test for this bias, respondents were asked if they would purchase a stock recommended by their friend who had heard about it through word of mouth. An inclination to purchase such a stock show herding as the tendency to not miss a good stock induces them to purchase it regardless of whether it is suitable for them or their portfolio. Evidence of this bias was not as strong as the others. In fact, only 47.7% respondents overall suffered from it. Relatively lesser females than males showed it. Herding in those with post graduate degrees was highest (60%). Across the age demographic, incidence was highest in those above 55 and lowest in those aged between 35 and 55.

Table 4 Incidence of herding across age

	Bias does not exist	Herding	Total
<25	36	31	67
>55	3	14	17
25–35	6	15	21
35–45	19	6	25
45–55	15	6	21
Grand total	79	72	151

Table 5 Incidence of conservatism across education level

	Bias does not exist	Conservatism	Total
Graduate	17	77	94
Postgraduate	15	26	41
School	2	14	16
Total	34	117	151

4.3 *Cognitive Biases*

4.3.1 Conservatism

Respondents were asked what they would do if they purchased stocks of Company X after independent rational decision-making but a few months later there was buzz of low efficiency in the company. Table 4 shows how 77% respondents exhibited the bias as they chose to hold the stock till prices started falling and then sold them rather than selling them immediately after received the news. This shows Conservatism, as there is an avoidance of changing prior rationally formed beliefs. The incidence was similar in males and females. An exception was found in post-graduates where only 63% respondents were affected by this bias compared to much higher levels of 87% in people who had only completed school (Table 5).

4.3.2 Representativeness

Respondents were asked if Eicher Motors was doing well given the economy conditions whether they would purchase stocks of other auto companies too. If the answer to this question was yes, it implied that they thought Eicher Motor was a "typical" item in the auto sector industry and its characters or performance would apply to all other auto stocks too. As visible from the pie chart below, a large portion of the sample exhibited this bias. It was observed more frequently in men. The bias was lowest for those who had completed school (Fig. 9).

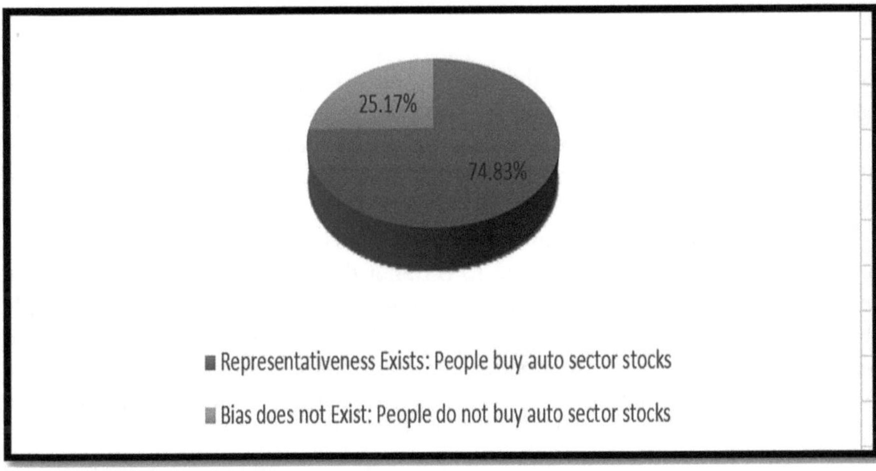

Fig. 9 Existence of representativeness

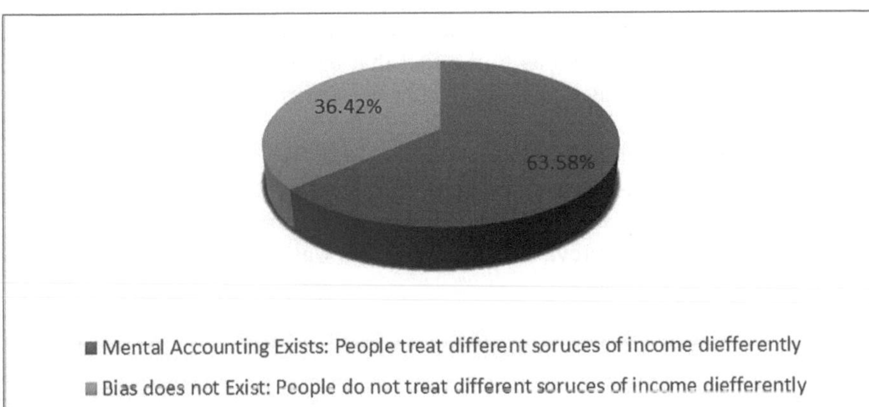

Fig. 10 Incidence of mental accounting

4.3.3 Mental Accounting

To check for the existence of this bias, the following question was posed—You have various sources of income-salary, bonus, and dividends. How would you use your money? According to Fig. 10, 63% people said they would invest the bonus and dividends and use the salary to fund their daily expenses. Across the education demographic, incidence varied between 60 and 68%. This bias was highest in old people which implies that they were most likely to treat sources of income in different ways.

4.3.4 Framing Bias

The last bias to be studied was the framing bias. Respondents were asked which statement out of the following statements would induce them to purchase a stock: *Statement 1* Earnings per Share (EPS) was $1.25, compared to expectations of $1.23, *Statement 2* Earnings per Share (EPS) was $1.25, compared to Q2, where it was $1.21.

The first statement demonstrates the framing bias by emphasizing the comparison between the actual and expected EPS rather than focusing on the comparison between Q3 and Q2 EPS. The fact that EPS was greater than expected makes people feel the stock has outperformed itself. Across the age demographic this was relatively low in older people. Distribution between men and women was similar. An inverse relation was seen between the existence of this bias and education levels. Overall, 75.5% respondents exhibited the bias (Fig. 11 and Table 6).

The results of the first 4 questions and last 4 questions were consolidated by taking weighted average. On conversion to percentage, it was observed that Cognitive Biases were relatively more prevalent among Indian investors than Emotional ones when it comes to financial decision-making. This can be seen from Fig. 12—Cognitive Biases prevailed 72.8% of the time while Emotional Biases impacted investors 55.9% only. This points to the fact that investors do suffer from logical inconsistencies while taking decisions and use heuristics to simplify their decision-making process.

The findings suggest that Indian investors unfortunately suffer from both cognitive and emotional biases. Hence, it can be said that they don't make wealth maximizing rational decisions as assumed by Traditional Finance theories. In the light of this information, the most prevalent emotional bias was loss aversion, and the least

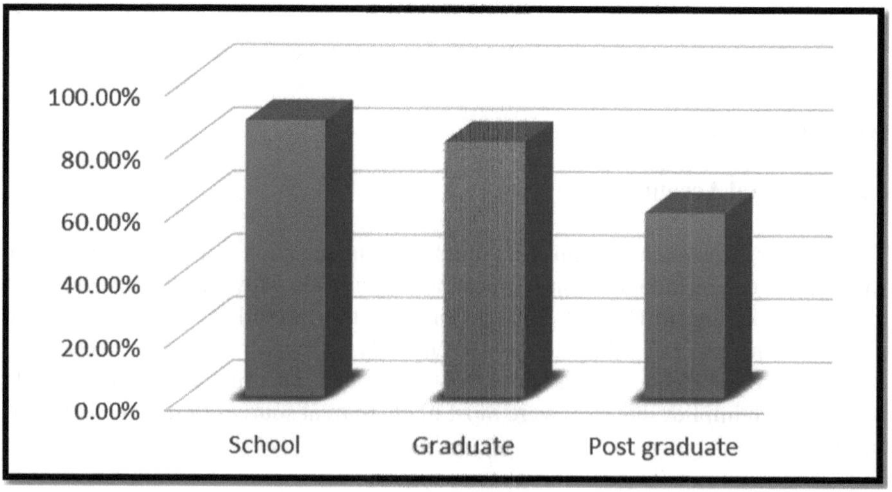

Fig. 11 Incidence of framing bias

Table 6 Incidence of framing bias

	Bias does not exist	Framing	Total
Graduate	18	76	94
Postgraduate	17	24	41
School	2	14	16
Total	37	114	151

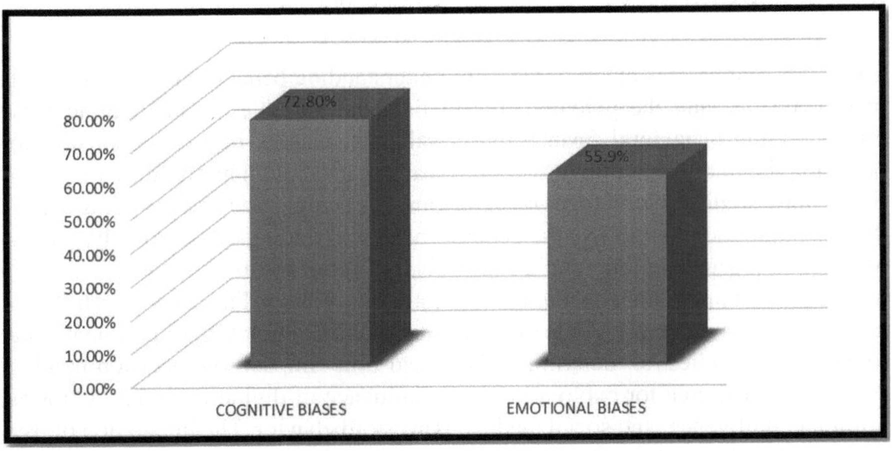

Fig. 12 Cognitive vs emotional biases

prevalent one was herding. On the other hand, the most evident cognitive bias was Conservatism and the one that impacted people the least was Mental Accounting. The incidence of cognitive biases overall was higher than that of emotional ones. Hence, we fail to reject our null hypothesis that Cognitive Biases are found extensively and there is a need to look for moderating variables to reduce their occurrence in financial decision-making.

5 Limitations and Scope of the Study

Since the data was gathered from primary sources, the conclusions are accurate to the extent that the data could be confirmed. The study was conducted only for investors in India's metropolitan cities. In the case of self-administered questionnaires, respondents are more likely to choose the first option on the list. As a result, there could be a confirmation bias in the evaluation process. Inaccurate feedbacks are often biased because of the exhaustive nature of the exercise. A majority of the 151 respondents that were considered for the analysis were students hence the results could be skewed. There are possibilities that respondents feel the pressure to offer opinions on certain issues when they truly have no attitudes. The questions being in the hypothetical forms may not necessarily put the respondents in that situation. Hypothetical situations give biased results. There is a chance that a question will be perceived ambiguously, in which case the respondents' opinions will vary. This study aims to identify trends, not make population-wide generalizations. Future research can build upon these findings with larger, more representative samples.

6 Conclusion

This study emphasizes the importance of understanding behavioral biases in investment decisions and the potential role of financial variables in moderating these effects. While behavioral finance offers valuable insights into irrational investor behavior, the findings highlight several research gaps that highlight further exploration. Future studies should focus on expanding the sample size and including a more diverse population to improve the generalizability of findings. Additionally, investigating how socioeconomic and cultural factors influence biases could provide a more comprehensive understanding of investor psychology. Further research should also explore the moderating role of financial variables, employing experimental and longitudinal studies to determine their real-time impact on decision-making. Another critical area for exploration is the influence of digital financial platforms, artificial intelligence, and social media on investor behavior. The integration of psychological and neurological methods, such as neurofinance approaches, could offer deeper insights into cognitive processing during financial decision-making. Moreover, intervention-based studies, such as behavioral nudges and decision aids, could be developed to help investors mitigate their biases. Behavioral finance remains an evolving field, and with continued empirical research, it holds the potential to equip investors with strategies that enhance rational decision-making and optimize financial outcomes.

References

Abhijeet, C., & Ravinder, K. (2012). Factors influencing Indian individual investor behaviour: Survey evidence. *Decision, 39*(3), 1–27.

Ahmad, F. (2020). Personality traits as predictor of cognitive biases: Moderating role of risk-attitude. *Qualitative Research in Financial Markets, 12*(4), 465–484.

Akerlof, G. A., & Shiller, R. J. (2009). *Animal spirits: How human psychology drives the economy, and why it matters for global capitalism*. Princeton University Press.

Athota, V. S., Pereira, V., Hasan, Z., Vaz, D., Laker, B., & Reppas, D. (2023). Overcoming financial planners' cognitive biases through digitalization: A qualitative study. *Journal of Business Research, 154*, 113291.

Barber, B. M., & Odean, T. (1999). The courage of misguided convictions: The trading behavior of individual investors. *Financial Analysts Journal, 55*(6), 41–55.

Barber, B. M., & Odean, T. (2000). Trading is hazardous to your wealth: The common stock investment performance of individual investors. *The Journal of Finance, 55*(2), 773–806.

Barber, B. M., & Odean, T. (2001). Boys will be boys: Gender, overconfidence, and common stock investment. *The Quarterly Journal of Economics, 116*(1), 261–292.

Barberis, N., & Huang, M. (2001). Mental accounting, loss aversion, and individual stock returns. *The Journal of Finance, 56*(4), 1247–1292.

Barberis, N., & Thaler, R. H. (2003). A survey of behavioral finance. In G. M. Constantinides, M. Harris, & R. M. Stulz (Eds.), *Handbook of the Economics of Finance* (Vol. 1, pp. 1053–1128). Elsevier.

Baumeister, R. F. (2002). Yielding to temptation: Self-control failure, impulsive purchasing, and consumer behavior. *Journal of Consumer Research, 28*(4), 670–676.

Benartzi, S., & Thaler, R. H. (2001). Naive diversification strategies in defined contribution saving plans. *American Economic Review, 91*(1), 79–98.

Biais, B., Hilton, D., Mazurier, K., & Pouget, S. (2005). Judgmental overconfidence, self-monitoring, and trading performance in an experimental financial market. *Review of Economic Studies, 72*(2), 287–312.

Bikhchandani, S., Hirshleifer, D., & Welch, I. (1992). A theory of fads, fashion, custom, and cultural change as informational cascades. *Journal of Political Economy, 100*(5), 992–1026.

Charles, A., & Kasilingam, R. (2015). Do investors' emotions determine their investment decisions? Drishtikon. *A Management Journal, 6*(2), 52–61.

Choi, J. J., Laibson, D., Madrian, B. C., & Metrick, A. (2004). For better or for worse: Default effects and 401(k) savings behavior. *Perspectives on the Economics of Aging, 81*, 81–121.

Coval, J. D., & Moskowitz, T. J. (1999). Home bias at home: Local equity preference in domestic portfolios. *The Journal of Finance, 54*(6), 2045–2073.

Coval, J. D., & Shumway, T. (2005). Do behavioral biases affect prices? *The Journal of Finance, 60*(1), 1–34.

Daniel, K., Hirshleifer, D., & Subrahmanyam, A. (1998). Investor psychology and security market under- and overreactions. *The Journal of Finance, 53*(6), 1839–1885.

De, S. (2016). The biases influencing an investor's behavior in India. *SSRN Electronic Journal.*

Fama, E. F. (1970). Efficient capital markets: A review of theory and empirical work. *The Journal of Finance, 25*(2), 383–417.

Forbes, W. (2009). *Behavioural finance*. Wiley.

French, K. R., & Poterba, J. M. (1991). Investor diversification and international equity markets. *American Economic Review, 81*(2), 222–226.

Gervais, S., & Odean, T. (2001). Learning to be overconfident. *The Review of Financial Studies, 14*(1), 1–27.

Grinblatt, M., Titman, S., & Wermers, R. (1995). Momentum investment strategies, portfolio performance, and herding: A study of mutual fund behavior. *The American Economic Review, 85*(5), 1088–1105.

Grinblatt, M., & Keloharju, M. (2001). What makes investors trade? *The Journal of Finance, 56*(2), 589–616.

Johnsson, M., Lindblom, H., & Platan, P. (2002). Behavioural finance and the change of investor behaviour during and after the speculative bubble at the end of the 1990s.

Joo, B. A., & Durri, K. (2018). Impact of psychological traits on rationality of individual investors. *Theoretical Economics Letters, 8*(11), 1973–1986.

Jyoti, K. (2019). A review of behavioral biases influencing investor decision making in India. *International Journal of Scientific & Technology Research, 8*(12), 367–372.

Kahneman, D., Knetsch, J. L., & Thaler, R. H. (1991). Anomalies: The endowment effect, loss aversion, and status quo bias. *Journal of Economic Perspectives, 5*(1), 193–206.

Kahneman, D., & Tversky, A. (1979). Prospect theory: An analysis of decision under risk. *Econometrica, 47*(2), 263–292.

Kaustia, M., Alho, E., & Puttonen, V. (2008). How much does expertise reduce behavioral biases? The case of anchoring effects in stock return estimates. *Financial Management, 37*(3), 391–412.

Khan, A. R., Azeem, M., & Sarwar, S. (2017). Impact of overconfidence and loss aversion biases on investment decision: Moderating role of risk perception. *International Journal of Transformation in Accounting, Auditing & Taxation, 1*(1), 14–28.

Kumar, S., & Goyal, N. (2015). Behavioural biases in investment decision making—a systematic literature review. *Qualitative Research in Financial Markets, 7*(1), 88–108.

Lakonishok, J., Shleifer, A., & Vishny, R. W. (1992). The impact of institutional trading on stock prices. *Journal of Financial Economics, 32*(1), 23–43.

Latif, M., Arshad, S., Fatima, M., & Farooq, S. (2011). Market efficiency, market anomalies, causes, evidences, and some behavioural aspects of market anomalies. *Research Journal of Finance and Accounting, 2*(9), 1–13.

Madaan, G., & Singh, S. (2019). An analysis of behavioural biases in investment decision-making. *International Journal of Financial Research, 10*(4), 55–67.

Malmendier, U., & Tate, G. (2008). Who makes acquisitions? CEO overconfidence and the market's reaction. *Journal of Financial Economics, 89*(1), 20–43.

Mitroi, M., & Oproiu, A. (2014). Behavioural finance and decision making: How investors manage their money. *Theoretical and Applied Economics, 21*(3), 35–52.

Mohapatra, A., & Samal, A. (2021). A study on the impact of behavioural biases on investment decisions of risk-seeking investors in India. *International Journal of Psychosocial Rehabilitation, 24*, 2020–2027.

Nair, V., & Antony, A. (2013). Evolutions and challenges of behavioural finance. *International Journal of Science and Research (IJSR), 4*, 1055–1059.

Nickerson, R. S. (1998). Confirmation bias: A ubiquitous phenomenon in many guises. *Review of General Psychology, 2*(2), 175–220.

Nofsinger, J. R. (2002). *The psychology of investing*. Prentice Hall.

Novianggie, V., & Asandimitra, N. (2019). The influence of behavioural bias, cognitive bias, and emotional bias on investment decisions for college students with financial literacy as the moderating variable. *Journal of Economics and Business, 2*(1), 92–107.

Odean, T. (1998). Are investors reluctant to realize their losses? *The Journal of Finance, 53*(5), 1775–1798.

Raheja, S., & Dhiman, B. (2017). Influence of personality traits and behavioural biases on the investment decisions of investors. *Asian Journal of Management, 8*(3), 819–826.

Ricciardi, V., & Simon, H. K. (2000). What is behavioral finance? *The Business, Education and Technology Journal, 2*(2), 1–9.

Sattaf, M. A., Toseef, M., & Sattar, M. F. (2020). Behavioural finance biases in investment decision-making. *International Journal of Accounting, Finance and Risk Management, 5*(2), 69–76.

Sewell, M. (2007). Behavioural finance. University of Cambridge, Technical Report. Retrieved from http://www.behaviouralfinance.net/.

Shefrin, H., & Statman, M. (1985). The disposition to sell winners too early and ride losers too long: Theory and evidence. *The Journal of Finance, 40*(3), 777–790.

Shiller, R. J. (2005). *Irrational exuberance*. Princeton University Press.

Statman, M., Fisher, K. L., & Anginer, D. (2008). Affect in a behavioral asset pricing model. *Financial Analysts Journal, 64*(2), 20–29.

Thaler, R. H. (1980). Toward a positive theory of consumer choice. *Journal of Economic Behavior & Organization, 1*(1), 39–60.

Thaler, R. H. (1985). Mental accounting and consumer choice. *Marketing Science, 4*(3), 199–214.

Thaler, R. H. (1999). Mental accounting matters. *Journal of Behavioral Decision Making, 12*(3), 183–206.

Tversky, A., & Kahneman, D. (1974). Judgment under uncertainty: Heuristics and biases. *Science, 185*(4157), 1124–1131.

Tversky, A., & Kahneman, D. (1981). The framing of decisions and the psychology of choice. *Science, 211*(4481), 453–458.

Tversky, A., & Kahneman, D. (1992). Advances in prospect theory: Cumulative representation of uncertainty. *Journal of Risk and Uncertainty, 5*(4), 297–323.

Weber, E. U., Weber, M., & Nosic, A. (2010). Who takes risks when and why? Determinants of changes in investor risk-taking. *Review of Finance, 14*(4), 611–635.

Cultivating Future Disruptors: A Study of Entrepreneurial Intentions in Emerging Markets

Md Monirul Islam

Abstract University students often generate innovative business ideas but rarely pursue them. Research has identified this issue in many emerging markets, but none have been found in the Cambodian market. This study identified key factors influencing university students' entrepreneurial intentions, such as motivations and personality traits. It also explored the moderating effects of variables like gender and years of study. A quantitative cross-sectional survey collected data from Cambodian university students. Based on the validated scale, a structured questionnaire was developed. A multiple regression was used to examine the relationship between variables. The findings revealed a significant correlation between entrepreneurial intention and key factors, including motivations, personality traits, university environment, and country situation. This study significantly contributes to our understanding by offering robust empirical evidence regarding the factors that drive entrepreneurial intentions among university students in emerging markets. It provides insights into creating effective strategies for policymakers, educators, and organizations that support entrepreneurship to assist students on their entrepreneurial journeys. Future research may explore longitudinal studies to track the evolution of entrepreneurial intentions over time and more profoundly investigate the driving forces of these intentions.

Keywords Entrepreneurial Intention · Motivations · Personality traits · University environment · Emerging markets

---

M. Monirul Islam (✉)
CamEd Business School, Phnom Penh, Cambodia
e-mail: moni@cam-ed.com; https://cam-ed.edu.kh

E. Lau et al. (eds.), *Economics and Finance Readings*,
https://doi.org/10.1007/978-981-96-6998-1_3

1 Introduction

Entrepreneurship is widely recognized as a significant contributor to the economy of every country, generating new jobs and fostering innovation and competitiveness in the labor market (Dimitrios Komninos et al., 2024). While entrepreneurship activities have gained significant attention in many Western nations, they are also becoming increasingly important in developing countries. Numerous studies have identified entrepreneurial intention as one of the most significant predictors of entrepreneurial activities and behaviors (Tian et al., 2022). As a result, contemporary research has shifted its focus from general entrepreneurship to exploring entrepreneurial intention (Huang & Huang, 2024). The number of studies using entrepreneurial intentions as a research framework has increased since the early 1990s, confirming its importance in various contexts (Maheshwari et al., 2022). Graduates must shift their mindset from seeking employment to creating jobs, as governments may need to provide more job opportunities for all tertiary-level graduates in the future (Ibrahim & Adeniyi, 2024). University students, therefore, should embrace the entrepreneurial revolution (Tomlinson, 2017).

It is essential to understand the factors influencing students' entrepreneurial intentions to promote their future entrepreneurial journeys. Many researchers have investigated the factors affecting the entrepreneurial intentions of higher education students. Personality traits, such as self-efficacy, individual attitudes, motivation, and behavioral control, significantly influence students' intentions toward entrepreneurship (Lee et al., 2022). Social and environmental influences, including educational experience, family background, country culture, and government support, have also been identified as key factors that impact students' entrepreneurial intentions (Bui et al., 2023). Moreover, entrepreneurial education plays a fundamental role in shaping students' EI by enhancing their foundational entrepreneurial knowledge and various cognitive and non-cognitive skills, stimulating their entrepreneurial activities (Brüne & Lutz, 2019). This motivates students toward entrepreneurship, improves the quality of their venture, and contributes to entrepreneurial success (Fan et al., 2024). Various frameworks and theories of entrepreneurship have been developed to examine the factors influencing an individual's entrepreneurial intentions.

However, many students in emerging markets give up on their entrepreneurial journeys while studying, representing a loss of valuable talent and ideas that could address social issues and create jobs. This is particularly concerning in Cambodia, where the rise of student-led startups is a promising trend, yet the specific factors influencing the entrepreneurial intentions of Cambodian students remain underexplored. This gap in understanding is crucial to address, as it hinders the development of effective support systems to enhance and sustain the country's entrepreneurial ecosystem. While Cambodia shares characteristics with other emerging markets, its unique socio-economic context, including its developing economy, cultural nuances, and evolving educational landscape, may significantly impact students' entrepreneurial aspirations. This study aims to explore students' entrepreneurial intentions in higher education institutions across Cambodia, explicitly addressing this critical gap. By identifying the independent and control variables related to personality traits, social and environmental influences, and entrepreneurial education, this research seeks to understand how these factors influence the dependent variable: the entrepreneurial intentions of Cambodian university students. This focus on Cambodian students is essential because it allows for a tailored understanding of their specific challenges and opportunities, enabling the development of targeted interventions. Understanding these factors is crucial for establishing effective support systems to enhance and sustain Cambodia's entrepreneurial ecosystem. With this insight, Cambodian universities can develop tailored programs to foster a thriving startup culture, which will, in turn, contribute to economic growth and poverty reduction.

This research significantly contributes to entrepreneurship by investigating the factors influencing entrepreneurial intentions (Bodolica & Spraggon, 2021) among emerging market university students. This study extends the theoretical understanding of entrepreneurial intention formation by identifying key determinants such as motivations, personality traits, university environment, and country situation. Moreover, the research explores the moderating effects of gender, years of study, significance, and institutional ownership on these relationships. The findings have practical implications for policymakers, educators, and entrepreneurship support organizations, enabling them to develop effective strategies (Adeel et al., 2023) to foster entrepreneurial aspirations and create a supportive entrepreneurial ecosystem. Unlike other emerging markets, Cambodia's post-conflict recovery, unique collectivist cultural norms, and nascent support systems for entrepreneurs create a distinct environment. This study addresses the critical gap in understanding how these localized factors shape entrepreneurial intentions, offering insights to foster Cambodia's economic development through youth entrepreneurship. This study fills a research gap by providing empirical evidence on entrepreneurial intentions in the Cambodian context. It contributes to a deeper understanding of the factors shaping entrepreneurial aspirations in emerging markets. This study aims to answer the following research question:

RQ: What factors influence the entrepreneurial intentions of university students in emerging markets, specifically in Cambodia?

2 Literature Review

I conducted this literature review by thoroughly searching relevant articles. The search process consisted of several steps; I looked at the keywords (Student Entrepreneurship, Entrepreneurial Intentions, Motivations, Personality Traits, University environment, and Country Situations) in my research questions in several search engines, including Google Scholar, JSTOR, Research Gate, Web of

Science, and Emerald. This literature review also aims to conceptualize what motivates students to become entrepreneurs during their university studies.

2.1 Entrepreneurial Intentions

Entrepreneurial intention refers to an individual's desire and determination to start a business in the future. This intention serves as a predictor of a person's future actions (Ajzen, 1991). Although someone may become an entrepreneur, entrepreneurial behavior only manifests when that intention is explicitly present (Neneh & Dzomonda, 2024). Understanding entrepreneurial intention is vital for grasping an individual's inclination and tendency to pursue entrepreneurship (Anjum et al., 2022). Many studies have examined the factors influencing the formation of entrepreneurial intention and how personality traits impact this process. Entrepreneurial intention is the crucial first step toward launching a new business venture (Shahzad et al., 2021).

Exploring entrepreneurial intention has become an active area of research within entrepreneurship. It effectively motivates individuals to engage in productive activities and initiate new ventures. Additionally, it reflects a person's commitment to starting a new business. Promoting entrepreneurial activities has become increasingly important in developing countries due to their significant role in creating employment opportunities and driving economic growth (Soluk et al., 2021).

2.2 Motivations

Individual motivation is crucial in starting and running a business (Dana et al., 2021). To start a business, motivated individuals can focus their behavior toward action. Motivation generates intensity, direction, and individual perseverance to achieve the desired goals. Intensity refers to how hard an individual tries to achieve their goals, but more is needed if the effort is directed toward a profitable goal. Perseverance significantly affects how long an individual can maintain their business (Rodrigo & Palacios, 2021). Individuals who are motivated tend to remain in their jobs for a longer duration until they achieve their goals. Motivation creates a situation within individuals that drives them to appear, direct, and maintain the behavior of fulfilling or satisfying their needs (Hajiali et al., 2022).

According to entrepreneurship research conducted by Hassan et al. (2021), entrepreneurial motivation is a critical factor that drives individuals to create new businesses and revolutionize industries. This motivation propels entrepreneurs to take risks, innovate, and succeed. Nurturing entrepreneurial motivation is essential for aspiring entrepreneurs as it enables them to pursue their dreams and build a better future. Fauzi (2021) states that cultivating an environment that fosters entrepreneurial motivation can lead to more opportunities for individuals to take charge of their lives, pursue their passions, and positively impact their communities.

Entrepreneurial intention recognizes the family's important role in encouraging children to start a business (Moindi Rose Meroka, 2023). Research has shown a positive relationship between family support and entrepreneurial intention. Family support strengthens individuals and helps them develop an entrepreneurial mindset (Osorio et al., 2017). The support provided by the family in various projects emphasizes the importance of family roles and the responsibilities that shape the interactions among family members and entrepreneurs (Cardella et al., 2020). In this context, entrepreneurs often leverage resources from their relatives and friends, which can enhance the overall success of their ventures (Arregle et al., 2013).

Family support has allowed entrepreneurs to engage in activities that help address business challenges and manage emotional distress related to financial difficulties (Shahzad et al., 2021). Starting a business often requires significant financial resources, which can take time for young graduates to secure. However, with financial assistance from family, friends, and relatives, they can more easily overcome these obstacles and embark on their entrepreneurial journeys (Manzi-Puertas et al., 2024).

H1. Higher levels of motivation positively influence the entrepreneurial intentions of university students from emerging markets.

2.3 *Personality Traits*

Several studies have suggested that personality traits are crucial in shaping an individual's entrepreneurial intentions (Karabulut, 2016). Research has indicated that these traits significantly predict entrepreneurial intention among university students (Bazkiaei et al., 2020). For instance, factors such as locus of control, need for achievement, and risk-taking propensity have been identified as significant predictors of entrepreneurial intention among university students from emerging markets (Uysal et al., 2021). It has been found to have a positive relationship between personality traits and entrepreneurial intention among university students in emerging markets (Li et al., 2022).

H2. A positive relationship exists between university students' personality traits and entrepreneurial intentions.

2.4 University Environment

Institutional support plays a significant role in encouraging young people to become entrepreneurs. It positively impacts job creation and establishes new entrepreneurial guidelines, improving economic growth (Shahzad et al., 2021). Recently, institutions have begun aligning academic degrees with professional requirements to inspire students and foster their desire to pursue entrepreneurship (Abu et al., 2024). This support enhances entrepreneurial intentions by organizing workshops and seminars for skill development, networking opportunities, and raising awareness (Shahzad et al., 2021).

Educational institutions have started focusing on aspiring entrepreneurs' attributes and skills rather than only imparting knowledge. In addition to educational support, these institutions can further enhance the entrepreneurial intentions of university students by facilitating resource creation that benefits entrepreneurship programs (Mohammad et al., 2024). To promote an entrepreneurial culture, it is essential to encourage active participation in co-curricular activities, such as business competitions, workshops, skills-based training sessions, and interactive events with successful business professionals (Pocek et al., 2021).

H3. There is a positive relationship between the supportive nature of the university environment and university students' entrepreneurial intentions.

2.5 Country Situation

Governments can foster the growth of new businesses by implementing effective entrepreneurship education programs, subsidizing enterprise advice and training, and providing financial support and incubation spaces (Panakaje et al., 2024). For these interventions to be successful, they should enhance the level of enterprise, entrepreneurship, and growth among small businesses, ultimately delivering the desired benefits. Support for entrepreneurship should motivate individuals to start businesses, offer solid opportunities for developing new ventures, and provide support structures to equip entrepreneurs with essential skills (Endang Sungkawati et al., 2023).

Additionally, social networks can provide access to vital resources needed to identify and seize opportunities, thereby increasing entrepreneurs' effectiveness, especially when resources are scarce (Park et al., 2017). These networks enable entrepreneurs to make quicker decisions, save valuable time, and benefit from their experiences and those of others (Liguori, 2019).

H4. A supportive entrepreneurial ecosystem positively affects the entrepreneurial intentions of university students.

Despite these insights, a gap remains in contextualizing these factors within Cambodia's entrepreneurial landscape. The country's startup ecosystem has grown

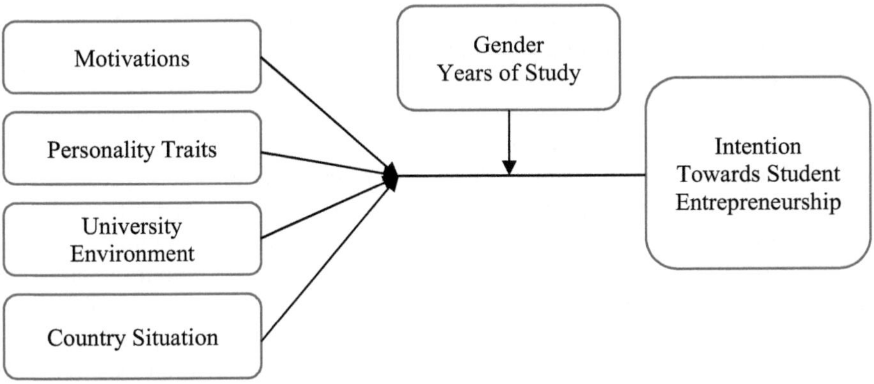

Fig. 1 Conceptual framework

with increased governmental and private sector support. However, challenges such as regulatory barriers, limited access to funding, and risk-averse cultural norms persist (Bui et al., 2023). By integrating these perspectives, this study enhances understanding of entrepreneurial intention within Cambodia's evolving business environment.

2.6 Conceptual Framework (Fig. 1)

The following text presents a conceptual framework illustrating the relationship between entrepreneurial intentions and other variables. It demonstrates a direct relationship between entrepreneurial intentions, including Motivations, Personality Traits, University Environment, and Country Situation. It also illustrates the moderating variables, including Gender and Years of Study.

3 Research Methodology

3.1 Research Design

This research investigates the factors influencing university students' entrepreneurial intentions in an emerging market. It seeks to understand how motivations, personality traits, the university environment, and the country's situation affect entrepreneurial intentions, focusing on how gender and years of study moderate these relationships.

This study will employ a quantitative research design to collect data and draw general conclusions about a specific segment of the target population known as the sample. A cross-sectional survey approach will be used to gather information from a representative group of Cambodian university students.

There are reasons for choosing a survey approach. First, surveys are an effective and efficient way to collect large amounts of data from a sizable population, essential for examining the diverse factors influencing entrepreneurial intentions across a broad demographic. This aligns with the theoretical framework, suggesting that various individual and environmental factors shape entrepreneurial intentions. By employing a survey, we can gather data on multiple variables, including motivations, personality traits, the university environment, and the country's situation, allowing for a comprehensive analysis. Second, surveys provide a standardized data collection method, ensuring consistency and reliability in the responses. This is crucial for testing the hypotheses outlined in the research, such as the positive relationships between motivation and entrepreneurial intentions (H1), personality traits and entrepreneurial intentions (H2), the university environment and entrepreneurial intentions (H3), and the supportive nature of the entrepreneurial ecosystem and entrepreneurial intentions (H4). A standardized survey allows us to measure these variables accurately and compare the results across different respondents.

I thoroughly reviewed the existing literature on entrepreneurial intentions and the factors that influence the development of the survey questions. The questions were designed to measure the key variables identified in the conceptual model: motivations, personality traits, the university environment, and the country's situation.

Motivations were assessed using items adapted from established scales that measure entrepreneurial motivation. These items were chosen for their relevance to the emerging market's context and their ability to capture different dimensions of motivation (Saeed et al., 2013). Personality traits were measured using items from well-validated personality inventories. These items were selected because they provide a comprehensive assessment of personality traits that have been shown to influence entrepreneurial intentions (Liñán & Chen, 2009). The university environment was evaluated using items that assess the support and resources available to students within their university. These items were adapted from surveys used in similar studies and tailored to reflect the specific characteristics of universities in emerging markets (Krueger et al., 2000). The country's situation was measured using items that capture students' perceptions of the entrepreneurial ecosystem in the emerging market. These items were derived from existing surveys on national entrepreneurial ecosystems and modified to fit the context of this research (Krueger et al., 2000).

3.2 Sampling

A simple random sampling technique will be employed to select participants from the target population of Cambodian university students enrolled in undergraduate programs. We will use a confidence level of 95% and a margin of error of ±5% to determine the required sample size. With a total population of 2500 students, a minimum sample size of 334 participants is needed (Krejcie & Morgan, 1970; Adam, 2020). This calculation ensures that the study's findings are statistically significant and represent the broader population.

3.3 Data Collection

A self-administered questionnaire will be developed to collect data on the variables of entrepreneurial intention, which will be measured using validated scales. The four key intentions identified in the paper, motivations, personality traits, university environment, and country situation, will be measured using validated scales or adapted items from existing research as independent variables. At the same time, gender and bachelor semesters will serve as control variables and can be measured through demographic questions. The questionnaire will be pilot-tested with a small group of students to ensure its clarity, reliability, and validity before being administered to the primary sample. It will be administered online through Qualtrics XM and distributed to university students for data collection.

The confidentiality of their personal information will be strictly maintained, and their anonymity will be guaranteed at all times. Any data collected during the research will be kept secure and only used for research purposes.

3.4 Data Analysis

This study will use descriptive statistics to summarize the data collected on all variables. Correlation analysis will be applied to identify the relationships between the independent and dependent variables. Additionally, multiple regression analysis will be used to assess the relative influence of each independent variable on entrepreneurial intentions while controlling for the effects of the control variables. These statistical techniques will provide a comprehensive understanding of entrepreneurial intentions. With this knowledge, targeted and effective interventions that can help foster and promote entrepreneurial intentions can be designed.

3.5 Data Coding, Cleaning, Transformation, and Management

Survey data will be automatically coded into numerical formats for statistical analysis using the SPSS software. Survey responses will be reviewed to identify and remove incomplete or inconsistent responses, and then the data will be cleaned and transformed into analyzable formats. For example, Likert scale responses will be converted into numerical scores. All data will be securely stored in an encrypted folder with restricted access to ensure confidentiality and comply with ethical guidelines.

3.6 Reliability and Validity of the Survey Instrument

A pilot test was conducted with a small sample of students to assess the reliability and validity of the survey instrument. Cronbach's alpha was used to assess the reliability of the survey items for each construct. The pilot data showed that Cronbach's alpha values for all constructs were 0.879, indicating that the survey items consistently measured the intended constructs.

4 Results

4.1 Demographics of the Respondents

Table 1 presents an overview of the demographic profile of the study's sample, which included 390 participants. Most of the sample was female, with 278 individuals (71.3%), while males comprised 112 participants (28.7%).

Regarding academic year distribution, the largest group consisted of first-year students, totaling 156 participants (40%). Fourth-year students followed, representing 86 participants (22.1%). Second-year and third-year students comprised smaller portions of the sample, with 78 participants (20%) and 70 participants (17.9%), respectively.

4.2 Descriptive Statistics

Table 2 presents the descriptive statistics for the study's key variables based on a sample of 390 participants. Gender was coded as 1 for females and 2 for males, resulting in a mean of 1.29 (SD = 0.453). This indicates a higher proportion of

Table 1 Demographic profile of the sample ($n = 390$)

Variable name	Category	Frequency	Percentage (%)
Gender	Female	278	71.3
	Male	112	28.7
Years of study	Year 01	156	40
	Year 02	78	20
	Year 03	70	17.9
	Year 04	86	22.1

Table 2 Descriptive statistics ($n = 390$)

Variable	n	Min	Max	Mean	SD	Skewness	Kurtosis
Gender	390	1	2	1.29	0.453	0.944	−1.114
Years of study	390	1	4	2.22	1.190	0.358	−1.417
Motivation	390	1	5	3.86	0.911	−0.556	−0.499
Personality traits	390	2	5	3.62	0.702	−0.296	0.033
University environment	390	2	5	3.63	0.770	−0.477	−0.121
Country situation	390	1	5	3.33	0.758	−0.123	0.448
Entrepreneurial intention	390	1	5	3.84	0.902	−0.626	0.025

female participants in the sample. The years of study ranged from the first year (coded as 1) to the fourth year (coded as 4), with a mean of 2.22 (SD = 1.190). This suggests that participants were distributed across all academic years, with a slight concentration in the earlier years.

Motivation, rated on a scale from 1 to 5, had a mean score of 3.86 (SD = 0.911), indicating moderately high motivation levels among participants. Personality traits were similarly rated favorably, with a mean of 3.62 (SD = 0.702). The university environment was viewed positively, with a mean score of 3.63 (SD = 0.770). The country situation received a mean score of 3.33 (SD = 0.758), indicating moderate socio-economic and institutional environment perceptions. Lastly, entrepreneurial intention, which is the central focus of the study, had a mean of 3.84 (SD = 0.902), suggesting that participants generally exhibited moderately high levels of intention toward entrepreneurship.

The skewness and kurtosis values for all variables suggest that the data are approximately normally distributed, with no extreme skewness or kurtosis observed. Motivation showed a skewness of −0.556 and a kurtosis of −0.499, while personality traits had a skewness of −0.296 and a kurtosis of 0.033. Entrepreneurial intention exhibited a skewness of −0.626 and a kurtosis of 0.025, indicating slight negative skews and a tendency toward higher ratings. Similarly, the university environment had a skewness of −0.477, and the country situation had a skewness of −0.123, suggesting favorable perceptions. In contrast, gender had a skewness of 0.944, which was positively skewed due to the higher proportion of female respondents. Overall, these results provide an initial overview of the sample's characteristics and the central variables of the study.

4.3 Correlations

Table 3 presents the Pearson correlation coefficients between the key variables in the study. The analysis reveals that gender did not correlate significantly with other variables, indicating that gender composition had minimal influence on motivation, personality traits, or entrepreneurial intention. Conversely, years of study displayed a significant negative correlation with motivation ($r = -0.260$, $p < 0.01$) and

Table 3 Correlations ($n = 390$)

Variable	1	2	3	4	5	6	7
1. Gender	1						
2. Years of study	−0.094	1					
3. Motivation	−0.030	−0.260**	1				
4. Personality traits	−0.025	−0.195**	0.586**	1			
5. University environment	0.068	−0.120*	0.177**	0.316**	1		
6. Country situation	−0.036	−0.114*	0.278**	0.469**	0.422**	1	
7. Entrepreneurial intention	0.000	−0.288**	0.831**	0.631**	0.115*	0.324**	1

personality characteristics ($r = -0.195$, $p < 0.01$). This suggests that as students advance in their academic years, their motivation and positive personality traits tend to decrease slightly.

Motivation exhibited a strong positive correlation with personality traits ($r = 0.586$, $p < 0.01$) and moderate correlations with the university environment ($r = 0.177$, $p < 0.01$) and the country situation ($r = 0.278$, $p < 0.01$). These findings imply that higher levels of motivation are associated with more favorable perceptions of personality traits, the university environment, and the broader socio-economic context. Additionally, personality traits showed significant positive correlations with the university environment ($r = 0.316$, $p < 0.01$), the country situation ($r = 0.469$, $p < 0.01$), and entrepreneurial intention ($r = 0.631$, $p < 0.01$). This emphasizes the role of personality traits in promoting entrepreneurial intention and positive perceptions of the surrounding environment.

Entrepreneurial intention, the primary variable of interest, was strongly positively correlated with both personality traits ($r = 0.631$, $p < 0.01$) and motivation ($r = 0.831$, $p < 0.01$), as well as showing a moderate correlation with the university environment ($r = 0.324$, $p < 0.01$). These results highlight the importance of personality traits, motivation, and perceived support from the university environment in fostering entrepreneurial intentions. The country's situation also displayed a small yet significant positive correlation with entrepreneurial intention ($r = 0.115$, $p < 0.05$), suggesting that a supportive socio-economic and institutional context plays a less pronounced role in encouraging entrepreneurial aspirations.

The correlational analysis reveals that motivational, environmental, and personality-related factors are key in shaping entrepreneurial intentions, particularly within emerging markets.

4.4 Regression Analysis

A multiple regression analysis was conducted to evaluate the extent to which motivation, personality traits, university environment, and country situation predict entrepreneurial intention. The results indicate that the model significantly explains a large proportion of the variance in entrepreneurial intention ($R^2 = 0.733$, adjusted

Table 4 Model summary

Model	*R*	R^2	Adjusted R^2	Std. error of the estimate
1	0.856	0.733	0.730	0.469

Table 5 ANOVA

Model		Sum of squares	*df*	Mean square	*F*	Sig.
1	Regression	232.115	4	0.58.029	263.818	<0.001
	Residual	84.684	385	0.220		
	Total	316.799				

Table 6 Coefficients and significance

Model	B	Std. error	Beta	*t*	Sig.
(Constant)	0.310	0.154		2.008	0.045
Motivation	0.694	0.032	0.700	21.533	<0.001
Personality traits	0.285	0.046	0.222	6.210	<0.001
University environment	−0.128	0.034	−0.109	−3.705	<0.001
Country situation	0.085	0.038	0.072	2.272	0.024

$R^2 = 0.730$), suggesting that 73.0% of the variation in entrepreneurial intention can be attributed to the combined influence of these predictors. The model was statistically significant, $F(4, 385) = 263.818$, $p < 0.001$, demonstrating that the independent variables reliably predict the dependent variable (Tables 4, 5, and 6).

The coefficients for the individual predictors reveal essential insights. Motivation was the most substantial predictor (B = 0.694, SE = 0.032, \beta = 0.700, $t = 21.533$, $p < 0.001$), indicating that higher motivation levels are strongly associated with greater entrepreneurial intention. Personality traits also significantly predicted entrepreneurial intention (B = 0.285, SE = 0.046, \beta = 0.222, $t = 6.210$, $p < 0.001$), suggesting that favorable personality characteristics positively influence entrepreneurial aspirations.

Unexpectedly, the university environment exhibited a significant but negative association with entrepreneurial intention (B = −0.128, SE = 0.034, $\beta = -0.109$, $t = -3.705$, $p < 0.001$). This counterintuitive finding suggests that more favorable perceptions of the university environment are linked to lower entrepreneurial intentions. It may indicate that individuals who perceive a strong institutional environment might feel more inclined to pursue traditional career paths rather than entrepreneurial ventures, warranting further investigation. The country's situation also had a small but statistically significant positive impact on entrepreneurial intention (B = 0.085, SE = 0.038, $\beta = 0.072$, $t = 2.272$, $p = 0.024$), highlighting the role of broader contextual factors in shaping entrepreneurial aspirations.

5 Discussion and Implications

This study contributes to understanding entrepreneurial intentions in emerging markets, particularly Cambodia. It finds that motivation and personality traits are the key predictors of entrepreneurial intentions, while the university environment shows a surprising negative correlation. This highlights the complex factors affecting how students in developing economies view entrepreneurship. A critical insight is that intrinsic motivations drive entrepreneurial intentions in Cambodia. Unlike more developed markets with structured support, Cambodian students depend more on personal drive and self-efficacy. This emphasizes the need to foster entrepreneurial mindsets at the individual level. The study notes that while a stable economy and supportive government initiatives can positively affect entrepreneurial intention, direct, personalized support is essential.

To enhance entrepreneurial motivation, policymakers should implement targeted initiatives, such as mentorship programs connecting students with local entrepreneurs, seed funding for promising business ideas, and regulatory reforms to ease startup creation. The Cambodian government should also improve its entrepreneurship education framework to promote entrepreneurial careers alongside traditional employment.

The negative relationship between the university environment and entrepreneurial intention suggests focusing on conventional career paths within academic structures. Many universities emphasize traditional jobs like accounting and law, leading students to view entrepreneurship as riskier. Limited hands-on training and a risk-averse culture further hinder entrepreneurial development. To address these issues, universities should incorporate experiential learning into entrepreneurship courses, fostering a supportive, risk-tolerant environment. Established business leaders can help build a robust entrepreneurial ecosystem by providing mentorship and advocating for policies that make entrepreneurship more accessible.

The unexpected negative correlation between university support and entrepreneurial intention requires a more profound analysis. Students may perceive a strong university focus on job security as discouraging entrepreneurship, and rigid academic structures may prioritize theoretical knowledge over practical experience. Additionally, a lack of entrepreneurial role models in academia may inhibit students from pursuing entrepreneurial paths. To address these challenges, universities should elevate entrepreneurship as a respected and viable career path, encourage faculty engagement with entrepreneurial ecosystems, and incorporate real-world insights into the classroom. This study sheds light on entrepreneurial intentions within Cambodia's emerging market context. The findings underscore the significant influence of motivation and personality traits while raising important questions about how the university environment contributes to cultivating entrepreneurship. Tackling these issues necessitates a comprehensive approach that involves policymakers, educators, and business leaders to foster a culture conducive to entrepreneurial aspirations.

6 Conclusion

This study investigated the factors influencing entrepreneurial intentions among university students in Cambodia, an emerging market context. The results highlighted the critical roles of motivation and personality traits in shaping entrepreneurial intentions. Motivation emerged as the most significant predictor, while personality traits also had a notable positive effect. Interestingly, the university environment showed a negative relationship with entrepreneurial intentions, suggesting that students who perceive a strong institutional support system may be more inclined toward traditional career paths than entrepreneurship. Conversely, the country's situation demonstrated a modest positive influence, indicating that favorable socio-economic conditions contribute to entrepreneurial aspirations.

Based on the findings of this study, several policy recommendations can be offered. For educators, integrating experiential learning opportunities, such as startup incubators or simulated business projects, within university curricula can better align institutional support with students' entrepreneurial aspirations, potentially mitigating the observed negative relationship between perceived strong institutional support and entrepreneurial intentions. For policymakers, developing targeted funding schemes for student entrepreneurs and efforts to reduce bureaucratic barriers to business registration and operation can create a more enabling environment for young ventures. Finally, for ecosystem builders, fostering stronger partnerships between universities and local industries can provide students with practical, real-world opportunities for venture development, mentorship, and networking, bridging the gap between academic learning and entrepreneurial practice.

Future research should address the study's limitations to provide a more comprehensive understanding of the factors shaping entrepreneurial intentions. A longitudinal study could track students' entrepreneurial journeys over time, providing insights into how intentions translate into actual ventures. Qualitative research, such as interviews and focus groups, could complement the quantitative findings by exploring the nuances of students' motivations and perceptions. Comparative studies across different emerging markets could identify cultural and institutional factors that moderate entrepreneurial intentions, enhancing the generalizability of the findings. Finally, future research could investigate the effectiveness of specific interventions, such as entrepreneurship boot camps, mentorship programs, or changes in university curricula, to improve entrepreneurial intention and ultimately drive entrepreneurial activity. These future directions will enrich the academic discourse and provide practical guidance for fostering a thriving entrepreneurial ecosystem in Cambodia and beyond.

References

Abu, M., Kazi, M., Yusof, M. F., Masud, A., Aminul Islam, M., Rahman, A., & Alamgir Hossain, M. (2024). Mediating role of entrepreneurial intention on the relationship between entrepreneurship education and employability: A study on university students from a developing country. *Cogent Business & Management, 11*(1). https://doi.org/10.1080/23311975.2023.2294514

Adam, A. M. (2020). Sample size determination in survey research. *Journal of Scientific Research and Reports, 26*(5), 90–97. https://doi.org/10.9734/jsrr/2020/v26i530263

Adeel, S., Daniel, A. D., & Botelho, A. (2023). The effect of entrepreneurship education on the determinants of entrepreneurial behaviour among higher education students: A multigroup analysis. *Journal of Innovation & Knowledge, 8*(1), 100324. https://doi.org/10.1016/j.jik.2023.100324

Ajzen, I. (1991). The theory of planned behavior. *Organizational Behavior and Human Decision Processes, 50*(2), 179–211. https://doi.org/10.1016/0749-5978(91)90020-T

Anjum, T., Amoozegar, A., Farrukh, M., & Heidler, P. (2022). Entrepreneurial intentions among business students: The mediating role of attitude and the moderating role of university support. *Education + Training, 65*(4). https://doi.org/10.1108/et-01-2021-0020

Arregle, J.-L., Batjargal, B., Hitt, M. A., Webb, J. W., Miller, T., & Tsui, A. S. (2013). Family ties in entrepreneurs' social networks and new venture growth. *Entrepreneurship Theory and Practice, 39*(2), 313–344. https://doi.org/10.1111/etap.12044

Bazkiaei, H. A., Heng, L. H., Khan, N. U., Saufi, R. B. A., & Kasim, R. S. R. (2020). Do entrepreneurial education and big-five personality traits predict entrepreneurial intention among universities students? *Cogent Business & Management, 7*(1). https://doi.org/10.1080/23311975.2020.1801217

Bodolica, V., & Spraggon, M. (2021). Incubating innovation in university settings: Building entrepreneurial mindsets in the future generation of innovative emerging market leaders. *Education + Training.*, ahead-of-print(ahead-of-print). https://doi.org/10.1108/et-06-2020-0145

Brüne, N., & Lutz, E. (2019). The effect of entrepreneurship education in schools on entrepreneurial outcomes: A systematic review. *Management Review Quarterly*. https://doi.org/10.1007/s11301-019-00168-3

Bui, D. T., Nghia Vu, T., Tran, T. V. H., Duong, C. D., & Loan Le, T. (2023). Impact of institutional environment on social entrepreneurial intentions. *Journal of Open Innovation: Technology, Market, and Complexity, 9*(3), 100120. https://doi.org/10.1016/j.joitmc.2023.100120

Cardella, G. M., Hernández-Sánchez, B. R., & Sánchez García, J. C. (2020). Entrepreneurship and family role: A systematic review of a growing research. *Frontiers in Psychology, 10*. https://doi.org/10.3389/fpsyg.2019.02939

Dana, L.-P., Tajpour, M., Salamzadeh, A., Hosseini, E., & Zolfaghari, M. (2021). The impact of entrepreneurial education on technology-based enterprises development: The mediating role of motivation. *Administrative Sciences, 11*(4), 105. https://doi.org/10.3390/admsci11040105

Fan, J., Hu, J., & Wang, J. (2024). How entrepreneurship education affects college students' entrepreneurial intention: Samples from China. *Heliyon*, e30776. https://doi.org/10.1016/j.heliyon.2024.e30776

Fauzi, R. U. (2021). The influence of business plan competition and loan provision on nurturing the spirit of entrepreneurship among students. Proceedings of the conference on international issues in business and economics research (CIIBER 2019). https://doi.org/10.2991/aebmr.k.210121.028.

Hajiali, I., Fara Kessi, A. M., Budiandriani, B., Prihatin, E., Sufri, M. M., & Sudirman, A. (2022). Determination of work motivation, leadership style, employee competence on job satisfaction and employee performance. Golden Ratio of. *Human Resource Management, 2*(1), 57–69. https://doi.org/10.52970/grhrm.v2i1.160

Hassan, A., Anwar, I., Saleem, I., Islam, K. M. B., & Hussain, S. A. (2021). Individual entrepreneurial orientation, entrepreneurship education and entrepreneurial intention: The mediating role of entrepreneurial motivations. *Industry and Higher Education, 35*(4), 403–418. https://doi.org/10.1177/09504222211007051

Huang, Z., & Huang, Z. (2024). Exploring entrepreneurial intention: The roles of proactive personality, education. *Opportunity and Planned Behavior. Heliyon, 10*(11), e31714. https://doi.org/10.1016/j.heliyon.2024.e31714

Ibrahim, I., & Adeniyi, A. (2024). Cultivating an entrepreneurial mindset to address unemployment through innovation, adaptability and interdisciplinary research. African Journal of Inter/Multidisciplinary. *Studies, 6*(1), 1–11. https://doi.org/10.51415/ajims.v6i1.1386

Karabulut, A. T. (2016). Personality traits on entrepreneurial intention. *Procedia: Social and Behavioral Sciences, 229*, 12–21. https://doi.org/10.1016/j.sbspro.2016.07.109

Komninos, D., Dermatis, Z., Anastasiou, A., & Papageorgiou, C. (2024). The role of entrepreneurship in changing the employment rate in the European Union. *Journal of the Knowledge Economy.* https://doi.org/10.1007/s13132-024-01841-z

Krejcie, R. V., & Morgan, D. W. (1970). Determining Sample Size for Research Activities. *Educational and Psychological Measurement, 30*(3), 607–610. https://doi.org/10.1177/001316447003000308

Krueger, N. F., Reilly, M. D., & Carsrud, A. L. (2000). Competing models of entrepreneurial intentions. *Journal of Business Venturing, 15*(5–6), 411–432.

Lee, S., Kang, M.-J., & Kim, B.-K. (2022). Factors influencing entrepreneurial intention: Focusing on individuals' knowledge exploration and exploitation activities. *Journal of Open Innovation: Technology, Market, and Complexity, 8*(3), 165. https://doi.org/10.3390/joitmc8030165

Li, L.-N., Huang, J.-H., & Gao, S.-Y. (2022). The relationship between personality traits and entrepreneurial intention among college students: The mediating role of creativity. *Frontiers in Psychology, 13*. https://doi.org/10.3389/fpsyg.2022.822206

Liguori, E. W. (2019). *Networks* (pp. 33–49). Emerald Publishing Limited EBooks. https://doi.org/10.1108/978-1-83867-871-520191003

Liñán, F., & Chen, Y.-W. (2009). Development and Cross-Cultural Application of a Specific Instrument to Measure Entrepreneurial Intentions. *Entrepreneurship Theory and Practice, 33*(3), 593–617. https://doi.org/10.1111/j.1540-6520.2009.00318.x

Maheshwari, G., Kha, K. L., & Arokiasamy, A. R. A. (2022). Factors affecting students' entrepreneurial intentions: A systematic review (2005–2022) for future directions in theory and practice. *Management Review Quarterly, 73*, 1903–1970. https://doi.org/10.1007/s11301-022-00289-2

Manzi-Puertas, M. A., Agirre-Aramburu, I., & López-Pérez, S. (2024). Navigating the student entrepreneurial journey: Dynamics and interplay of resourceful and innovative behavior. *Journal of Business Research, 174*, 114524. https://doi.org/10.1016/j.jbusres.2024.114524

Moindi Rose Meroka. (2023). Role of the family in fostering student's entrepreneurial intention. *IntechOpen EBooks.* https://doi.org/10.5772/intechopen.110026

Mohammad, S. S., Md Sharif Hassan, Md Aminul Islam, Farid Ahammad Sobhani, & Md Touhidul Islam. (2024). Entrepreneurial intention among university students of a developing economy: the mediating role of access to finance and entrepreneurship program. *Cogent Business & Management, 11*(1). https://doi.org/10.1080/23311975.2024.2322021

Neneh, B. N., & Dzomonda, O. (2024). Transitioning from entrepreneurial intention to actual behaviour: The role of commitment and locus of control. *The International Journal of Management Education, 22*(2), 100964. https://doi.org/10.1016/j.ijme.2024.100964

Osorio, A. E., Settles, A., & Shen, T. (2017). The influence of support factors on entrepreneurial attitudes and intentions of college students. *Academy of Management Proceedings, 2017*(1), 10901. https://doi.org/10.5465/ambpp.2017.10901abstract

Panakaje, N., Bhagwath, A. A., Riha Parvin, S. M., Madhura, K., & Kambali, U. (2024). Accelerating entrepreneurship: Evidence from the incubation centers of management institutes of Dakshina Kannada. *Heliyon, 10*(14), e34312. https://doi.org/10.1016/j.heliyon.2024.e34312

Park, J., Sung, C., & Im, I. (2017). Does social media use influence entrepreneurial opportunity? A review of its moderating role. *Sustainability, 9*(9), 1593. https://doi.org/10.3390/su9091593

Pocek, J., Politis, D., & Gabrielsson, J. (2021). Entrepreneurial learning in extra-curricular start-up programs for students. *International Journal of Entrepreneurial Behavior & Research.*, ahead-of-print(ahead-of-print). https://doi.org/10.1108/ijebr-04-2020-0206

Rodrigo, L., & Palacios, M. (2021). What antecedent attitudes motivate actors to commit to the ecosystem of digital social innovation? *Technological Forecasting and Social Change, 162*, 120394. https://doi.org/10.1016/j.techfore.2020.120394

Saeed, R., Mussawar, S., Lodhi, R. N., Iqbal, A., Nayab, H. H., & Yaseen, S. (2013). Factors affecting the performance of employees at work place in the banking sector of Pakistan. *Middle-East Journal of Scientific Research, 17*(9), 1200–1208.

Shahzad, M. F., Khan, K. I., Saleem, S., & Rashid, T. (2021). What factors affect the entrepreneurial intention to start-ups? The role of entrepreneurial skills, propensity to take risks, and innovativeness in open business models. *Journal of Open Innovation: Technology, Market, and Complexity, 7*(3), 173.

Soluk, J., Kammerlander, N., & Darwin, S. (2021). Digital entrepreneurship in developing countries: The role of institutional voids. *Technological Forecasting and Social Change, 170*, 120876. https://doi.org/10.1016/j.techfore.2021.120876

Sungkawati, E., Usmiyatun, U., & Karim, S. (2023). "Improving" food processing skills by creating new entrepreneurs. *Revenue Journal Management and Entrepreneurship, 1*(1), 10.61650/rjme.v1i1.273.

Tian, H., Akhtar, S., Qureshi, N. A., & Iqbal, S. (2022). Predictors of entrepreneurial intentions: The role of prior business experience, opportunity recognition, and entrepreneurial education. *Frontiers in Psychology, 13*. https://doi.org/10.3389/fpsyg.2022.882159

Tomlinson, M. (2017). Forms of graduate capital and their relationship to graduate employability. *Education and Training, 59*(4), 338–352. https://doi.org/10.1108/et-05-2016-0090

Uysal, Ş. K., Karadağ, H., Tuncer, B., & Şahin, F. (2021). Locus of control, need for achievement, and entrepreneurial intention: A moderated mediation model. *The International Journal of Management Education, 20*(2), 100560. https://doi.org/10.1016/j.ijme.2021.100560

Digital and Sustainable Trade Facilitation in ASEAN Countries

Weng Chi Lei, Katerina Toshevska-Trpchevska, and Viktor Stojkoski

Abstract The pandemic exposed weaknesses in the global trade system, making it clear that climate actions are the priority in the recovery. International organizations are urging countries to seize this opportunity and integrate climate-friendly trade and investment rules to promote sustainable development. Trade is recognized as a powerful tool for tackling climate change, offering economies ways to both reduce emissions and adapt to environmental changes. In this paper, we investigate the digital and sustainable trade facilitation measures implemented in ASEAN countries, namely Brunei, Cambodia, Indonesia, Laos, Malaysia, Myanmar, the Philippines, Singapore, Thailand, and Vietnam. We use a well-established trade model, the gravity model, to assess the impacts of trade facilitation efforts, particularly those that leverage digital technologies and promote sustainability. The data for this analysis comes from the UN Global Survey on digital and sustainable trade facilitation in 2017, 2019, and 2021. The results show that trade facilitation measures are crucial to increasing trade among the ASEAN countries. Measures of transparency of trade procedures, trade formality alleviation, and cross-border paperless trade have significant positive impacts on bilateral trade between ASEAN countries.

Keywords ASEAN · Digital and sustainable trade facilitation · Gravity model · Paperless trade · UN global survey on digital and sustainable trade facilitation

W. C. Lei (✉)
Faculty of Business and Law, University of Saint Joseph, Macao, China
e-mail: florence.lei@usj.edu.mo; http://www.usj.edu.mo

K. Toshevska-Trpchevska
Department of International Trade, Faculty of Economics, Ss. Cyril and Methodius University, Skopje, Republic of North Macedonia
e-mail: Katerina.Tosevska@eccf.ukim.edu.mk; http://www.ukim.edu.mk

V. Stojkoski
Department of Mathematics and Statistics, Faculty of Economics, Ss. Cyril and Methodius University, Skopje, Republic of North Macedonia
e-mail: vstojkoski@eccf.ukim.edu.mk; http://www.ukim.edu.mk

E. Lau et al. (eds.), *Economics and Finance Readings*,
https://doi.org/10.1007/978-981-96-6998-1_4

1 Introduction

The 12th Ministerial Conference of the World Trade Organization (WTO) held in 2022 called for member countries' actions against environmental challenges. The conference drew attention to the attribution of the world's multilateral trading system toward the United Nations (UN) 2030 Agenda and the Sustainable Development Goals (SDGs). The COP28 UN Climate Change Conference in 2023 proposed critical global climate actions that relied on the collaboration of governments and private sectors. Subsequently, the WTO (2023) published the "Trade Policy Tools for Climate Action," covering 10 policy measures that governments can adopt to facilitate climate-friendly cross-border flow of goods and services. Number one of the 10 policy areas is trade facilitation, which can improve the efficiency of customs clearance and reduce GHG emissions during the procedures. Examples are electronic documentation that reduces paper use, speeds up border crossing, and lowers the associated energy consumption. The WTO (2023) cited a reduction of 85% in GHG emissions at the Port of Nogales-Mariposa due to shorter vehicle queues and crossing times. It was also estimated that paperless, electronic invoicing could lower GHG emissions in Finland's trading processes by as much as 63% (WTO, 2023).

The progress of implementing environmental-friendly trade policy measures differs across countries and regions. The Framework Agreement on Facilitation of Cross-border Paperless Trade in Asia and the Pacific (CPTA) is a UN treaty that aims to expedite digital trade facilitation in Asia and the Pacific regions. The UN Economic and Social Commission for Asia and the Pacific (ESCAP) conducted a survey in 2023 to assess the implementation of digital and sustainable trade facilitation of the Association of Southeast Asian Nations (ASEAN), whose member states include Brunei, Cambodia, Indonesia, Laos, Malaysia, Myanmar, the Philippines, Singapore, Thailand, and Vietnam (UN, 2023a). The ESCAP found that in terms of the 40 general digital and sustainable trade facilitation measures, the average implementation rate across ASEAN member states increased from 79% in 2021 to 81% in 2023, which was remarkable growth after the Covid-19 pandemic. Specifically, ASEAN countries achieved an 81% implementation rate in "Paperless trade" and a 60% implementation rate in "Cross-border paperless trade" (UN, 2023a). The report further highlighted that full implementation of paperless and cross-border trade measures could reduce trade costs by more than 9% (UN, 2023a). This presents substantial potential and opportunities for ASEAN's improvement in the future.

Besides, the study of digital and sustainable trade in ASEAN is particularly relevant, given the region's dynamic economic landscape. ASEAN has a total GDP of US$3.8 trillion in 2024, and it is forecasted to become the world's fourth-largest economy by 2030; with total trade of US$3.5 trillion, it is ranked the third largest trading bloc (ASEAN, 2024). The digital economy of ASEAN is predicted to reach US$2 trillion in 2030, showing evidence of continuous digitalization and green transformation (ASEAN, 2024). However, as open economies that rely heavily on trade with the rest of the world, ASEAN faced both internal and external opportunities and challenges in the implementation of digital and sustainable trade policy measures. The creation of policies that align with global standards will reinforce ASEAN's competitive position in digital and sustainable economies in the coming decades. As will be identified in the literature review of this paper, there is a lack of empirical studies that focus on digital and sustainable trade facilitation among ASEAN countries. Therefore, we aim to investigate the status of digital and sustainable trade facilitation among ASEAN countries and how such measures improve trade flow and economic integration in the region. Filling this research gap will be a contribution to the literature. The academic contribution will be beyond the scope of this study. For example, in our previous study, Toshevska-Trpchevska et al. (2024), we applied the same methodology in studying the digital and sustainable trade facilitation among Western Balkans Countries. Having some of the fastest-growing digital and sustainable economies, ASEAN's experiences serve as an important lesson for other economic communities with similar pursuits.

To achieve the research objectives, this paper collects data on measures of digital and sustainable trade facilitation from the UN Global Survey on Digital and Sustainable Trade Facilitation and applies the standard gravity model to analyze international trade flows and their influencing factors. The added value of this research is the fact that it provides a more detailed analysis of the digital and sustainable component of trade facilitation in the region of the 10 ASEAN countries as very active participants in international trade from the whole Asia-Pacific region.

The structure of the paper is as follows. Following the introduction, we provide a review of the literature on trade facilitation in ASEAN, particularly on studies that used a gravity model as the analytical tool. Some recent literature that focused on digital and sustainable trade is also discussed. In the third section of the paper, we explain the model and the data used for the research. The fourth section provides a detailed analysis of the results of the regressions with a short discussion of them. In the last section, we provide a short conclusion together with some recommendations for future policy creators.

2 Literature Review

To investigate the state-of-the-art of the literature, we performed a search in Scopus, a widely used multidisciplinary database of peer-reviewed literature, including journal articles, book chapters, and conference papers. Another widely used source is the Web of Science, but a subscription is required for access. Table 1 shows the terms used in the title searches, the number of papers found, and the references of the recent studies. A total of 116 studies were identified. 25 studies researched trade facilitation in ASEAN countries, 54 applied the gravity model to analyze trade of ASEAN countries, 7 covered digital trade of ASEAN countries, and 30 focused on sustainable trade of the ASEAN countries. However, there are no studies that investigate digital or sustainable trade facilitation in ASEAN countries, nor do any of them predict digital or sustainable trade among ASEAN countries using a gravity model. These remain research gaps to be filled by the present study.

Table 1 Searches for literature

Search terms	Number of studies	References of studies between 2021 and 2025
"Trade facilitation" AND (*)	25	Fang (2021, 2023), Hien and Quang (2022), Hong (2022), Huong et al. (2023), Sun (2021), Nguyen (2021), Putranti (2024), Sarisae et al. (2023), Tan (2022), Wu (2022), and Zaman (2022)
"Digital" AND "trade" AND (*)	7	Burri (2022), Corning (2022), Detros (2023), Jones et al. (2024), Vu (2023)
"Sustainable" AND "trade" AND (*)	30	Chien (2023), Downs et al. (2022), Giuliani et al. (2021), Li et al. (2021), Limenta (2022), Ma (2024), Nahib et al. (2024), Nijman et al. (2024), Omeje (2024), Phompida and Yu (2022), Ramlee (2021), Ruan (2023), Santoso (2022), Sicurelli (2023), and Wang and Chen (2025)
"Gravity model" AND (*)	54	Abdullah et al. (2024), Dung (2024), Hasan et al. (2024), Herianingrum et al. (2024), Heriqbaldi et al. (2023), Hoan and Hung (2024), Huong et al. (2023), Ikasari et al. (2022), Khati (2023), Pan (2022), Minh (2024), Nguyen (2022), Pham et al. (2022), Pratiwi (2021), Quang (2024), Rangkakulnuwat and Weravess (2022), Taguchi (2021), Tang (2024), Thuong (2021), Utama et al. (2023), Wang (2025), Zainuddin et al. (2021), Zhang (2022), and Zhai (2023)
"Sustainable" AND "trade facilitation" AND (*)	0	
"Digital" AND "trade facilitation" AND (*)	0	
"Sustainable" AND "gravity model" AND (*)	0	
"Digital" AND "gravity model" AND (*)	0	

Note: (*) indicates ("ASEAN" OR "Brunei" OR "Cambodia" OR "Indonesia" OR "Lao" OR "Laos" OR "Malaysia" OR "Myanmar" OR "Burma" OR "Philippines" OR "Singapore" OR "Thailand" OR "Vietnam" OR "Viet Nam")

In the following sections, we focus on the 55 recent studies published between 2021 and 2025 in the four strands of literature found, of which the references are listed in Table 1.

2.1 *Trade Facilitation in ASEAN Countries*

Trade facilitation is crucial in reducing trade costs and improving the efficiency of cross-border transactions. Recent studies on trade facilitation of ASEAN countries found that the scope of trade facilitation varied across ASEAN countries and sectors. While logistics, infrastructure, and customs efficiency remained key determinants of trade, policy harmonization, technological advancements, and regional cooperation were also essential for optimizing trade facilitation.

Nguyen (2021) examined the effectiveness of trade facilitation measures in ASEAN, highlighting the variation in trade facilitation performance across member states. The study identified logistics-related costs as a significant factor affecting competitiveness and suggested harmonizing logistics policies to advance the ASEAN Economic Community. Zaman (2022) found a positive correlation between intra-ASEAN trade openness and poverty alleviation, with variations in income inequality impacts among member states. The research also revealed that institutional development, infrastructure, and technological readiness significantly contributed to trade efficiency. Putranti et al. (2024) explored the evolution of ASEAN's trade agreements, particularly the ASEAN Trade in Goods Agreement (ATIGA). The studies highlighted challenges such as environmental issues, food security, and human rights concerns, emphasizing the need for balanced trade policies that integrate oversight mechanisms with economic liberalization.

A few studies focused on individual ASEAN member countries. Hien and Quang (2022) and Huong et al. (2023) focused on Vietnam's trade facilitation efforts following its ratification of the WTO's Trade Facilitation Agreement (TFA). Hien and Quang (2022) found that small and medium-sized enterprises (SMEs) faced compliance obstacles. Huong et al.'s (2023) gravity model confirmed a positive impact of trade facilitation on Vietnam's imports and exports, especially after 2017. Sarisae et al. (2023) examined Thailand's automotive exports, revealing that infrastructure, tracking, and timeliness significantly impacted trade, while other logistics components showed limited influence. Tan (2022) assessed Cambodia's customs administration, identifying IT systems, risk management, and legislative barriers against trade facilitation at Sihanoukville International Port.

A number of studies examined the trade relations between ASEAN and China. Sun (2021) discussed the strengthening of China-ASEAN trade relations following the Belt and Road Initiative (BRI) and the establishment of an upgraded free trade area. The research employed a measurement model comprising four categories and 19 sub-indices to assess the trade facilitation level between China and ASEAN, underscoring its importance in economic and trade exchanges. Fang (2021) explored the role of international road transport in China-ASEAN trade growth, which saw an increase despite the COVID-19 pandemic. The study drew lessons from the European Union (EU) and recommended infrastructure improvements, transportation cooperation, and emergency response mechanisms to enhance regional trade efficiency. Wu et al. (2022) emphasized the role of China's Outward Foreign Direct Investment (OFDI) in ASEAN. The study employed a principal component analysis method to assess investment facilitation and found that Singapore led in providing a conducive investment environment. Infrastructure and logistics improvements were critical factors in attracting OFDIs.

Hong (2022) and Fan (2023) analyzed the impact of trade facilitation on China's agricultural exports to ASEAN. In particular, Hong (2022) attributed exports to growth in infrastructure efficiency, customs, and regulatory environments. On the other hand, Fan (2023) employed a gravity model to confirm that economic freedom, trade across borders, and infrastructure quality positively influenced agricultural trade.

2.2 *Digital Trade in ASEAN Countries*

Studies on digital trade in ASEAN countries emphasized the growing complexity of digital trade governance and the strategic adjustments made by regional actors. Despite their similar focuses, the studies provided different perspectives regarding the legal framework of digital trade in ASEAN countries.

According to Burri (2022), digital trade rulemaking had become a crucial aspect of free trade agreements, though approaches differed across states, leading to a fragmented data governance regime. Burri (2022) highlighted the legal and institutional aspects of digital trade rulemaking, contrasting US and EU approaches.

Corning (2022) emphasized the Digital Economy Partnership Agreement (DEPA) as a model for regional digital trade cooperation and examined how ASEAN countries, specifically Singapore, Vietnam, and Indonesia, navigated between US and Chinese regulatory models. Corning (2022) adopted a political economy lens to assess ASEAN members' strategic navigation of digital trade governance.

Jones et al. (2024) employed a legal coding methodology to track normative changes in trade agreements. Jones et al. (2024) identified Singapore as a key "norm entrepreneur" in digital trade, actively shaping rulemaking through agreements covering AI governance, e-invoicing, and e-payments. Jones et al. (2024) found that Singapore-led agreements expanded the scope of digital trade beyond traditional areas to include emerging technologies, reinforcing the notion of evolving digital trade norms.

Two studies focused on specific ASEAN member states. Detros (2023) highlighted the Philippines' readiness for digital economy collaborations, particularly with Singapore. Vu (2023) estimated the impact of digital trade facilitation on Vietnam's exports, concluding that improvements in information availability measures positively affected trade.

2.3 *Sustainable Trade in ASEAN Countries*

Studies that focused on sustainable trade of ASEAN countries, while different in methodologies and industries of focus, had similar interests in investigating environmental sustainability in the context of trade, economic growth, and policy implementation.

Chien et al. (2023) used an ARDL model to analyze eco-innovation's effects on sustainability. Ruan (2023) applied the Lotka-Volterra model to assess trade competition. Ma (2024) employed the MMQR technique to evaluate trade diversification and sustainability. Nahib et al. (2024) integrated TSD with the MGWR model to study watershed management. There were studies that focused on specific industries, including palm oil (Sicurelli 2023; Downs et al. 2022), aquatic products (Wang and Chen (2025), energy and natural resources (Phompida and Yu (2022) and Ma (2024)), illegal wildlife trade (Nijman et al. (2024), and eco-tourism (Ramlee (2021)).

Some studies highlighted environmental challenges and policy responses. Giuliani et al. (2021) focused on biodiversity and traditional knowledge protection. Nijman et al. (2024) investigated the failure of Indonesia to meet SDG targets concerning illegal wildlife trade. Sicurelli (2023) studied how EU sustainability criteria clashed with ASEAN palm oil regulations. Phompida and Yu (2022) identified trade risks in China's energy cooperation under the Belt and Road Initiative. Omeje (2024) emphasized governance, corruption, and political stability in ASEAN trade competitiveness.

Several studies focused on trade relationships and their economic impact. Limenta (2022) explored EU-ASEAN trade relations. Wang and Chen (2025) examined China-Vietnam aquatic trade. Santoso (2022) and Ruan (2023) analyzed broader ASEAN-China trade relations, highlighting competition and cooperation.

2.4 *Applications of the Gravity Model to Study Trade in ASEAN Countries*

The gravity model is widely employed in international trade studies to assess the impacts of economic size, distance, policy measures, and other structural constraints on trade flows. There were a relatively large number of studies that employed the gravity model to evaluate trade in ASEAN countries. These studies recognized the significance of economic size, infrastructure, trade policies, and regulatory measures in shaping trade and tourism flows. Some recent studies further assessed the adverse economic impacts of the Covid-19 pandemic and stressed the need for adaptive policies.

Thuong et al. (2021) examined how technical barriers to trade (TBT) affected Vietnam's tea exports from 2001 to 2019. The study found that GDP, population, distance, tariffs, and participation in the WTO significantly influenced Vietnam's tea exports. However, TBT measures imposed by importing countries had a negative impact, indicating that developed countries' stricter regulations significantly impeded Vietnam's tea trade.

Zainuddin et al. (2021) analyzed the effects of the Covid-19 pandemic on Malaysia's bilateral sectoral exports using the Poisson Pseudo Maximum Likelihood (PPML) method. Zainuddin et al. (2021) found that while some sectors experienced a decline in exports due to the pandemic, others saw an increase. The severity of Covid-19 in Malaysia negatively impacted numerous sectors, whereas severe outbreaks in trading partners positively influenced exports in some sectors. Zainuddin et al. (2021) concluded that Malaysia benefited from increased demand for imported goods in countries facing supply chain disruptions.

Ikasari et al. (2022) investigated the impact of Covid-19 on Indonesia's tourism sector using panel data analysis. The study found that the GDP per capita of the origin countries, the "Wonderful Indonesia" nation branding, and Indonesia's tourism development policies positively influenced tourist arrivals. However, Covid-19, distance, and relative prices negatively affected tourism. These results highlighted the importance of strategic marketing and international cooperation in mitigating tourism losses during crises.

Hasan et al. (2024) conducted a study on landslide-prone areas in Batu City, Indonesia, using gravity anomaly measurements from the GGMplus satellite. The results identified Trunojoyo Road as a high-risk landslide area due to its low rock density. Hasan et al. (2024) pointed to the need for local government intervention to implement effective landslide mitigation strategies, demonstrating the relevance of geophysical methods in urban planning and disaster management.

Pham et al. (2022) applied various gravity filtering techniques to delineate structural lineaments in the Southwest Sub-basin of the East Vietnam Sea. The findings confirmed the presence of recognized faults and provided new insights into the region's tectonic framework. The study underscored the effectiveness of modern gravity analysis techniques in geological mapping and resource exploration.

Nguyen (2022) employed the stochastic frontier gravity model to assess factors affecting Vietnam's rice and coffee exports. Nguyen (2022) revealed that "behind-the-border" constraints significantly lowered export potential. Nguyen (2022) recommended policy interventions to eliminate domestic trade barriers and enhance export efficiency.

Dung (2024) analyzed Vietnam's rice export performance from 2011 to 2021 using panel data regression. The results showed that global rice prices, the importing country's population, and participation in trade agreements positively impact export values. However, factors such as the importing country's GDP, self-sufficiency in food production, and Vietnam's inflation negatively affect rice exports. Maintaining stable domestic economic conditions was crucial for sustaining export growth.

Pratiwi (2021) examined Indonesia's palm oil export competitiveness using the Revealed Competitiveness Advantage (RCA) index and panel data regression. The study found that Indonesia had a strong comparative advantage in palm oil exports, particularly to China, the USA, India, the Netherlands, and Spain. Key determinants include economic distance, real GDP per capita of partner countries, free trade agreements (FTA), non-tariff measures (NTMs), and real exchange rates. Pratiwi (2021) suggested that Indonesia should strengthen trade diplomacy and bilateral cooperation to sustain its competitive edge.

Abdullah et al. (2024) investigated the relationship between freight transport services and international trade in Malaysia using three gravity model variations. The study found that economic scale and infrastructure significantly influenced Malaysia's freight transport, while distance had only a marginal effect. The volume of container handling at ports emerged as the most critical determinant of both export and import freight. The findings highlighted the need for Malaysia to invest in robust port infrastructure and logistical facilities to enhance its trade competitiveness.

3 Methodology

The study utilizes a gravity model to perform a quantitative analysis of the bilateral trade relationships among ASEAN countries, following the methodology used in Toshevska-Trpchevska et al. (2024). This model assumes that the trade volume between two countries is directly proportional to their economic sizes and inversely proportional to the geographical distance between them (Yotov, 2022). It has been expanded to include additional determinants, such as trade policies and historical factors like colonial ties, that either facilitate or hinder trade flows between countries (Yotov et al., 2016).

Here, we use the gravity model to investigate the impact of digital and sustainable trade facilitation measures on the trade relations between the ASEAN member countries. The dataset spans annual data for the years 2017, 2019, and 2021, as these are the years for which the UN Global Survey provides relevant data for the selected countries. The dataset covers bilateral trade between the countries across 21 Harmonized System Sections (sectoral definitions are available at the Observatory of Economic Complexity (OEC, 2024)), resulting in a total of 5670 observations. We employ a gravity model estimation within a panel data framework, originally proposed by Linder (1961) and Linnemann (1966), inspired by Newton's law of gravitation. The estimates are derived using the Ordinary Least Squares (OLS). The gravity model is specified as follows:

$$\ln EXPij_{ijp,t} = \beta_0 + \beta_1 \ln DISTANCE_{ij} + \beta_2 \ln GDP_{i,t} + \beta_3 \ln GDP_{j,t} + \\ + \beta_4 BORD_{ij} + \beta_5 LANG_{ij} + \beta_5 SMCTRY_{ij} + \beta_6 \left(TFX_{Xij} *\right) + \varepsilon_{ij,t}. \quad (1)$$

In Eq. (1), the dependent variable $ln\ EXPij_{ijp,\ t}$ is the natural logarithm of exports from country i to country j in product p in year t, expressed in USD, with export data sourced from the OEC (2024).

As independent variables, we include the geographical distance ($lnDISTANCE_{ij}$) between the largest cities of countries *i* and *j*, measured in kilometers sourced from Conte (2022). Economic size, measured by the GDP of the exporter and importer countries ($lnGDP_{i,t}$) and ($lnGDP_{j,t}$), is in PPP constant 2017 USD, with data taken from the World Development Indicators (World Bank, 2024). Additional binary variables account for common borders ($BORD_{ij}$), common official language ($LANG_{ij}$), and historical political unity ($SMCTRY_{ij}$), with data also sourced from CEPII's gravity dataset.

We also relate trade flows to the economic size of the exporter ($lnGDP_{i,t}$) and importer ($lnGDP_{j,t}$). We also add three binary variables accounting for a common border ($BORD_{ij}$), common official language ($LANG_{ij}$), and a variable indicating whether the exporter and importer were part of the same country in the past ($SMCTRY_{ij}$). These data were also taken from CEPII's gravity dataset.

Due to the high correlation among trade facilitation measures, separate regressions are run to determine the significance of each measure for trade. This approach is adopted to achieve more accurate and stable results (Wilson, 2010). Initially, a regression is conducted for the overall trade facilitation (TF) score of the countries, followed by five separate regressions for the categories of trade facilitation measures: transparency, formalities, institutional arrangements and cooperation, paperless trade, and cross-border paperless trade. Each regression estimates the linear relationship with the respective TFX_{Xij}measure. These measures are the natural logarithm of the product of the specific trade facilitation measures for both trading partners.

Data on trade facilitation measures is sourced from the UN Global Survey on Digital and Sustainable Trade Facilitation, available at untfsurvey.org. For the countries analyzed, the measures are available for the years 2017, 2019, and 2021 for the above-mentioned five categories of trade facilitation measures. The measures, originally in percentages, are rescaled to a 0–10 range for this model. The variable $TFX_{Xij}$is calculated as the natural logarithm of the product of specific TFX measures for both importer and exporter:

$$TFX_{Xij} = TFX_{Xj} * TFX_{Xi}. \tag{2}$$

By using this variable, the model aims to examine how changes in specific groups of trade facilitation measures jointly affect both exporters and importers in bilateral trade relationships.

Figure 1 provides a graphical explanation of the gravity model. The sizes of the bubbles are proportional to the sizes of the economies, measured by their GDP, of the ASEAN member countries in 2021. For example, Thailand's economy is larger than that of Cambodia, but the countries have relatively close distances to Singapore, and neither country shares a border, an official language, nor historical political unity with Singapore. Other things equal, the gravity model should predict Singapore's exports to Thailand to be larger than the exports to Cambodia. In addition to the standard gravity model, the present paper further incorporates various digital and sustainable trade facilitation measures in an attempt to assess the

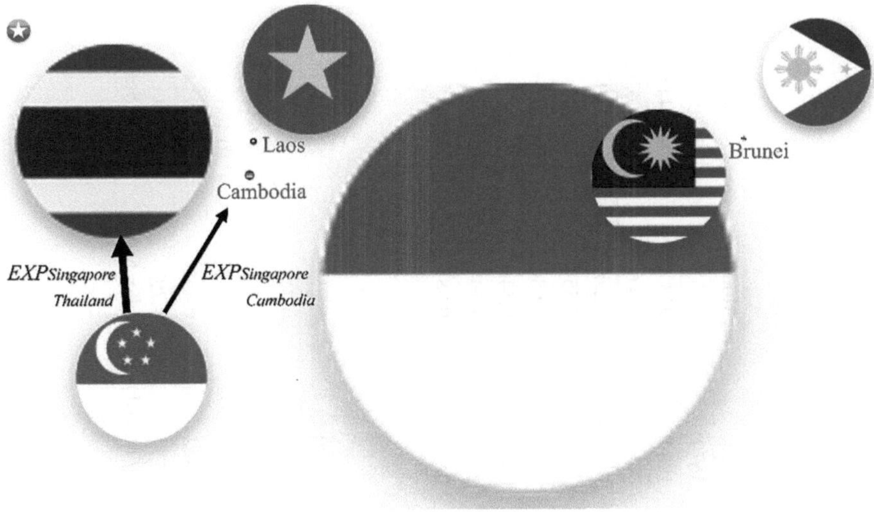

Fig. 1 The gravity model

possible impacts of such measures on the trade relationships between each pair of ASEAN member countries.

4 Results

For the purposes of our research, we have run seven regressions. There is strong multicollinearity among the data, and to avoid it, first, we run an "empty" regression with only the classical gravity model variables: GDP of the home country, GDP of the destination country, distance, and the three dummy variables. After that, in the second regression, we put all trade facilitation data or the so-called "TF score" of the countries to receive the overall importance of all 60 trade facilitation measures on trade. Then, from regression 3 until regression 7, we run separately each set of available trade facilitation measures combined, such as transparency, formalities, institutional arrangements and cooperation, paperless trade, and cross-border paperless trade. We want to check their influence on ASEAN countries' mutual trade.

Besides dealing with multicollinearity, running seven regressions enables us to check the robustness of the results and their stability. From the data provided in Table 2, it is visible that all "classical" gravity model variables: distance, GDP from the home country, GDP from the destination country, sharing a common border, sharing a common language, and previously being part of the same country are all stable, significant, and approximately with the same value in all regressions.

The results indicated that countries that are closer to each other tend to trade more easily, as opposed to countries which are more distant between themselves. For them, distance has a negative effect on their mutual trade. GDP, on the other

Table 2 Results of regression of ASEAN trade on UN trade facilitation and paperless trade, 2021

	Model 1	Model 2	Model 3	Model 4	Model 5	Model 6	Model 7
No of observations	5670	5670	5670	5670	5670	5670	5670
Constant	215.88**	698.161**	512.918**	540.78**	198.827*	273.48**	943.445**
	(78.788)	(114.046)	(90.081)	(93.582)	(89.578)	(94.656)	(145.626)
log(dist)	−2.460**	−2.238**	−2.252**	−2.344**	−2.473**	−2.437**	−2.149**
log(gdp_iso_o)	2.576**	2.453**	2.519**	2.487**	2.571**	2.554**	2.399**
log(gdp_iso_d)	1.706**	1.583**	1.649**	1.617**	1.700**	1.684**	1.529**
Border	0.521*	0.777**	0.750**	0.700**	0.496*	0.546*	0.801**
Language	1.248**	0.519†	0.639*	0.722**	1.290**	1.141**	0.668*
Same country	0.916**	1.163**	0.909**	1.020**	0.925**	0.981**	1.056**
log(TFScore)		**6.522****					
log(transparency)			**7.544****				
log(formalities)				**4.699****			
log(InstArrangements)					−0.315		
log(PaperlessTrade)						0.743	
log(CrossborderPaperless)							**7.688****
R^2	0.462	0.466	0.467	0.466	0.462	0.463	0.466
Adjusted R^2	0.462	0.465	0.466	0.466	0.462	0.462	0.465
Residual Std. Error	4.793 ($df = 5662$)	4.779 ($df = 5661$)	4.774 ($df = 5661$)	4.776 ($df = 5661$)	4.793 ($df = 5661$)	4.793 ($df = 5661$)	4.779 ($df = 5661$)

Source: Author's calculations. Note: $^{**}p < 0.01$, $^{*}p < 0.05$, and $^{\dagger}p < 0.1$

hand, has a positive effect on mutual trade among the ASEAN countries. Countries tend to trade more when their GDP is higher. When the GDP is higher in the home country, trade tends to increase even more than the GDP in the destination country. The results from the dummy variables are also significant and positive. They indicate that ASEAN countries that share a common border or a common language or have previously been part of the same country have a strong statistical and positive influence on increasing their mutual trade.

The result provided in the second regression shows that the overall influence of the Trade Facilitation Scores of these countries has a positive and significant statistical influence over trade. This result indicates that if there is a 1% improvement in the overall set of all 60 trade facilitation measures, a 6.52% increase in mutual trade among the ASEAN countries could happen. This coefficient shows that trade facilitation is a space where these countries could work more and should not be underestimated in the creation of future trade policies.

From the third to the seventh regression, we have presented the results of each of the five sets of digital and sustainable trade facilitation measures. Only three sets of trade facilitation measures are significant and can have a positive influence on increasing ASEAN's trade. Those are the measures that encompass the trade facilitation measures on improving transparency, alleviating formalities, and applying cross-border paperless measures. The trade facilitation measures that encompass the institutional arrangements and cooperation and paperless trade have resulted as insignificant for increasing ASEAN mutual trade.

We can see that the coefficients are high and significant, and that a 1% improvement in the application of trade facilitation measures that enable cross-border paperless trade could lead to a 7.69% increase in their mutual trade. A 1% improvement in the transparency of the trade procedures among the ASEAN countries could lead to a 7.54% increase in their trade. Also, it is worth mentioning that improving the formalities to trade for 1% could lead to an increase in the ASEAN mutual trade of approximately 4.7%.

The results that we have obtained indicate that digital and sustainable trade facilitation is important for improving trade in the ASEAN region. We have obtained results that show that out of all trade facilitation measures analyzed, cross-border paperless measures have the highest significance and could lead to the highest increase in trade. These measures are laws and regulations for electronic transactions, recognized certification authority, electronic exchange of customs declarations, electronic exchange of certificates of origin, electronic exchange of sanitary and phytosanitary certificates, and paperless collection of payment from a documentary letter of credit. After that, improving the transparency of the trading procedures and enhancing the formalities could also have a positive effect on improving and facilitating their mutual trade. These results should be considered in the creation of future trade policies as to measures which, if appropriately implemented, could lead to the highest increase in their trade.

Additional research and insight are needed to check for the insignificance of the measures that capture the influence of institutional arrangements and cooperation, especially the paperless trade measures, as they are mostly directed at enabling digital and sustainable trade facilitation. This can be considered a limitation to our study and a challenge for additional research in the future to investigate the reasons behind these results. In this context, for example, we could mention that for Singapore, all paperless trade measures have been fully implemented. Singapore has 100% of the set of measures for paperless trade. These measures are an automated customs system, internet connection available to Customs and other trade control agencies, electronic Single Window system, electronic submission of customs declarations, electronic submission of a sea cargo manifest, electronic submission of air cargo manifests, electronic application and issuance of import and export permits and preferential certificates of origin, e-payment of customs duties and fees, and electronic application for customs refunds (UN, 2023c). On the other hand, we have Lao with 62.96% of the implementation of paperless trade measures. Lao does not have any paperless trade facilitation measures fully implemented. Most of the paperless trade measures are partly implemented in Lao (UN, 2023b). What we want to point out is the fact that the big discrepancy in the implementation of paperless trade measures has probably led to the insignificance of the result that paperless trade measures are not statistically significant for their mutual trade increase. The same can be said for institutional arrangement and cooperation.

4.1 Robustness Checks: Trade in Six Product Groups

To check the sensitivity of the obtained results, we decided to run the gravity model by differentiating the products into six separate groups. We have used the 22 sections of the Harmonized System and then grouped them into the following six groups: group 1 consisted of animal products, vegetable products, animal and vegetable bi-products, and foodstuffs; group 2 consisted of mineral products, stone and glass, precious metals, and metals; group 3 of animal hides, wood products, paper goods, textiles, and footwear and headwear; group 4 consisted of machines, transportation, instruments, and weapons; group 5 of miscellaneous products, arts and antiques, and unspecified products; and group 6 of chemical products, plastics, and rubber. In order not to overload the paper, we will only present the main results and significance of the trade facilitation measures for each of the product groups that we have analyzed. However, the tables with regression results (seven regressions for each of the six product groups) can be made available on request.

The results for the products differentiated in group 1 show that the trade facilitation measures are important for increasing countries' mutual trade, and all separate sets of trade facilitation measures are positive and statistically significant with high coefficients, even above the value of 10. A 1% improvement of the cross-border paperless trade facilitation measures could lead to a 19.33% increase in the ASEAN mutual trade in animal products, vegetable products, animal and vegetable by-products, and foodstuffs. There is one exception: the coefficient for institutional arrangements and cooperation is significant but with a negative sign. This result was very often obtained in our previous analysis of digital and sustainable trade facilitation measures in the region of Western Balkan countries. This result should be further analyzed, possibly in future research.

For the products differentiated in group 2, the results from the gravity model have shown that all analyzed sets of trade facilitation measures are statistically significant with a positive sign, except for the coefficient showing the influence of institutional arrangements and cooperation, which is insignificant in this case. The results for group 3 are mostly insignificant for their mutual trade, with two exceptions. Improving transparency could lead to increased mutual trade of animal hides, wood products, paper goods, textiles, footwear and headwear, and paperless trade appears to be significant in this case but with a negative sign.

The results for group 4, containing machines, transportation, instruments, and weapons, provide mixed results from the gravity model regressions. The overall significance of trade facilitation measures is important for improving ASEAN's mutual trade, and from the specific sets of trade facilitation measures statistically significant and with positive signs are the measures for transparency and cross-border paperless measures. The other three sets of trade facilitation measures appear to be insignificant for improving trade in the products differentiated in group 4. The analysis of the importance of digital and sustainable trade facilitation measures for the products in group 5, miscellaneous products, arts and antiques, and unspecified products, is approximately the same as the situation with the products in group 4. The coefficient measuring the overall importance of all trade facilitation measures is significant and positive, and so are the coefficients of the two sets of measures covering transparency of the trading procedures and cross-border paperless trade facilitation measures. The other three coefficients measuring the influence of the other sets of trade facilitation measures are insignificant.

The results for group 6—chemical products, plastics, and rubber—indicate that increasing ASEAN trade in these products has a positive and significant influence on the trade facilitation measures connected to transparency, formalities, and cross-border paperless trade facilitation measures.

As a summary of results from the gravity model regressions that we have run through all products differentiated into six groups, we can say that overall, the results confirm the results presented in Table 2, where we analyzed all products. This resemblance of the results from the regressions serves as a check of the sensitivity of the results and confirms their robustness. Additionally, from the results of the differentiated groups of products, we could observe that the highest importance of trade facilitation measures with the highest positive, coefficients was acknowledged in the regressions of the first group of products, consisting of animal products vegetable products, animal and vegetable by-products, and foodstuffs. This means that for these products, the application of trade facilitation measures could have the highest influence on improving their mutual trade among the ASEAN countries. Also, what is visible from these differentiated results is the fact that in almost all situations, the importance of trade facilitation measures is significant, and among the separate sets of trade facilitation measures, in almost every group, two sets of trade facilitation measures are statistically significant with positive signs. Those are the measures covering transparency of the trading procedures and cross-border paperless measures.

5 Conclusion

The purpose of our research was to analyze the importance of digital and sustainable trade facilitation measures in the context of improving and facilitating trade among the ASEAN countries as a regional group. Many recent studies done for the Asia-Pacific region, and especially by the UN regional commission, have shown that there is considerable improvement in the application of trade facilitation measures in the Southeast Asian region. Nevertheless, our research provides additional value to the research and practice as it specifically tests the newest results from the UN Global survey on digital and sustainable trade facilitation of the ten ASEAN countries in the region of Southeast Asia.

The results from the research have shown that, in general, trade facilitation measures could have a positive influence on increasing ASEAN mutual trade. An approximately 6.5% increase in the ASEAN mutual trade could happen if there is a 1% improvement in all trade facilitation measures analyzed. This is a considerable increase in trade that could happen through the improvement of trade facilitation measures applied by these countries. An especially positive effect could be expected with the improvement of cross-border paperless trade measures, measures that improve the transparency of the trading procedures, and measures that enhance the trading formalities. A 7.69% increase in ASEAN's mutual trade could happen if a 1% improvement of the cross-border paperless measures happens, a 7.54% increase in trade if there is a 1% improvement in the transparency of the trading procedures, and a 4.7% increase in trade if there is an enhancement of the formalities in trade. Besides obtaining these high coefficients for the importance of the specific digital and sustainable trade facilitation measures to improve countries' mutual trade, we think that these results should be considered in the future creation of trade policies of these countries and especially for knowing which measures deserve priority. This means that policy creators in the ASEAN countries should pay more attention to improving cross-border paperless trade procedures, increasing transparency, and enhancing trade formalities.

5.1 Limitations and Recommendations for Future Research

Although the results of the research and the robustness checks that we have done in the analysis confirm the importance of applying digital and sustainable trade facilitation measures in the region of ASEAN and provide us with insights on the level of importance and priority that each set of trade facilitation measures should deserve, we are completely aware of the few limitations that this research has.

One limitation is the lack of ASEAN member country-specific analysis. Each ASEAN member country has unique characteristics in sizes of economies, levels of economic development, and levels of implementation of each trade facilitation measure. The cross-sectional analysis takes averages over the 10 ASEAN member countries, allowing insights to be given to all of ASEAN as a whole. With panel data of longer time periods, future research can explore the differences and similarities across ASEAN member countries.

Another limitation of our study is the insufficiency of measures that capture the influences of institutional arrangements and cooperation, especially the paperless trade measures, which are mostly directed at enabling digital and sustainable trade facilitation. Future research can delve into the specifics of these two sets of digital and sustainable trade facilitation measures and their impact on trade among the ASEAN countries.

Acknowledgments Supported by the Education Fund of the Macao Special Administrative Region.

References

Abdullah, A., Zamzuri, Z. H., & Miswan, N. H. (2024). An application of gravity models to freight data in Malaysia. *Journal of Transport and Supply Chain Management, 18*, 1–11.

Association of Southeast Asian Nations (ASEAN). (2024). *Annual Report 2024—ASEAN: Enhancing Connectivity and Resilience*. https://asean.org/wp-content/uploads/2024/12/ASEAN-AR-2024_e-pub_web.pdf.

Burri, M. (2022). Approaches to digital trade and data flow regulation across jurisdictions: Implications for the future ASEAN-EU agreement. *Legal Issues of Economic Integration, 49*(2), 149–168., ISSN 1566-6573. https://doi.org/10.54648/LEIE2022007

Chien, F. S. (2023). The impact of eco-innovation, trade openness, financial development, green energy and government governance on sustainable development in ASEAN countries. *Renewable Energy, 211*, 259–268., ISSN 0960-1481. https://doi.org/10.1016/j.renene.2023.04.109

Chien, F., Paramaiah, C., Pham, H. C., Phan, T. T. H., & Ngo, T. Q. (2023). The impact of eco-innovation, trade openness, financial development, green energy and government governance on sustainable development in ASEAN countries. *Renewable Energy, 211*, 259–268.

Conte, M., Cotterlaz, P. & Mayer T. (2022, July). *The CEPII gravity database* (working paper no. 2022-05). https://www.cepii.fr/CEPII/en/bdd_modele/bdd_modele_item.asp?id=8.

Corning, G. P. (2022). ASEAN and the regime complex for digital trade in the Asia-Pacific. *Journal of World Trade, 56*(6), 915–938., ISSN 1011-6702. https://doi.org/10.54648/trad2022038

Detros, K. (2023). Philippines: Digital payments, identification, and paperless trade pose challenges. In P. Cheung & X. Taojun (Eds.), *The ASEAN digital economy: Towards an integrated regional framework* (pp. 97–113). Routledge https://doi.org/10.4324/9781003308751-6

Downs, S. M., Nicholas, K., Linn, K. K., & Fanzo, J. (2022). Examining the trade-offs of palm oil production and consumption from a sustainable diets perspective: Lessons learned from Myanmar. *Public Health Nutrition, 25*(4), 964–976.

Dung, L. C. (2024). Vietnam rice value: Gravity model for transitional export period 2011–2021. *International Journal on Food System Dynamics, 15*(4), 388–396, ISSN 1869-6945. https://doi.org/10.18461/ijfsd.v15i4.L4

Fan, H. (2023). The influence of trade facilitation on agricultural product exports of China: Empirical evidence from ASEAN countries. *Economic Research-Ekonomska Istrazivanja, 36*(2) ISSN 1331-677X. https://doi.org/10.1080/1331677X.2022.2143845

Fang, T. (2021). Analysis on promoting the belt and road international road transport for economic cooperation and trade facilitation in China-ASEAN area. Proceedings—2021 international conference on public management and intelligent society, PMIS 2021, (pp. 17–21). https://doi.org/10.1109/PMIS52742.2021.00011.

Giuliani, A., Undurraga, J. T., Dunkel, T., & Aung, S. M. (2021). Access and benefit sharing and the sustainable trade of biodiversity in Myanmar: The case of Thanakha. *Sustainability, 13*(22), 12372.

Hasan, M. F. R., Susilo, A., Suryo, E. A., Agung, P. A. M., Idmi, M. H., Suaidi, D. A., & Aprilia, F. (2024). Mapping of landslide potential in Payung, Batu City, Indonesia, using global gravity model plus (GGMplus) data as landslide mitigation. *The Iraqi Geological Journal*, 159–168.

Herianingrum, S., Alan Nur, M., Rusgianto, S., Hapsari, M. I., Huseyin, E., Firmansyah, F., & Febriyanti, A. R. (2024). Gravity model of trade approach: What drives Indonesia's seafood export and its halal market potency in OIC (Organization of Islamic Cooperation) countries. *Journal of Islamic Marketing, 15*(8), 2016–2035.

Heriqbaldi, U., Esquivias, M. A., & Agusti, K. S. (2023). The role of cultural distance in boosting international tourism arrivals in ASEAN: A gravity model. *Consumer Behavior in Tourism and Hospitality, 18*(1), 97–109.

Hien, P. T. T., & Quang, B. T. (2022). Enhancing trade compliance to benefit small and medium-sized enterprises (SMEs) in Trade Facilitation Agreement (TFA) implementation in Vietnam. *World Customs Journal, 16*(1), 49–60.

Hoan, P. T., & Hung, P. X. (2024). Determinants of Vietnam's textile exports: An analysis by gravity model. *Journal of Economic Cooperation & Development, 45*(2), 41–64.

Hong, P. (2022). Influence of trade facilitation level on China s agricultural exports: Based on empirical evidence from 10 ASEAN importing countries. *Journal of Chinese Agricultural Mechanization, 43*(2), 188–195., ISSN 2095-5553. https://doi.org/10.13733/j.jcam.issn.2095-5553.2022.02.026

Huong, T. T. T., Tuan, N. T., & Le, H. (2023). The impacts of trade facilitation on Vietnam's imports and exports: Evidence from a gravity model. *The Journal of Social, Political, and Economic Studies, 47*(3/4), 269–307.

Ikasari, H., Sugiyanto, F. X., & Kurnia, A. S. (2022). Model of International tourism demand in Indonesia during the Covid-19: Gravity model approach. *E-review of Tourism Research, 19*(2), 237–260.

Jones, E., Kira, B., & Tavengerwei, R. (2024). Norm entrepreneurship in digital trade: The Singapore-led wave of digital trade agreements. *World Trade Review, 23*(2), 208–241.

Khati, P. (2023). Impact of India's free trade agreement with ASEAN on its goods exports: A gravity model analysis. *Economies, 11*(1) ISSN 2227-7099. https://doi.org/10.3390/economies11010008

Li, P., Agusdinata, D. B., Suditha, P. H., & Zhang, Y. (2021). Ecosystem services and trade-offs: Implications for land dynamics and sustainable livelihoods in Northern Lombok, Indonesia. *Environment, Development and Sustainability, 23*, 4321–4341.

Limenta, M. (2022). Toward an ASEAN-EU FTA: Examining the trade and sustainable development chapter in the prospective Indonesia-EU CEPA. *Legal Issues of Economic Integration, 49*(2), 191–216., ISSN 1566-6573. https://doi.org/10.54648/LEIE2022009

Linder, S. B. (1961). *Essay on trade and transformation*. John Wiley & Sons.

Linnemann, H. (1966). *An econometric study of international trade flows*. Holland Publishing.

Ma, X. (2024). Sustainable development in ASEAN: The role of trade diversification, government revenue, and natural resources. *Natural Resources Forum*, ISSN 0165-0203. https://doi.org/10.1111/1477-8947.12526

Minh, P. L. E. N. (2024). Is Vietnam's tourism demand model compatible with the extended gravity model? *Geojournal of Tourism and Geosites, 54*, 784–793, ISSN 2065-0817. https://doi.org/10.30892/gtg.542spl02-1253

Nahib, I., Widiatmaka, W., Tarigan, S., Ambarwulan, W., & Ramadhani, F. (2024). Exploring ecosystem service trade-offs and synergies for sustainable urban watershed management in Indonesia – a case study of the Citarum River Basin, West Java, Indonesia. *Ecological Engineering & Environmental Technology (EEET), 25*(12), 315.

Nguyen, A. T. (2021). Trade facilitation performance influences on ASEAN trade flows. *Economic Horizons, 23*(3), 263–275., ISSN 1450-863X. https://doi.org/10.5937/ekonhor2103275N

Nguyen, D. D. (2022). Determinants of Vietnam's rice and coffee exports: Using stochastic frontier gravity model. *Journal of Asian Business and Economic Studies, 29*(1), 19–34, ISSN 2515-964X. https://doi.org/10.1108/JABES-05-2020-0054

Nijman, V., Abdullah, A., Adinda, E., Ardiansyah, A., Campera, M., Chavez, J., et al. (2024). Indonesia's sustainable development goals in relation to curbing and monitoring the illegal wildlife trade. *Sustainable Development, 32*(5), 5393–5403.

Observatory of Economic Complexity. (2024). Harmonized system (HS) products. https://oec.world/en/product-landing/hs.

Omeje, A. N. (2024). Institutional quality and trade competitiveness in ASEAN region: Implication for inclusive and sustainable development. *Journal of Asian and African Studies*, ISSN 0021-9096. https://doi.org/10.1177/00219096241303938

Pan, H. I. (2022). An analysis of determinants of foreign direct Investment in Banking Industry from Taiwan to ASEAN countries with gravity model. *Asia-Pacific Financial Markets, 29*(4), 631–649., ISSN 1387-2834. https://doi.org/10.1007/s10690-022-09363-x

Pham, L. T., Oliveira, S. P., Le, M. H., Trinh, P. T., Vu, T. V., Duong, V. H., et al. (2022). Delineation of structural lineaments of the Southwest Sub-basin (East Vietnam Sea) using global marine gravity model from CryoSat-2 and Jason-1 satellites. *Geocarto International, 37*(25), 7681–7698.

Phompida, S., & Yu, D. (2022). China-Laos economic and trade cooperation and construction of sustainable energy cargo channel under the background of "One Belt, One Road". *Scientific Programming, 2022*(1), 9048584.

Pratiwi, I. E. (2021). The predictors of indonesia's palm oil export competitiveness: A gravity model approach. *Journal of International Studies, 14*(3), 250–262, ISSN 2071-8330. https://doi.org/10.14254/2071-8330.2021/14-3/16

Putranti, I. R. (2024). Assessing inclusivity vs. Exclusivity: Impacts on Asean trade facilitation and human security. *Indonesian Journal of International Law, 22*(1), 27–60., ISSN 1693-5594. https://doi.org/10.17304/ijil.vol22.1.1898

Putranti, I. R., Warsono, H., Paganizza, V., Hadi, D., & Alfian, M. (2024). Assessing inclusivity vs. exclusivity: Impacts on ASEAN trade facilitation and human security. *Indonesian Journal of International Law, 22*(1), 27–60, ISSN 1693-5594. https://doi.org/10.17304/ijil.vol22.1.1898

Quang, P. T. (2024). Investigating the determinants of macroeconomic factors on outward FDI of Vietnam: The gravity model approach. *Revista de Gestao Social e Ambiental, 18*(8), e06134. ISSN 1981-982X. https://doi.org/10.24857/rgsa.v18n8-079

Ramlee, M. N. A. (2021). Redefine green economy and sustainable development: A trade-off analysis approach on Tasik Kenyir, Terengganu, Malaysia. In M. T. Abdullah, C. V. Bartholomew, & A. Mohammad (Eds.), *Resource use and sustainability of Orang Asli: Indigenous communities in Peninsular Malaysia* (pp. 225–235). Springer. https://doi.org/10.1007/978-3-030-64961-6_15

Rangkakulnuwat, P., & Weravess, R. (2022). The gravity model for rice exports: The cases of India and Thailand. *Economics Bulletin, 42*(3), 1432–1473.

Ruan, W. X. (2023). Exploration of China–ASEAN trade relations in the context of sustainable economic development—based on the Lotka–Volterra model. *Sustainability (Switzerland), 15*(1), 517. ISSN 2071-1050. https://doi.org/10.3390/su15010517

Santoso, Y. N. (2022). Achieving sustainable development goals by 2030: Reducing the gap of inequality through ASEAN-China trade relations. *Digital Economy and the Sustainable Development of ASEAN and China*, 69–83. https://doi.org/10.1142/9789811257896_0004

Sarisae, S., Ariffin, M. I., & Alavi, R. (2023). The impact of trade facilitation on automotive export performance of Thailand. *International Journal of Economic Policy in Emerging Economies, 17*(4), 505–523.

Sicurelli, D. (2023). Conflicting standards of sustainable biofuel in the EU- ASEAN trade negotiations. *Standardizing the World: EU Trade Policy and the Road to Convergence*, 195–215. https://doi.org/10.1093/oso/9780197681886.003.0009

Sun, L. (2021). Measurement Analysis of Trade Facilitation in China-ASEAN Free Trade Area. *E3S Web of Conferences, 251*, ISSN 2555-0403, https://doi.org/10.1051/e3sconf/202125101023.

Taguchi, H. (2021). Quantitative linkage between global value chains' backward participation and logistics performance in the host country: A structural gravity model analysis of emerging ASEAN economies. *Asia-Pacific Journal of Regional Science, 5*(2), 453–475., ISSN 2509-7954. https://doi.org/10.1007/s41685-020-00187-z

Tan, A. (2022). Strengthening customs control and trade facilitation: A case study of Sihanoukville International Port, Cambodia. *World Customs Journal, 16*(2), 99–114.

Tang, C. (2024). The comparison of bilateral trade between China and ASEAN, China and EU: From the aspect of trade structure, trade complementarity and structural gravity model of trade. *Applied Economics, 56*(9), 1077–1089. ISSN 0003-6846,. https://doi.org/10.1080/00036846.2023.2174940

Thuong, N. T. T. (2021). Do technical barriers to trade measures affect Vietnam's tea exports? Evidence from the gravity model. International. *Journal on Food System Dynamics, 12*(2), 164–176, ISSN 1869-6945. https://doi.org/10.18461/ijfsd.v12i2.82.

Thuong, N. T. T., Thinh, D. T. H., Long, N. T., & Linh, D. H. (2021). Do technical barriers to trade measures affect Vietnam's Tea Exports? Evidence from the gravity model. *International Journal on Food System Dynamics, 12*(2), 164–176.

Toshevska-Trpchevska, K., Lei, W. C. F., & Stojkoski, V. (2024). Digital and sustainable trade facilitation in Western Balkans countries. *European Scientific Journal, ESJ, 20*(13), 46.

United Nations. (2023a). Digital and sustainable trade facilitation in the Association of Southeast Asian Nations (ASEAN) 2023. https://repository.unescap.org/rest/bitstreams/72c73135-23c8-4b85-9b12-2c19cc6e98ed/retrieve.

United Nations. (2023b). Trade facilitation and paperless trade in LAO P.D.R. https://www.untfsurvey.org/economy?id=LAO.

United Nations. (2023c). Trade facilitation and paperless trade in Singapore. https://www.untfsurvey.org/economy?id=SGP.

Utama, W., Putra, D. P. N., Garini, S. A., & Indriani, R. F. (2023). Optimizing surface lithology interpretation from global gravity model and landsat 8 satellite imagery in Semeru Mountain, Indonesia. *IOP Conference Series: Earth and Environmental Science, 1276*(1), 012048. IOP Publishing.

Vu, T. H. (2023). An Empirial study on Vietnam's trade facilitation in the digital economy. *Journal of Global Business and Trade, 19*(2), 97–117, ISSN 1946-5130. https://doi.org/10.20294/jgbt.2023.19.2.97

Wang, L. (2025). The impact of trade liberalization on China–ASEAN trade relations along the belt and road: An augmented gravity model analysis. *Finance Research Letters*, 71., ISSN 1544-6123. https://doi.org/10.1016/j.frl.2024.106418

Wang, L., & Chen, K. (2025). The impact of trade liberalization on China–ASEAN trade relations along the belt and road: An augmented gravity model analysis. *Finance Research Letters, 71*, 106418.

Wilson, N. (2010). Examining the effect of certain customs and administrative procedures on trade. In *OECD trade policy studies, overcoming border bottlenecks: The costs and benefits of trade facilitation*. OECD Publishing.

World Bank. (2024). GDP per capita, PPP (constant 2021 international $). https://data.worldbank.org/indicator/NY.GDP.PCAP.PP.KD.

World Trade Organization. (2023). Policy tool #1 Trade facilitation. https://www.wto.org/english/res_e/booksp_e/tptfca_05_01_trade_facilitation_e.pdf.

Wu, J. (2022). An assessment of trade facilitation impacts on China's outward foreign direct investment to ASEAN countries. *Business, Industry, and Trade in the Tropics*, 97–113. https://doi.org/10.4324/9781003153580-6

Wu, J., Wood, J., & Jang, H. (2022). An assessment of trade facilitation impacts on China's outward foreign direct investment to ASEAN countries. In J. Wood, T. Chaiechi, & K. Thirumaran (Eds.), *Business, Industry, and Trade in the Tropics* (pp. 97–113). Routledge.

Yotov, Y. V. (2022). On the role of domestic trade flows for estimating the gravity model of trade. *Contemporary Economic Policy, 40*(3), 526–540.

Yotov, Y. V., Piermartini, R., & Larch, M. (2016). An advanced guide to trade policy analysis: The structural gravity model. *WTO iLibrary*.

Zainuddin, M. R. K. V., Shukor, M. S., Zulkifli, M. S., & Abdullah, A. H. (2021). Dynamics of Malaysia's bilateral export post Covid-19: A gravity model analysis. *Jurnal Ekonomi Malaysia, 55*(1), 51–69.

Zaman, K. A. U. (2022). SDGs' indicators for trade facilitation and the regional comprehensive economic partnership (RCEP) in ASEAN. *Sustainable Development Goals and Pandemic Planning: Role of Efficiency Based Regional Approaches*, 505–541. https://doi.org/10.1007/978-981-16-6734-3_12

Zhai, H. (2023). Evaluation of China-ASEAN trade status and trade potential: An empirical study based on a gravity model. *PLoS One, 18*(9) ISSN 1932-6203. https://doi.org/10.1371/journal.pone.0290897

Zhang, W. (2022). A gravity model analysis of China's trade in renewable energy goods with ASEAN countries as well as Japan and South Korea. *Frontiers in Environmental Science, 10.*, ISSN 2296-665X. https://doi.org/10.3389/fenvs.2022.953005

Does Human Capital Reduce Poverty in Indonesia? Evidence from System-GMM District Dynamic Panel Data

B. S. Nazamuddin, Putri Bintusy Syathi, Riswandi Riswandi, Fitriyani Fitriyani, and Asri Diana

Abstract The varying rates of human capital development across regions present a significant challenge for Indonesia. This study examines the role of education and health in reducing poverty in Indonesia. Utilizing data from 417 districts between 2019 and 2023, we employed the system-GMM approach. Our findings indicate that the contemporaneous effect of the logarithm of the human capital index is negative, suggesting that greater human capital accumulation results in lower poverty within the same period; however, this effect is not long-lasting unless education and health explanatory variables are considered separately. The impacts of both the logarithms of years of schooling and life expectancy are significant, although their directions differ. This implies that the quality of educational services has not kept pace with the increased accessibility to education. Therefore, priority should be given to improving the quality of education in disadvantaged areas.

Keywords Human capital · Regional disparities · Poverty · System-GMM · Indonesia

1 Introduction

Indonesia's poverty rate dropped significantly from 17.47% in 1996 to 9.03% in 2024. However, there is a variation in the rate of decline across districts, significantly influenced by factors such as economic development (BPS, 2023a), access to quality education and health services (BPS, 2024; Nugroho et al., 2021), and infrastructure development. Economic opportunities greatly vary between regions due to disparities in human capital development, particularly in education and health.

B. S. Nazamuddin (✉) · P. B. Syathi · R. Riswandi · F. Fitriyani · A. Diana
Department of Development Economics, Faculty of Economics and Business, Banda Aceh, Aceh, Indonesia
e-mail: nazamuddin@usk.ac.id; putri_syathi@usk.ac.id; riswandi@usk.ac.id; fitriyani@usk.ac.id; asridiana@usk.ac.id

E. Lau et al. (eds.), *Economics and Finance Readings*,
https://doi.org/10.1007/978-981-96-6998-1_5

Java's population aged 15 and above has higher average years of education and longer life expectancy than those in the outer islands. While the national poverty rate decreases, economic disparities persist. There remains a remarkable disparity in infrastructure across Indonesia's municipalities and districts (Adriana & Suparyati, 2023; Wiratama et al., 2023). In Java island's provinces, which account for 57% of Indonesia's 2023 GDP (BPS, 2024), poverty rates are comparatively lower than in eastern Indonesian provinces (BPS, 2023a). Greater efforts are needed to improve human capital and achieve a more equitable distribution of economic opportunities. Enhancing human capital requires investment in both education and health. Indonesia's major obstacles to enhancing human capital include subpar education quality (Bilad et al., 2024) and childhood stunting under age 2 (Supadmi et al., 2024). However, studies on the human capital-poverty relationship in Indonesia are scarce and limited to cross-sectional data analysis (Tantriana, 2024) and error correction approach using panel data on underdeveloped districts of Indonesia (Wau, 2022). Moreover, most studies on Indonesia have focused on the relationship between human capital and economic growth (Simatupang et al., 2024; Suparman & Muzakir, 2023), human development index and poverty (Arwani et al., 2023; Diniati & Permana, 2024; Sayyidina et al., 2023), knowledge and poverty (Nizar et al., 2024), life expectancy and schooling (Setyadi et al., 2023), whereas dynamic analyses are scant due to data availability limitation. Consequently, previous studies have only used cross-sectional data to estimate the relationship using a simple regression (Dahliah, 2023) and calculated human capital indices and provided a descriptive analysis of the spatial disparities in the human capital across Indonesian provinces and districts (Sari & Tiwari, 2024). Those studies were limited by data availability to analyze the dynamics of the relationship. Moreover, the country-specific and cross-country evidence of the causality relationship between education and health and economic growth has been shown by extensive recent studies (Bos et al., 2024; Dhrifi et al., 2021; Kustanto, 2021; Liu et al., 2023; Spada et al., 2023). However, the bulk of the recent literature is based on cross-country and country-scale data. While studies that consider region-specific heterogeneity are lacking, this study provides a unique contribution to the body of existing literature by using subnational panel data to investigate the relationship between human capital and poverty in Indonesia.

Previous studies on poverty in Indonesia using subnational panel data have examined economic growth and public investment (Wau, 2022), inequality (Rohmatilah, 2023), fiscal efficiency (Tirtosuharto, 2022), and crime rates (Sugiharti et al., 2023). Wau (2022) focused on underprivileged regions through a panel data error correction model. Research specifically linking human capital to poverty in various Indonesian regions is limited due to a lack of time series data. There is a notable gap in studies utilizing a system-GMM approach to investigate the dynamic impacts of education and health on poverty. This study is unique in employing the system-GMM method to analyze both short-run and long-run dynamics using panel data, which is suitable given the limited time dimensions of the available Indonesian data.

2 Literature

Human capital represents the collective skills, expertise, and intangible assets of individuals, contributing to economic benefits for society. It refers primarily to investments in education, on-the-job training, and healthcare. Enhanced economic productivity and earnings can be linked to education and skill level (Becker, 1964). Since Becker's pioneering work, extensive research has been devoted to studying the effect of human capital on economic growth and poverty reduction. Human capital investments, in accordance with Becker (1995), are crucial for eradicating poverty. According to Sen (1999), poverty hampers the acquisition of justice, health, education, and productive resources. The impoverished are unable to acquire essential resources and liberties. A fulfilling life is seldom attainable without it. In poverty, insufficient resources hinder personal freedom. Human capital development significantly enhances an individual's capabilities and determines the trajectory of their life and financial sustainability (Fahad et al., 2023).

Investments in education, training, and health by individuals or society often compete with other needs at the household level (Naurin & Pourpourides, 2023) as well as at the aggregate level (Dhrifi et al., 2021; Mincer, 1981; Raghupathi & Raghupathi, 2020). The poor may invest inadequately in their children because of borrowing constraints and tradeoff between immediate economic needs and long-term education investments (Dhrifi et al., 2021; Naurin & Pourpourides, 2023). More equal education opportunities significantly reduce income inequality (Sağlam, 2021). The inadequacy of education and health perpetuates poverty intergenerationally due to the lack of economic opportunities associated with low human capital. Parents' education and health knowledge significantly influence their children's future health and human capital (Handayani et al., 2023). Health effects extend across generations, with income losses from poor health often exceeding healthcare costs. Ineffective health spending may fail to alleviate poverty. However, data from low- and middle-income countries indicates that public health insurance significantly aids poverty reduction (O'Donnell, 2024). Low educational attainment, skills, and health status lead to low productivity. The educational attainment gap among cohorts narrows as the overall level of education improves (Blanden & Macmillan, 2016). In Indonesia, as a result of extensive school construction in the 1970s, intergenerational market outcomes have improved due to better access to schooling (Akresh et al., 2023).

Productivity in the secondary sector is typically higher than in the primary sector (Fazaalloh, 2024). The structural changes that accompany economic growth require a more educated and trained workforce. A shift from primary economic activities to secondary economic activities like manufacturing does not only enhance productivity, but also reduces poverty (Erumban & de Vries, 2024). Improvements in education and health as well as the interaction between the two contribute significantly to growth (Abdelgany & Saleh, 2022; Dhrifi et al., 2021; Fonseca et al., 2020; Fumagalli et al., 2024; Ullah et al., 2019; Widarni & Bawono, 2021). This is because workers with higher educational attainment and better health become more productive, and thereby reduce poverty (Jibir et al., 2023; Ochi et al., 2024; Permana et al., 2024).

Work experience and education enhance productivity by equipping individuals with essential skills and knowledge (Folloni & Vittadini, 2010). Measuring and tracking human capital is a complex task. Human capital, an intangible asset, constantly evolves through an individual's employment history. The measurement can be taken retrospectively or prospectively. Because of differing interpretations of what constitutes human capital, an agreed-upon approach to quantifying it remains elusive. The term human capital encompasses numerous attributes linked to individuals. Representing all dimensions accurately in a single measure is a challenging task. Challenges arise in comparing study findings based on varying research methods. In developing countries, dependable long-term data on human capital attributes is sparse.

Abraham and Mallatt (2022) and Arokiasamy et al. (2023) examined a comprehensive body of literature on human capital measurement methodologies. They highlighted both challenges and opportunities for achieving consistency. The three primary methods for calculating human capital are indicators, costs, and income. Studies such as Wang et al. (2022) utilized a single indicator, either average years of schooling or aggregated education and health indices. Cost approach studies assess the expenses incurred (Teterinets, 2022). Some research methods, like that of Jacobsen et al. (2024), concentrate on the differences in future expected income. Égert et al. (2022) introduced mean years of schooling for the working-age population to quantify education and a cohort-weighted average of past PISA scores to evaluate education quality. They discovered that the elasticity of human capital stock concerning education quality is three to four times greater than that related to education quantity. Furthermore, education quality is strongly linked to potential productivity. Recent studies emphasize the significance of education quality (Choi et al., 2024; Sari & Tiwari, 2024), highlighting it as a crucial component of human capital. However, data on student achievement quality, such as PISA scores for developing countries like Indonesia, is not consistently available, and subnational data is lacking. Education quality enhances productivity and income, making it a suitable measure of human capital. Abraham & Mallatt (2022) observe that earnings-based measures, which correlate with educational attainment, provide higher estimates of human capital value than spending or cost-based approaches. Increased educational spending does not guarantee improvements in human capital. Suwandaru et al. (2021) demonstrated that public education expenditures have an insignificant impact on Indonesia's economic growth in both the short and long term. Similarly, increased expenditure on the education of children does not consistently lead to a corresponding enhancement of educational outcomes (Jin & Peng, 2024).

The World Bank uses the human capital index as a broad measure of the human capital potential that a child born today can look forward to attaining by the age of 18 (Kraay, 2018). It incorporates educational and health indicators, assessing both their quantity and quality. The index signifies measurable elements of education and health, i.e., chances of survival, anticipated years of education, and odds of survival, forecasted years of education, and the standard of educational quality. The human capital index offers a measure from zero to one that represents the potential productivity of an average future worker born today. Nevertheless, calculating and assessing a human capital index is challenging due to the inconsistent availability of data for subnational regions.

A study in Indonesia (Sari & Tiwari, 2024) evaluated human capital indices at the district level using Kraay's methodology. However, the analysis focused mainly on the geographic distribution of the human capital index across provinces and districts and its national trends from 2013 to 2018. Limitations arose due to insufficient data for dynamic analysis. Avitabile et al. (2020) also highlighted several issues in human capital index research. The national focus and data time gap do not adequately reflect economic disparities within the country, particularly between wealthier and poorer regions and households. The latest available national human capital index data for Indonesia is from 2020, and limited access to human capital index data hampers the integration of dynamic changes in human capital, affecting policy recommendations based on index analysis. A composite index that combines years of education and life expectancy provides a straightforward method for comparing human capital improvements across regions. Subnational data on education and health status facilitate the analysis of human capital development in relation to broader variables like poverty rates. Additionally, this composite index simplifies the assessment of overall human capital trends at both national and subnational levels.

Education and health are essential components of human capital and serve as reliable indicators of societies' productive capabilities. The accumulation of human capital is linked to labor market returns on education, which enhances workers' skills and leads to better economic outcomes (Botev et al., 2019; Huntington-Klein, 2021; Runde et al., 2017; Y. Wang & Liu, 2016). Similarly, health directly affects productivity and economic growth (Jayadevan, 2021; Stein & Sridhar, 2019; Yang, 2020). Recent studies have utilized education and health variables to assess poverty alleviation (Cerf, 2023; Spada et al., 2023; Sugiharti et al., 2023).

Many studies on poverty in Indonesia have highlighted the significant impacts of human capital, education, and health on poverty levels. However, conducting dynamic analyses in both the short and long term can provide deeper insights into poverty in Indonesia, especially by employing panel data at the district level. Given Indonesia's diverse socio-economic landscape, it is crucial to recognize regional inequalities, as the factors affecting poverty can vary greatly among districts, underscoring the need for tailored strategies. Ultimately, leveraging a dynamic analysis of human capital investments will not only enhance our understanding of poverty in Indonesia but also inform effective strategies that promote equitable growth and sustainable development.

3 Methodology

3.1 Data

We employed a panel dataset consisting of 417 out of Indonesia's 514 districts, which includes both regencies and municipalities, from 2019 to 2023. We focused exclusively on districts with available time series data for the variables in our model. All data were obtained from the Indonesian Central Agency for Statistics (BPS). Table 1 presents the variables used in this study.

The dependent variable in this study is the logarithm of the poverty rate, specifically the percentage of the population living below the poverty line. The selection

Table 1 Description of variables

Variable	Definition	Source	Base unit of measurement
The logarithm of poverty (LPOV)	Poverty is a head count percentage of population who live under poverty line	BPS (Indonesian Central Agency for Statistics)	Percentage
The logarithm of human capital index (LHCI)	HCI is a composite index computed as geometric mean of Normalized Years of Schooling (NYS) and Normalized Life Expectancy (NLE)	BPS (Indonesian Central Agency for Statistics)	Index
The logarithm of Gross Regional Domestic Product per capita (GRDPP)	GRDPP is per capita GRDP of regencies/municipalities at 2010 constant market prices	BPS (Indonesian Central Agency for Statistics)	Thousand Rupiah
The logarithm of years of schooling (LYS)	Years of schooling is the average number of completed years of education for individuals aged 25 and older	BPS (Indonesian Central Agency for Statistics)	Years
Normalized years of schooling (NYS)	Normalized years of schooling, calculated as the ratio of individual years of schooling to the max value of years of schooling in the dataset	BPS (Indonesian Central Agency for Statistics)	Ratio ranging from 0 to 1
The logarithm of life expectancy (LLE)	Life expectancy is the average number of years a newborn is expected to live, given the mortality rates of a specific year	BPS (Indonesian Central Agency for Statistics)	Years
Normalized life expectancy (NLE)	Normalized life expectancy, calculated as the ratio of individual life expectancy to the max value of life expectancy in the dataset	BPS (Indonesian Central Agency for Statistics)	Ratio ranging from 0 to 1
Covid-19 dummy (DUM)	The Covid-19 dummy is assigned a value of 1 for the years 2020 to 2022, during which the Indonesian government enforced movement restrictions, and a value of 0 for the years 2019 and 2023	Authors	0, 1

of poverty rates is guided by data availability, comparability across districts, and its established use in poverty literature. Utilizing the poverty headcount ratio as a dependent variable is quite common in contemporary poverty research, both in developed and developing nations (Panyi et al., 2025; Wu et al., 2024). Applying the logarithm of these values reduces heteroscedasticity and improves estimation performance. The explanatory variable is human capital. This study utilizes two measurements of human capital: a composite index of human capital and specific measures, namely years of schooling and life expectancy. All explanatory variables are presented in normalized values for ease of interpretation and transformed into logarithmic form. Equations (1) to (3) below detail the calculations for these variables. Additionally, this study incorporates the logarithm of gross regional domestic product per capita as a control variable, along with a Covid-19 dummy to account for the structural break caused by the coronavirus pandemic that impacted Indonesia from 2020 to 2022.

The World Bank defines poverty as the percentage of individuals living on less than \$2.15 per day, adjusted for 2017 purchasing power (World Bank, 2024). In contrast, Indonesia defines poverty as the percentage of the population living below its national poverty line. Poverty is defined as an individual's inability to meet basic needs (BPS, 2023b). A person is deemed poor if their average monthly expenditure falls below the poverty line. Two thresholds are established: one for food poverty and another for non-food poverty. The food poverty line varies by region and is affected by living costs and economic conditions, as indicated by the consumer price index for essential items, including food staples, clothing, housing, and services like education and healthcare. The food poverty line is established by evaluating a reference population's spending on 52 essential commodities, ensuring an intake of 2100 kilocalories per person daily. The non-food poverty line is computed based on expenditures excluding food. Poverty lines are then assessed for each province, distinguishing between urban and rural areas (Adji et al., 2020). District poverty rates are additionally calculated using provincial poverty lines.

We developed a human capital index (HCI) by combining years of schooling (YS) and life expectancy (LE) into a single composite index. First, we standardized both indicators for comparability. We applied Eqs. 1 and 2 to calculate Normalized Years of Schooling (NYS) and Normalized Life Expectancy (NLE), then computed their geometric mean to represent the Human Capital Index (HCI) using Eq. 3.

$$NYS_{it} = \frac{YS_{it}}{YS^{max}} \tag{1}$$

$$NLE_{it} = \frac{LE_{it}}{LE^{max}} \tag{2}$$

$$HCI_{it} = \sqrt{NYS_{it} \times NLE_{it}} \tag{3}$$

3.2 The Baseline Model

To capture the effects of human capital formation, educational attainment, and health, we employ the following baseline System-GM dynamic model:

$$LPOV_{it} = \alpha_{1,q} \sum_{i,t-q}^{q} LPOV_{i,t-q} + \alpha_2 LHCI_{it} + \alpha_3 LGRDPP_{it} + \alpha_4 DUM_{it} + \mu_i + v_{it} \quad (4)$$

where LPOV_{it} represents poverty rates in district i at time t, LHCI_{it} is the human capital index for district i at time t, LGRDPP_{it} is the gross regional domestic product per capita of district i at time t. DUM_{it} is the Covid-19 dummy variable constructed not only as a control variable but also to account for structural breaks caused by the Covid-19 pandemic. u_i denotes the individual-specific-district effect error term, and v_{it} is the idiosyncratic effect error term. q denotes the lag length. The System-GMM approach, an extension of GMM, combines first differences and level equations to produce efficient and robust estimates by utilizing more instruments. It constructs instruments from within the system, using lagged values of endogenous variables and their differences, effectively addressing endogeneity and omitted variable bias. Blundell and Bond (2000) and Markakkaran and Sridharan (2022) demonstrated that the system-GMM method is suitable for dynamic panel data, providing efficient and robust estimates.

Due to the limited time dimension of our panel, we restrict LPOV to a one-period lag. Consequently, we specify the model as follows.

$$\mathrm{LPOV}_{it} = \alpha_1 \mathrm{LPOV}_{i,t-1} + \alpha_2 \mathrm{LHCI}_{it} + \alpha_3 \mathrm{LGRDPP}_{it} + \alpha_4 \mathrm{DUM}_{it} + \mu_i + v_{it} \quad (5)$$

We assume that idiosyncratic errors are correlated over time, with human capital and poverty significantly influenced by their past levels. This indicates the presence of heteroscedasticity and autocorrelation within individuals, but not between districts. A fixed-effects model may produce biased results, as it assumes that past values have constant effects on the current state. The dynamic panel model in Eq. 5 effectively captures these temporal dependencies by including the lagged dependent variable as a regressor, resulting in a more accurate representation of the relationship between human capital and poverty.

We further estimate Eq. 5 by decomposing LHCI_{it} into two components: LYS_{it} for the logarithm of years of schooling and LLE_{it} for the logarithm of life expectancy. This modifies Eqs. 5 to 6 as follows:

$$\mathrm{LPOV}_{it} = \beta_1 \mathrm{LPOV}_{i,t-1} + \beta_2 \mathrm{LYS}_{it} + \beta_3 \mathrm{LLE}_{it} + \beta_4 \mathrm{LGRDPP}_{it} + \beta_5 \mathrm{DUM}_{it} + \mu_i + v_{it} \quad (6)$$

where LYS_{it} is the logarithm of years of schooling for district i at time t. LLE_{it} is the logarithm of life expectancy for district i at time t.

Equations 4 to 6 represent models with direct effects. Estimating the model using fixed effects leads to Nickell bias, which is most apparent in short dynamic panels with a small T and a relatively large N. A Nickell bias arises when the lagged dependent variable is used as an explanatory variable, leading to inconsistencies in standard panel data estimators such as fixed effects, random effects, and first differences, especially in studies with short time period and large cross-sections (Nickell, 1981). This bias occurs due to the correlation between the lagged dependent variable and the unobserved individual-specific effect, resulting in endogeneity. System-GMM estimation addresses this problem by using lagged values as instruments for the endogenous variables. Therefore, we employ the System-GMM method proposed by Arellano and Bond (1991) to adjust for Nickell bias. The method yields strong estimates as it employs both level and difference equations, which aids in eliminating the Nickell bias.

3.3 Validity Testing

We conduct two essential tests to verify the robustness and reliability of GMM estimates. Firstly, we use the J-statistic (Hansen test) to ensure that the instruments are uncorrelated with the error term and robust to heteroscedasticity. While more instruments can increase efficiency, overidentification may lead to biased and inconsistent estimates, so we carefully select an appropriate number of lagged dependent variables. Secondly, we apply the Arellano-Bond test to examine for serial correlation in the residuals, as its presence would invalidate the instruments used in the first-differenced equation.

4 Results and Discussion

4.1 Descriptive Statistics

Table 2 provides a descriptive statistical summary of the base variables utilized in this study. Table 3 displays the summary statistics in logarithmic form. The poverty variable exhibits a mean of 11.95, indicating a significant dispersion, as shown by a standard deviation of 7.179 and a range that spans from the minimum to the maximum values. Not only is the data widely dispersed overall, but it also indicates significant variability in poverty rates within each district over time. In 2019, the Badung district of Bali recorded the lowest poverty rate at 1.78 percent. Conversely, in 2021, Supiori district in Papua registered the highest poverty rate, close to 40 percent. Contrarily, the overall mean of the human capital index indicates a low level of dispersion. The high overall standard deviation suggests a significant variance in human capital across Indonesian districts. The lowest human capital index was recorded in Nduga district, Papua, in 2019, while the highest was observed in Banda Aceh municipality in 2022.

Table 2 Statistical summary of the variables

Variable	Observations	Sample	Mean	Std.Dev.	Min.	Max.
POV	$N = 2085$	Overall	11.95	7.179	1.78	39.91
	$n = 417$	Between		0.941	2.25	38.06
	$T = 5$	Within				
HCI	$N = 2085$	Overall	0.76	0.086	0.23	0.96
	$n = 417$	Between		16.006	0.27	0.95
	$T = 5$	Within				
YS	$N = 2085$	Overall	8.40	1.61	0.97	13.04
	$n = 417$	Between		3.59		
	$T = 5$	Within				
LE	$N = 2085$	Overall	69.73	3.47	55.08	78.01
	$n = 417$	Between		7.73		
	$T = 5$	Within				
GRDPP	$N = 2085$	Overall	36,459	38,678	2434	498,605
	$n = 417$	Between		84,863		
	$T = 5$	Within				

Sources: Authors' computations

Table 3 Statistical summary of the variables in logarithm (overall sample)

	LPOV	LHCI	LYS	LLE	LGRDPP
Mean	2.321487	−0.287815	2.105843	4.243385	10.24375
Median	2.322388	−0.286913	2.112635	4.248209	10.18244
Maximum	3.686627	−0.039600	2.568022	4.356837	13.11957
Minimum	0.576613	−1.473266	−0.030459	4.008787	7.797291
Std. Dev.	0.564501	0.127493	0.230523	0.050638	0.655013
Sum	4840.300	−600.0952	4390.682	8847.457	21358.21
Sum Sq. Dev.	664.0908	33.87435	110.7455	5.343835	894.1248
Observations	2085	2085	2085	2085	2085

Sources: Authors' computations

The average length of education is 9 years, which is nearly equivalent to completing junior high school, and has a standard deviation of 1.61. This notable difference in standard deviation indicates a broad range of educational accessibility. In the meantime, the average life expectancy is around 70 years, which also demonstrates considerable variation among districts. The Gross Regional Domestic Product per Person (GRDPP) exhibits an unequal distribution, underscored by the substantial standard deviations, both overall and across districts, with a marked contrast between the minimum and maximum values.

By examining the wide spectrum of minimum and maximum human capital indicators and their considerable between-standard deviations, we can deduce that there are notable differences in human capital accumulation throughout Indonesia's districts. There is no doubt that overall human capital differs significantly between regions in Indonesia (Sari & Tiwari, 2024). High levels of poverty are mainly present in geographically isolated areas, like Papua province and other provinces in eastern Indonesia. Still, many provinces outside of Java Island also demonstrate poverty rates that are higher than the national average.

4.2 Results of Panel Common Unit Root Tests and Cross-Section Dependence

In this study, the Breitung test (Breitung & Pesaran, 2005) is employed for panel unit root testing due to its compatibility with our data structure. Our dataset is a short panel where the number of panels is large while the time dimension is short. Consequently, the panel-based Breitung unit root test yields robust results. This test not only assumes common unit roots across all panels but also accounts for cross-sectional dependence. It is particularly suitable for data exhibiting trends that differ across panels (Moon et al., 2006). Table 4 provides the results of Breitung panel unit root results. All variables indicate strong evidence of common unit roots in all panels, i.e., they are all nonstationary and display stochastic trends over time. The results are robust because the Breitung test considers cross-sectional dependence among various cross-sectional units (Breitung & Das, 2003).

4.3 Results of System-GMM Estimation

To address the nonstationarity inherent in our panel series and the cross-sectional dependence among their residuals, as noted in Sect. 4.2, we employed the dynamic panel model outlined in Sect. 3.2, which also mitigates endogeneity (Arellano & Bond, 1991). In the system-GMM model, both first-differenced and level equations are used simultaneously. Therefore, it ensures the consistency and efficiency of the resulting estimates.

In Model 1, we used the logarithm of the composite human capital index (LHCI), whereas in Model 2, we individually applied the logarithm of years of schooling (LYS) and the logarithm of life expectancy (LLE) to denote human capital. We

Table 4 Results of panel unit root tests

Variable	Test statistics	*p*-value	Result
LPOV	13.7161	1.0000	Common unit root process
LHCI	13.2955	1.0000	Common unit root process
LYS	7.68809	1.0000	Common unit root process
LLE	24.9363	1.0000	Common unit root process
LGRDPP	17.1816	1.0000	Common unit root process

Source: Authors' computations
417 cross-sections and 1251 balanced observations

included the logarithm of gross regional domestic product per capita (GRDPP) as a control variable in both models, along with a COVID-19 pandemic dummy (DUM) to account for the structural break. To ensure reliable estimation results, we included LHCI(-1) within Model 1. To verify the validity of the instruments, we implemented the LPOV lagged by one and two periods in Model 1, whereas in Model 2, we exclusively used the two-period lag.

Table 5 presents the results of the system-GMM estimation. In Model 1, the one-period lag of the logarithm of the poverty rate (LPOV) does not significantly influence current poverty. However, in Model 2, its effect is significantly negative. This suggests that when a composite index of human capital is employed, any exogenous intervention or shock aimed at reducing poverty will have an immediate impact rather than depending on its previous values. Changes in poverty rates will not produce lasting effects. The insignificant results may stem from the limited one-period lag used in the estimation, while time-specific factors within each district, such as productivity growth, could have a significant effect. Due to the short panel, these factors might not be fully captured. Nevertheless, when human capital is represented by two distinct indicators—the log of years of schooling and the log of life expectancy—its lagged effect is significantly negative. An exogenous shock in one

Table 5 Results of system-GMM dynamic estimates of Log of Poverty (LPOV)

	Coefficient	
Variable	Model 1	Model 2
LPOV(-1)	0.134537 *(0.121683)*	−1.504946[a] *(0.561785)*
LHCI	−21.34139[a] *(6.823333)*	–
LHCI(-1)	17.19240[a] (4.129169)	–
LYS	–	7.160990[a] *(1.891885)*
LLE	–	−20.03953[b] *(8.374746)*
LGRDPP	0.576522 *(1.442253)*	−1.105475 *(0.761079)*
DUM	−0.016299 *(0.027331)*	0.052167 *(0.059085)*
Mean dependent var	−0.009728	−0.009728
S.E. of regression	0.189242	0.194030
J-statistic	0.553495	1.821828
Prob(J-statistic)	0.456893	0.177096
S.D. dependent var	0.055938	0.055938
Sum squared resid	44.62242	46.90906
Instrument rank	6	6

Source: Authors' computation

Note: GMM two-step iteration with White period weights from final iteration—Robust standard errors

Source: Authors' computation (2024)

Standard errors in parentheses

[a] Significant at 1%

[b] Significant at 5%

period would reduce poverty in the following period, and this effect would be enduring.

The coefficients of the logarithm of the human capital index (LHCI) and its one-period lag in Model 1 are significant. However, the direction of effects differs. The contemporaneous effect of LHCI is negative, indicating that higher human capital accumulation leads to lower poverty, while its one-period lag suggests a positive association. Increased human capital accumulation immediately influences productivity and, in turn, reduces poverty. This finding is consistent with recent studies. Enhanced education, training, and health care quality lead to improved economic opportunities for certain segments of the population (Nunoo et al., 2024; Sağlam, 2021). In the short term, human capital creates jobs and thereby decreases unemployment (Mushtaq et al., 2022). Human capital decreases income inequality in the short run (Vo et al., 2024). The positive coefficient of LHCI(-1) implies that the increase in human capital stock in a particular year leads to a rise in poverty in the subsequent year. This could occur because, over time, inequality may rise. As the economy expands due to human capital enhancement, inequality increases in the following period, thereby elevating poverty levels (Marrero & Servén, 2022). While increased human capital reduces income inequality in the short term, this effect may be reversed in the long term. Consequently, while human capital improvement immediately boosts productivity and narrows the income gap, the subsequent effect may lead to higher poverty rates (Vo et al., 2024). In addition, the finding indicates that funding education and health may cause temporary financial stress for certain groups within the population, which could raise poverty levels. For example, financial inclusion has a modest impact on decreasing moderate poverty (Saha & Qin, 2023). Moreover, the benefits of human capital can only be realized once a certain investment threshold is reached (Dai et al., 2022).

In Model 2, where human capital is broken down into two components, the effects of both the logarithm of years of schooling (LYS) and the logarithm of life expectancy (LLE) are significant. However, the directions of the effects differ. Only LLE affects LPOV negatively, suggesting improved society's health results in lower poverty, whereas high schooling leads to higher poverty. The first is consistent with previous studies (Jibir et al., 2023; Ochi et al., 2024; Permana et al., 2024). The positive impact of years of schooling appears to contradict general theoretical predictions. However, in the context of Indonesia, several explanations can be offered. Firstly, the government's allocation of financial resources to education has indeed increased schooling accessibility; however, the quality of educational services remains problematic. Despite significant improvements in enrollment, educational outcomes have not progressed uniformly across the country (Jasmina & Oda, 2022). The disparity in access to quality education among districts is a crucial factor affecting the differences in poverty reduction (BPS, 2024). The quality of education holds considerable importance in Indonesia (Choi et al., 2024; Sari & Tiwari, 2024).

Secondly, as shown in Table 2, the mean years of schooling in Indonesia is 8.4, equivalent to nearly junior high school completion. This level of average educational attainment is considered low and has not reached a threshold beyond which education begins to bring about positive effects. The impact of higher education on

GDP growth and poverty alleviation becomes apparent once the threshold is reached (Li et al., 2024). Only after a threshold of educational attainment is surpassed, its effect becomes apparent (Dai et al., 2022). In 2023, only 13 percent of Indonesian adults attained the tertiary level of education (Rachel, 2024), lower than several other southeast Asian countries (OECD, 2023). Thirdly, the high rate of teacher absenteeism in Indonesia also significantly affects the quality of education and student learning outcomes (World Bank, 2020). The effects of absenteeism on educational achievements and life opportunities are detrimental (Sosu et al., 2021). Moreover, Bilad (2024) indicates that, based on the 2022 Program for International Student Assessment (PISA) results, the academic performance of Indonesian 15-year-olds in mathematics, reading, and science has declined, and the disparity between various socioeconomic groups has increased. Therefore, greater educational attainment does not automatically result in enhanced human capital and, in turn, reduced poverty levels.

The logarithm of gross regional domestic product per capita (LGRDPP) is statistically insignificant. Within the context of the model, we included the control variable to confirm the reliability of the estimates regarding the relationship between human capital indicators and poverty. There are several reasons that can explain the insignificant impact of LGRDPP on poverty. The overall average poverty level across Indonesian districts is relatively low, accompanied by a high standard deviation (refer to Table 2). When the poverty rate is low, the effect on output growth is not significant (Marrero & Servén, 2022). In subnational regions with notably high inequality, the growth of GRDPP fails to benefit the poorer segments of the population, and therefore does not contribute to poverty reduction. Another vital factor is financial inclusion. The increase in GRDP per capita may not necessarily result in better access to financial services for the poor, whereas financial inclusion effectively reduces poverty by ensuring a more equitable distribution of the benefits of growth (Omar & Inaba, 2020; Ochi et al., 2024).

Furthermore, the Covid-19 dummy variable (DUM) is also insignificant. The vulnerable portions of the population received substantial food, health, and financial aid from the government during the Covid-19 pandemic, making them less susceptible to severe impacts from COVID-19. In addition, Indonesian economy recovered relatively swiftly in mid-2021 during the pandemic's peak. This helped ease the negative effects of the Covid-19 pandemic on poverty in Indonesia (Tantriana, 2024).

4.4 Results of the Validity Test for Instruments and the Arellano-Bond Correlation Test

In Table 5, we demonstrate that the Hansen J-statistic in both models is insignificant, indicating that the instruments employed in the system-GMM estimation are not correlated with the residuals. Thus, the GMM estimates obtained are valid. In Table 6, we present the findings of the Arellano-Bond tests for serial correlation,

Table 6 Results of Arellano-bond serial correlation test

Test order	m-Statistic	rho	SE (rho)	Prob.
Model 1				
AR(1)	−2.499084	−9.974616	3.991308	0.0125
AR(2)	−0.828155	−0.471909	0.569831	0.4076
Model 2				
AR(1)	1.259832	5.031011	3.993397	0.2077
AR(2)	1.599271	1.519504	0.950123	0.1098

Source: Authors' computations

which reveal no serial correlation in the differenced residuals. The rho statistics for AR(2) in Model 1 and Model 2 are not significant, suggesting that the first-differenced residuals are uncorrelated with their own first and second lags. Therefore, the models are robust to model specifications.

5 Conclusion and Policy Implications

This study examined the dynamic relationship between human capital and poverty in Indonesia using a system-GMM approach, which has been underexplored in recent empirical literature. Utilizing a panel dataset comprising 417 districts from 2019 to 2023, two equations were estimated: one employing the logarithm of the composite human capital index and the other using the logarithms of years of schooling and life expectancy separately. A comparison was then made. When the human capital index was used as a measure of human capital stock, the one-period lag of the logarithm of the poverty rate had no significant effect on current poverty. However, when two separate measures of human capital stock were utilized, its effect was significantly negative. This implies that when a composite index of human capital is employed, any exogenous intervention or shock aimed at reducing poverty will have an immediate impact rather than depending on its previous values. Consequently, to uplift districts with relatively higher poverty incidence, the Indonesian government's short-term policy should prioritize the more disadvantaged poor districts, in addition to the long-term poverty eradication programs that have successfully reduced overall poverty in Indonesia over the past few decades.

This study also found that the coefficients of the logarithm of the human capital index and its one-period lag in Eq. 1 are both significant, but they exhibit different directions of effects. The contemporaneous effect of the logarithm of the human capital index is negative, indicating that higher human capital accumulation leads to lower poverty in the same period. This finding aligns with recent studies on the human capital-poverty relationship in Indonesia, where enhanced human capital results in reduced poverty. However, the positive effect of the one-period lag of the logarithm of the human capital index suggests that an increase in human capital stock in a given year leads to a rise in poverty in the following year. This may occur due to rising inequality among segments of the population, so that as the economy expands due to human capital enhancement, the gap in poverty levels between districts widens in the subsequent period. Consequently, poverty may instead increase. Although increased human capital reduces income inequality in the short term, its long-term effect may be reversed. The policy implication of this finding is that long-term poverty alleviation strategies should consider affirmative actions to improve the quality of education and health services for less advantaged districts and the marginalized socioeconomic groups within the population.

In the second equation, where two measures of human capital accumulation are utilized, the effects of both the logarithm of years of schooling and the logarithm of life expectancy are significant, yet their directions differ. The negative effect of the first explanatory variable indicates that improved societal health leads to lower poverty, while the positive effect of the second explanatory variable suggests that higher schooling correlates with increased poverty. The negative health-poverty relationship is straightforward and aligns with previous studies. However, the positive education-poverty relationship is more complex. In the context of Indonesia, the quality of educational services has not kept pace with the increased accessibility to education nationwide. The disparity in access to quality education among districts significantly influences the variations in poverty reduction across those regions. Therefore, the Indonesian government should focus more on enhancing education quality in under-performing districts, particularly those remote from growth centers that experience low-quality educational service delivery. It is crucial to prioritize and enhance these districts to reach an educational threshold level, ensuring that education produces positive impacts on productivity, growth, and ultimately, poverty reduction.

Our findings also underscore the importance of improving the quality of education across all districts in addition to healthcare, so that advancement in years of schooling leads to enhanced human capital. In turn, it will equally benefit all segments of the population in terms of higher productivity and growth.

Finally, we highlight the necessity of improving the quality of education, encompassing teachers' professional development, school management, and school infrastructure, in all districts, with particular focus on disadvantaged areas. Such enhancements will ensure that increases in years of schooling, paired with better healthcare, lead to improved human capital. This will benefit all population segments and regions by enhancing productivity and growth.

Our study findings and recommendations can be generalized and are relevant to other developing countries with similar levels of human capital development and comparable demographic and socioeconomic conditions, particularly nations with large multi-ethnic and geographically dispersed populations like Indonesia. However, policy environments may differ; therefore, both short-term and long-term poverty eradication interventions should consider the broader contexts of education, health, and other human capital enhancements specific to each country.

Acknowledgments The authors express their gratitude to colleagues at the Department of Development Economics, Faculty of Economics and Business, Universitas Syiah Kuala for their valuable suggestions to enhance the quality of the paper.

Limitations of the Study We acknowledge several limitations of the current study. First, we utilized only the available time series data from 2019 to 2023. Employing a longer time dimension in future research could enhance the applicability of findings in poverty research using panel data. Second, we used aggregated district-level data, which overlooks the likely distinct behaviors of the poor across various socioeconomic contexts in investing in human capital. Future research utilizing longitudinal household data can provide a more valuable and comprehensive explanation of the relationship between human capital and poverty. Third, we employed a complex system-GMM approach. Although we assessed the validity of the instruments utilized in this approach and its inherent robustness, future research employing panel data analysis could provide deeper insights into the long- and short-run relationships between human capital and poverty by using the panel vector error correction model (VECM) and the panel autoregressive distributed lags (ARDL) approach.

Declaration of Competing Interest The authors declare that they have no known competing interests or personal relationships that could have appeared to influence the work reported in this paper.

Funding This research was funded by the Directorate of Research, Technology, and Community Service (Contract number 094/E5/PG.02.00.PL/2024, dated 11 June 2024) via the Institute for Research and Community Development, Universitas Syiah Kuala (Contract Number 655/UN11.2.1/PG.01.03/SPK/DRTPM/2024, dated 12 June 2024).

Data Availability Data used in this study will be made available on request.

References

Abdelgany, M. F., & Saleh, A. A. (2022). Human capital and labour productivity: Empirical evidence from developing countries. *International Journal of Economics, 10*(4), 173–184. https://doi.org/10.11648/j.ijefm.20221004.13

Abraham, K. G., & Mallatt, J. (2022). Measuring Human Capital. *Journal of Economic Perspectives, 36*(3), 103–130. https://doi.org/10.1257/jep.36.3.103

Adji, A., Hidayat, T., Asmanto, P., Tuhiman, H., Kurniawati, S., & Maulana, A. (2020). Measurement of poverty line in Indonesia. *Theoretical Review and Proposed Improvements*. .

Adriana, M., & Suparyati, A. (2023). *Regional inequality analysis in Papua* (pp. 453–464). https://doi.org/10.2991/978-94-6463-350-4_44

Akresh, R., Halim, D., & Kleemans, M. (2023). Long-term and intergenerational effects of education: Evidence from school construction in Indonesia. *The Economic Journal, 133*(650), 582–612. https://doi.org/10.1093/ej/ueac058

Arellano, M., & Bond, S. (1991). Some tests of specification for panel data: Monte Carlo evidence and an application to employment equations. *The Review of Economic Studies, 58*(2), 277. https://doi.org/10.2307/2297968

Arokiasamy, L., Fujikawa, T., Piaralal, S. K., & Arumugam, T. (2023). A systematic review of literature on human capital investment and its significance for human resource development. *International Journal of System Assurance Engineering and Management, 14*(5), 1810–1826. https://doi.org/10.1007/s13198-023-01985-2

Arwani, A., Safi'i, M. A., Zawawi Tamara, K., & Masrur, M. (2023). Development of the economic growth model reducing poverty in Central Java Indonesia. *International Journal of Professional Business Review, 8*(3), e01134. https://doi.org/10.26668/businessreview/2023.v8i3.1134

Avitabile, C., D'Souza, R., Gatti, R. V., & Chapman, E. W. (2020). Insights from disaggregating the human capital INDEX.

Becker, G. S. (1964). Human capital: A theoretical and empirical analysis with special reference to education.

Becker, G. S. (1995). *Human capital and poverty alleviation* (HROWP 52).

Bilad, M. R., Zubaidah, S., & Prayogi, S. (2024). Addressing the PISA 2022 results: A call for reinvigorating Indonesia's education system. *International Journal of Essential Competencies in Education, 3*(1), 1–12. https://doi.org/10.36312/ijece.v3i1.1935

Blanden, J., & Macmillan, L. (2016). Educational inequality, educational expansion and intergenerational mobility. *Journal of Social Policy, 45*(4), 589–614. https://doi.org/10.1017/S004727941600026X

Blundell, R., & Bond, S. (2000). GMM estimation with persistent panel data: An application to production functions. *Econometric Reviews, 19*(3) .

Bos, J. M., Shonchoy, A. S., Ravindran, S., & Khan, A. (2024). Early childhood human capital formation at scale. *Journal of Public Economics, 231*, 105046. https://doi.org/10.1016/j.jpubeco.2023.105046

Botev, J., Égert, B., Smidova, Z., & Turner, D. (2019). *A new macroeconomic measure of human capital with strong empirical links to productivity*. www.oecd.org/eco/workingpapers.

BPS. (2023a). Data dan Informasi Kemiskinan Kabupaten/Kota Tahun 2023.

BPS. (2023b). Penghitungan dan Analisis Kemiskinan Makro Indonesia Tahun 2023.

BPS. (2024). *Gross regional domestic product of provinces in Indonesia by industry 2019–2023.*

Breitung, J., & Das, S. (2003). Panel unit root tests under cross sectional dependence.

Breitung, J., & Pesaran, M. H. (2005). *Unit roots and cointegration in panels* (42; 1).

Cerf, M. E. (2023). The social-education-economy-health nexus, development and sustainability: Perspectives from low- and middle-income and African countries. *Discover Sustainability, 4*(1), 37. https://doi.org/10.1007/s43621-023-00153-7

Choi, S., Li, H., Ogawa, K., & Tanaka, Y. (2024). Secondary vocational education and decent work in Indonesia: Differences between urban and rural areas. *International Journal of Training Research, 22*(2), 125–146. https://doi.org/10.1080/14480220.2023.2222939

Dahliah. (2023). The effect of human capital and unemployment on poverty through economic growth and the moderating role of investment. *Jurnal Ekonomi Kuantitatif Terapan, 16*(1), 45–66.

Dai, X., Yan, L., Jianping, L., & Wu, J. (2022). A research on the threshold effect of human capital structure upgrading and industrial structure upgrading—based on the perspective of path dependence. *Quality & Quantity, 56*(4), 2645–2674. https://doi.org/10.1007/s11135-021-01230-7

Dhrifi, A., Alnahdi, S., & Jaziri, R. (2021). The causal links among economic growth, education and health: Evidence from developed and developing countries. *Journal of the Knowledge Economy, 12*(3), 1477–1493. https://doi.org/10.1007/s13132-020-00678-6

Diniati, B. T., & Permana, D. A. (2024). The influence of population size, economic growth, human development index, unemployment on poverty in Indonesia from 1998 to 2022. https://proceedingsiches.com/index.php/ojs/article/view/172.

Égert, B., De La Maisonneuve, C., & Turner, D. (2022). *A new macroeconomic measure of human capital exploiting PISA and PIAAC: Linking education policies to productivity*. www.RePEc.org.

Erumban, A. A., & de Vries, G. J. (2024). Structural change and poverty reduction in developing economies. *World Development, 181*, 106674. https://doi.org/10.1016/j.worlddev.2024.106674

Panyi, A., Whitacare, B., & Young, A. (2025). The shifting relationship between educational attainment and poverty: Analysis of seven deep southern states. *The Annals of Regional Science, 74*(1), 1–25. https://doi.org/10.1007/s00168-024-01344-4

Fahad, S., Nguyen-Thi-Lan, H., Nguyen-Manh, D., Tran-Duc, H., & To-The, N. (2023). Analyzing the status of multidimensional poverty of rural households by using sustainable livelihood framework: Policy implications for economic growth. *Environmental Science and Pollution Research, 30*(6), 16106–16119. https://doi.org/10.1007/s11356-022-23143-0

Fazaalloh, A. M. (2024). FDI and economic growth in Indonesia: A provincial and sectoral analysis. *Journal of Economic Structures, 13*(1), 3. https://doi.org/10.1186/s40008-023-00323-w

Folloni, G., & Vittadini, G. (2010). Human capital measurement: A survey. *Journal of Economic Surveys, 24*(2), 248–279. https://doi.org/10.1111/j.1467-6419.2009.00614.x

Fonseca, R., Michaud, P.-C., & Zheng, Y. (2020). The effect of education on health: Evidence from national compulsory schooling reforms. *SERIEs, 11*(1), 83–103. https://doi.org/10.1007/s13209-019-0201-0

Fumagalli, E., Pinna Pintor, M., & Suhrcke, M. (2024). The impact of health on economic growth: A narrative literature review. *Health Policy, 143*, 105039. https://doi.org/10.1016/j.healthpol.2024.105039

Handayani, N. S., Huriyati, E., & Hasanbasri, M. (2023). Association of maternal education with nutritional outcomes of poor children with stunting in Indonesia. *Asia Pacific Journal of Public Health, 35*(5), 373–380. https://doi.org/10.1177/10105395231185980

Huntington-Klein, N. (2021). Human capital versus signaling is empirically unresolvable. *Empirical Economics, 60*(5), 2499–2531. https://doi.org/10.1007/s00181-020-01837-z

Jacobsen, J., Khamis, M., & Yuksel, M. (2024). Demography, human capital investment, and lifetime earnings for women and men. *Eastern Economic Journal, 50*(3), 259–277. https://doi.org/10.1057/s41302-024-00273-6

Jasmina, T., & Oda, H. (2022). *Nonlinear relation between government spending and education: Theoretical and empirical evidence from districts in Indonesia* (pp. 1–36).

Jayadevan, C. M. (2021). Impacts of health on economic growth: evidence from structural equation modelling. Asia-Pacific Journal of Regional Science, 5(2), 513–522. https://doi.org/10.1007/s41685-020-00182-4

Jibir, A., Abdu, M., & Buba, A. (2023). Does human capital influence labor productivity? Evidence from Nigerian manufacturing and service firms. *Journal of the Knowledge Economy, 14*(2), 805–830. https://doi.org/10.1007/s13132-021-00878-8

Jin, R., & Peng, D. (2024). Does educational mismatch affect human capital investment in children? Evidence from China. *Applied Economics*, 1–22. https://doi.org/10.1080/00036846.2024.2331968

Kraay, A. (2018). Methodology for a World Bank human capital index. http://www.worldbank.org/research.

Kustanto, A. (2021). The prevalence of stunting, poverty, and economic growth in Indonesia: A panel data dynamic causality analysis. *Journal of Developing Economies, 6*(2), 150. https://doi.org/10.20473/jde.v6i2.22358

Li, J., Xue, E., Wei, Y., & He, Y. (2024). How popularising higher education affects economic growth and poverty alleviation: Empirical evidence from 38 countries. *Humanities and Social Sciences Communications, 11*(1), 520. https://doi.org/10.1057/s41599-024-03013-5

Liu, W., Li, J., & Zhao, R. (2023). The effects of rural education on poverty in China: A spatial econometric perspective. *Journal of the Asia Pacific Economy, 28*(1), 176–198. https://doi.org/10.1080/13547860.2021.1877240

Markakkaran, S., & Sridharan, P. (2022). Impact of export diversification on economic growth: A system GMM approach. *International Journal of Development Issues, 21*(2), 309–320. https://doi.org/10.1108/IJDI-10-2021-0210

Marrero, G. A., & Servén, L. (2022). Growth, inequality and poverty: A robust relationship? *Empirical Economics, 63*(2), 725–791. https://doi.org/10.1007/s00181-021-02152-x

Mincer, J. (1981). Human capital and economic growth. NBER working paper series, November. https://www.nber.org/papers/w0803.pdf.

Moon, H. R., Perron, B., & Phillips, P. C. B. (2006). On the Breitung test for panel unit roots and local asymptotic power. *Econometric Theory, 22*(6), 1179–1190.

Mushtaq, M., Ahmed, S., Fahlevi, M., Aljuaid, M., & Saniuk, S. (2022). Globalization and employment nexus: Moderating role of human capital. *PLoS One, 17*(10), e0276431. https://doi.org/10.1371/journal.pone.0276431

Naurin, A., & Pourpourides, P. M. (2023). On the causality between household and government spending on education: Evidence from a panel of 40 countries. *Empirical Economics, 65*(2), 567–585. https://doi.org/10.1007/s00181-022-02345-y

Nickell, S. (1981). Biases in dynamic models with fixed effects. *Econometrica, 49*(6), 1417. https://doi.org/10.2307/1911408

Nizar, N. I., Nuryartono, N., Juanda, B., & Fauzi, A. (2024). Can knowledge and culture eradicate poverty and reduce income inequality? The evidence from Indonesia. *Journal of the Knowledge Economy, 15*(2), 6425–6450. https://doi.org/10.1007/s13132-023-01398-3

Nugroho, A. P., Handayani, S., & Effendi, D. E. (2021). Health citizenship and healthcare access in Indonesia, 1945-2020. *Jurnal Ilmu Sosial Dan Ilmu Politik, 24*(3), 284. https://doi.org/10.22146/jsp.54618

Nunoo, J., Taale, F., Ofori, I. K., Mwinlaaru, P. Y., & Adama, A. Y. S. (2024). Human capital and income inequality in Africa: Robust governance synergies and thresholds. *Cogent Economics & Finance, 12*(1). https://doi.org/10.1080/23322039.2024.2417757

Ochi, A., Labidi, M. A., & Saidi, Y. (2024). The nexus between pro-poor growth, inequality, institutions and poverty: Evidence from low and middle income developing countries. *Social Indicators Research, 172*(2), 703–739. https://doi.org/10.1007/s11205-024-03326-7

O'Donnell, O. (2024). Health and health system effects on poverty: A narrative review of global evidence. *Health Policy, 142*, 105018. https://doi.org/10.1016/j.healthpol.2024.105018

OECD. (2023). OECD skills strategy Southeast Asia. *OECD*. https://doi.org/10.1787/923bfd03-en

Omar, M. A., & Inaba, K. (2020). Does financial inclusion reduce poverty and income inequality in developing countries? A panel data analysis. *Journal of Economic Structures, 9*(1), 37. https://doi.org/10.1186/s40008-020-00214-4

Permana, P. D., Larasati, L., Hati, C. M. P., & Amrina, D. H. (2024). The influence of education and training on labor productivity in Indonesia. *Journal of International Conference Proceedings, 6*(6), 369–379. https://doi.org/10.32535/jicp.v6i6.2705

Rachel, L. (2024). Education at a glance 2024: OECD indicators.

Raghupathi, V., & Raghupathi, W. (2020). The influence of education on health: An empirical assessment of OECD countries for the period 1995–2015. *Archives of Public Health, 78*(1), 20. https://doi.org/10.1186/s13690-020-00402-5

Rohmatilah, D. A. (2023). The role of gender equality on poverty alleviation: Case of Indonesia. *Jurnal Perencanaan Pembangunan: The Indonesian Journal of Development Planning, 7*(2), 272–287. https://doi.org/10.36574/jpp.v7i2.450

Runde, D. F., Rice, C., & Yayboke, E. (2017). Education and human capital development. In *Innovation-led economic growth (transforming tomorrow's developing economies through technology and innovation)*. Center for Strategic and International Studies (CSIS). http://www.jstor.org/stable/resrep23182.6.

Sağlam, B. B. (2021). Educational inequality versus income inequality: An empirical investigation. *The Economics and Social Review, 52*(3), 269–299.

Saha, S. K., & Qin, J. (2023). Financial inclusion and poverty alleviation: An empirical examination. *Economic Change and Restructuring, 56*(1), 409–440. https://doi.org/10.1007/s10644-022-09428-x

Sari, V. A., & Tiwari, S. (2024). The geography of human capital: Insights from the subnational human capital index in Indonesia. *Social Indicators Research, 172*(2), 673–702. https://doi.org/10.1007/s11205-024-03322-x

Sayyidina, N. A., Iranto, D., & Suparno, S. (2023). The effect of government expenditure in the education sector, human development index, and economic growth on poverty rate in eastern Indonesia. *Journal of Business and Economics Research, 4*(2), 186–193. https://doi.org/10.47065/jbe.v4i2.3559

Sen, A. (1999). *Development as freedom*. Oxford University Press.

Setyadi, S., Kustanto, A., & Widiastuti, A. (2023). Life expectancy in Indonesia: The role of health infrastructure, political, and socioeconomic status. *Iranian Economic Review, 27*(3), 965–1005. https://doi.org/10.22059/ier.2021.85012

Simatupang, D., Anggia, Y., Sari, R., & Sari, I. (2024, May 3). Analysis of the influence of education and health on economic growth in Indonesia. https://doi.org/10.4108/eai.22-9-2022.2337484.

Sosu, E. M., Dare, S., Goodfellow, C., & Klein, M. (2021). Socioeconomic status and school absenteeism: A systematic review and narrative synthesis. *Review of Education, 9*(3). https://doi.org/10.1002/rev3.3291

Spada, A., Fiore, M., & Galati, A. (2023). The impact of education and culture on poverty reduction: Evidence from panel data of European countries. *Social Indicators Research*. https://doi.org/10.1007/s11205-023-03155-0

Stein, F., & Sridhar, D. (2019). Back to the future? Health and the World Bank's human capital index. BMJ, l5706. https://doi.org/10.1136/bmj.l5706

Sugiharti, L., Esquivias, M. A., Shaari, M. S., Jayanti, A. D., & Ridzuan, A. R. (2023). Indonesia's poverty puzzle: Chronic vs. transient poverty dynamics. *Cogent Economics & Finance, 11*(2). https://doi.org/10.1080/23322039.2023.2267927

Supadmi, S., Laksono, A. D., Kusumawardani, H. D., Ashar, H., Nursafingi, A., Kusrini, I., & Musoddaq, M. A. (2024). Factor related to stunting of children under two years with working mothers in Indonesia. *Clinical Epidemiology and Global Health, 26*, 101538. https://doi.org/10.1016/j.cegh.2024.101538

Suparman, S., & Muzakir, M. (2023). Regional inequality, human capital, unemployment, and economic growth in Indonesia: Panel regression approach. *Cogent Economics & Finance, 11*(2). https://doi.org/10.1080/23322039.2023.2251803

Suwandaru, A., Alghamdi, T., & Nurwanto, N. (2021). Empirical analysis on public expenditure for education and economic growth: Evidence from Indonesia. *Economies, 9*(4). https://doi.org/10.3390/economies9040146

Tantriana, A. (2024). Poverty and vulnerability transitions in Indonesia before and during the COVID-19: Insights from synthetic panels. *Quality & Quantity, 58*(4), 3215–3249. https://doi.org/10.1007/s11135-023-01785-7

Teterinets, T. A. (2022). Assessment of human capital from the perspective of investment costs. *Studies on Russian Economic Development, 33*(2), 157–162. https://doi.org/10.1134/S1075700722020150

World Bank. (2020). *Measuring the quality of MoRA's education services*. www.worldbank.org.

Tirtosuharto, D. (2022). The impact of fiscal efficiency on poverty reduction in Indonesia: Institutional factor and geographical differences. *Journal of Geographical Systems, 24*(1), 67 93. https://doi.org/10.1007/s10109-021-00359-1

Ullah, S., Nauman Malik, M., & Ul Hassan, M. (2019). Impact of health on labour productivity: Empirical evidence from Pakistan. *European Online Journal of Natural and Social Sciences, 8*(1), 139–147. http://www.european-science.com.

Vo, D. H., Vo, A. T., & Ho, C. M. (2024). The short- and long-run effect of human capital on income inequality: Empirical evidence in the ASEAN region. *PLoS One, 19*(7), e0304678. https://doi.org/10.1371/journal.pone.0304678

Wang, S., Lin, X., Xiao, H., Bu, N., & Li, Y. (2022). Empirical study on human capital, economic growth and sustainable development: Taking Shandong Province as an example. *Sustainability, 14*(12), 7221. https://doi.org/10.3390/su14127221

Wang, Y., & Liu, S. (2016). Education, human capital and economic growth: Empirical research on 55 countries and regions (1960-2009). *Theoretical Economics Letters, 6*(2), 347–355. https://doi.org/10.4236/tel.2016.62039

Wau, T. (2022). Economic growth, human capital, public investment, and poverty in underdeveloped regions in Indonesia. *Jurnal Ekonomi & Studi Pembangunan, 23*(2), 189–200. https://doi.org/10.18196/jesp.v23i2.15307

Widarni, E. L., & Bawono, S. (2021). Human capital, technology, and economic growth: A case study of Indonesia. *Journal of Asian Finance, 8*(5), 29–0035. https://doi.org/10.13106/jafeb.2021.vol8.no5.0029
Wiratama, B. F., Kurniawan, R., Mulyanto, Isnaeni, M. A., Sumargo, B., & Gio, P. U. (2023). Measuring the physical infrastructure development as poverty reduction program in Kalimantan, Indonesia. *Cities, 141*, 104515. https://doi.org/10.1016/j.cities.2023.104515
World Bank. (2024). Poverty, prosperity, and planet report 2024: Pathways out of the polycrisis. https://doi.org/10.1596/978-1-4648-2123-3.
Wu, Y., Naqvi, S. M. M. A., & Yasin, I. (2024). Dynamic relationship between social factors and poverty: A panel data analysis of 23 selected developing countries. *Journal of the Knowledge Economy.* https://doi.org/10.1007/s13132-024-01843-x
Yang, X. (2020). Health expenditure, human capital, and economic growth: an empirical study of developing countries. International Journal of Health Economics and Management, 20(2), 163–176. https://doi.org/10.1007/s10754-019-09275-w

Cross Taiwan Strait Trade and Low-Temperature Logistics

Zhuo Chen

Abstract This article examines one aspect of the cross-strait trade between Taiwan and mainland China from 2000 to 2019, categorizing it into three stages: the trade of tangible goods, the trade of services, and the dissemination of knowledge. Initially, trade focuses on agricultural products, particularly tropical fruits, transported through low-temperature logistics. As trade progresses, Taiwan's logistics companies specializing in low-temperature transport begin to provide services in the mainland, representing the second stage. The final stage involves the dissemination of knowledge including the technology and management driving these logistics systems. A case study on Tianjin's food low-temperature logistics plan illustrates Taiwan's role in enhancing mainland China's logistics capacity.

Keywords Taiwan Strait · Low-temperature logistics · Service trade · Technology dissemination

1 Introduction

1.1 Time Frame of the Research

Cross-strait trade here refers to economic exchanges across the Taiwan Strait. These exchanges, along with all other forms of civil interaction, almost ceased after the Chinese Civil War concluded in 1949. From 1949 to 1979, the Taiwan Strait represented a militarized boundary between the two sides. In 1979, mainland China issued the Message to Compatriots in Taiwan, advocating for the normalization of

Z. Chen (✉)
Munk School of Global Affairs and Public Policy, University of Toronto, Toronto, ON, Canada
e-mail: zo.chen@mail.utoronto.ca; http://www.utoronto.ca/

E. Lau et al. (eds.), *Economics and Finance Readings*,
https://doi.org/10.1007/978-981-96-6998-1_6

cross-strait relations, including the establishment of the "three direct links"—direct mail, trade, and transportation across the Strait—to facilitate civilian exchanges. The Taiwan government initially responded with a conservative "Three-Noes Policy" (no contact, no compromise, and no negotiation). However, under pressure from Taiwanese business stakeholders attracted by the economic potential of mainland China's "reform and opening up" period, the government eventually acquiesced to civilian trade and investment on the mainland.

We make the study start at 2000 when two sides started to trade directly. In the early 1990s, stringent regulations required all cross-strait trade to transit through Hong Kong or Japan, incurring additional costs and logistical delays. By 2003, shipments were permitted to pass through the Taiwan controlled islands of Kinmen and Matsu, located closer to the mainland, though transport capacity remained limited. Following extensive negotiations, an agreement on the "three direct links" was finalized on November 4, 2008. Cross-strait relations were warm during the government of Ma Ying-jeou from 2008 to 2016. The 2010 Economic Cooperation Framework Agreement (ECFA) marked a significant milestone in cross-strait relations, shifting Taiwan's position from passive acquiescence to active support of economic integration. Through the ECFA, both sides opened their goods, investment, and services markets reciprocally to foster mutual benefits. The substantial and growing movement of people and goods across the strait brings considerable welfare benefits to populations on both sides.

We select 2019 as the endpoint for this study because cross-strait trade dynamics underwent significant political disruptions after this time, making it increasingly difficult to analyze the trade evolution solely through market mechanisms. One of the most critical turning points was the sharp deterioration in cross-strait relations following the election of Tsai Ing-wen from the Democratic Progressive Party (DPP) in 2016. The DPP government's refusal to recognize the "1992 Consensus" resulted in growing tensions with Beijing, which directly impacted economic agreements. The Cross-Strait Service Trade Agreement (CSSTA) has halted since 2014. Originally signed in 2013, the CSSTA aimed to deepen economic integration, particularly in service sectors such as logistics and cold-chain transport. However, due to political opposition within Taiwan, including the large-scale Sunflower Movement protests, the agreement never came into effect (Haime, 2024). Without this framework, further expansion of cross-strait service trade faced structural obstacles, limiting opportunities for Taiwanese firms in the mainland market. By 2019, the economic integration envisioned in earlier agreements had largely stalled due to these unresolved political tensions.

Additionally, the outbreak of the COVID-19 pandemic in early 2020 caused major disruptions in global trade, particularly in sectors dependent on cross-border logistics. Taiwan and the mainland implemented strict border controls, significantly reducing in-person business activities (Hsu et al., 2021). These restrictions disrupted supply chains, including the low-temperature logistics sector examined in this study. Cross-strait trade declined by 10.4% in the second quarter of 2020 compared to the same period in 2019 (Hsu et al., 2021), reflecting the widespread impact of pandemic-related restrictions. At the same time, the Chinese government increasingly employed economic measures as a tool to influence Taiwan's political stance.

Agricultural goods, which are the main goods in low-temperature logistics, became a major target of Beijing's economic sanctions, particularly because many Taiwanese farmers are considered supporters of the DPP. In 2021, for instance, China imposed import bans on Taiwanese pineapples, sugar apples, and wax apples, citing pest concerns, though these measures were widely interpreted as politically motivated (Dong, 2021). These post-2019 developments illustrate a shift away from market-driven trade patterns toward politically driven trade restrictions. Since this study focuses on trade evolution under normal market conditions, the inclusion of post-2019 data would introduce distortions that fall outside the scope of economic analysis. Ending the sample period in 2019 ensures that the findings remain grounded in economic mechanisms rather than political interventions that are beyond the reach of this paper.

2 Industry Information

2.1 A Pilot Industry of Cross-strait Exchange

The trade of agricultural products, supported by low-temperature logistics infrastructure, provides a prime example of cross-strait economic cooperation. To strengthen future economic collaboration across the Strait, Taiwan's Ministry of Economic Affairs launched the "cross-strait bridge-building project" in 2008, selecting three pilot industries to develop cooperative models for future engagement. This project aims to enhance communication and collaboration between Taiwanese and mainland enterprises, intellectuals, and government agencies in areas such as market access, regulatory frameworks, and technology transfer. Government agencies serve as intermediaries ("bridge builders") to facilitate these cross-strait connections, while private stakeholders take advantage of the opportunities provided. The low-temperature logistics sector was selected as a pilot industry due to its substantial demand and its potential to encompass the trade of goods, services, and ideas, aligning with the future trajectory of economic cooperation.

The "cross-strait bridge-building project" for the low-temperature logistics sector has four principal objectives:

- Establish Taiwanese low-temperature logistics bases at three mainland ports to serve inland areas, primarily facilitating the transport of Taiwanese products. The bases are situated in Tianjin, serving northeast, northern, and northwest China; Shanghai/Kunshan, serving central China with extended coverage along the Yangtze River; and Guangxi, serving southwest China and Southeast Asia.
- Provide low-temperature logistics services to the mainland Chinese food industry, with the goal of enhancing the capacity and quality of domestic food distribution. This objective encompasses transporting vegetables from the south to the

north, fruits from the west to the east, and optimizing the use of freezer trucks through two-way logistics (transporting imported products inland and exporting local products).

- Expand into other stages of low-temperature logistics. Taiwanese logistics companies offer end-to-end services, from raw material tracking and customs clearance to distribution and retail, tailored to the specific requirements of fruit trading firms.
- Promote Taiwan–mainland collaboration in international markets. Taiwanese enterprises, leveraging bonded ports, can process raw materials from mainland China using modern technology, enabling exports to international markets with higher profit margins.

2.2 Introduction to Low-Temperature Logistics

Low-temperature logistics refers to a system that maintains goods within a specified low-temperature range (refrigerated or frozen) throughout production, storage, transportation, and retail stages, thereby preserving food quality and integrity while minimizing spoilage. Enabled by advances in refrigeration technology, low-temperature logistics encompasses a series of interconnected processes that must be meticulously coordinated.

Numerous goods require low-temperature logistics, including fruits and vegetables, meat, poultry, eggs, live or frozen aquatic products, horticultural items, processed foods, quick-frozen products, packaged cooked foods, dairy products, fast-food raw materials, pharmaceuticals, and other temperature-sensitive items. Given that low-temperature logistics involves handling perishable goods under carefully controlled conditions across multiple processes, it is inherently more complex and costly than standard logistics in terms of control systems, specialized equipment, and labor. Rather than consisting solely of isolated vehicles or warehouses, low-temperature logistics functions as an integrated, complex system.

Time is critical in all stages of low-temperature logistics. Beyond its impact on product quality, time also influences transportation costs. Product quality diminishes over time, making expedited shipping vital yet costly. However, slower transportation can also be expensive due to the increased energy costs associated with maintaining a cold environment for extended periods. Thus, an optimal balance between speed and cost is essential to the efficiency of low-temperature logistics systems (Figure 1).

The study of the British milk trade after the introduction of railways (Rioux, 2014) demonstrates that modern transportation led to a "growing social-spatial separation between producers and consumers." When studying the movement of goods, particularly perishable goods such as food, it is crucial not to treat them as fixed and unchanging. The transportation of food should be considered through three dimensions: space, time, and material properties. As Rioux notes, "In a capitalist economy, where the vast majority of people are dependent on the market to obtain their

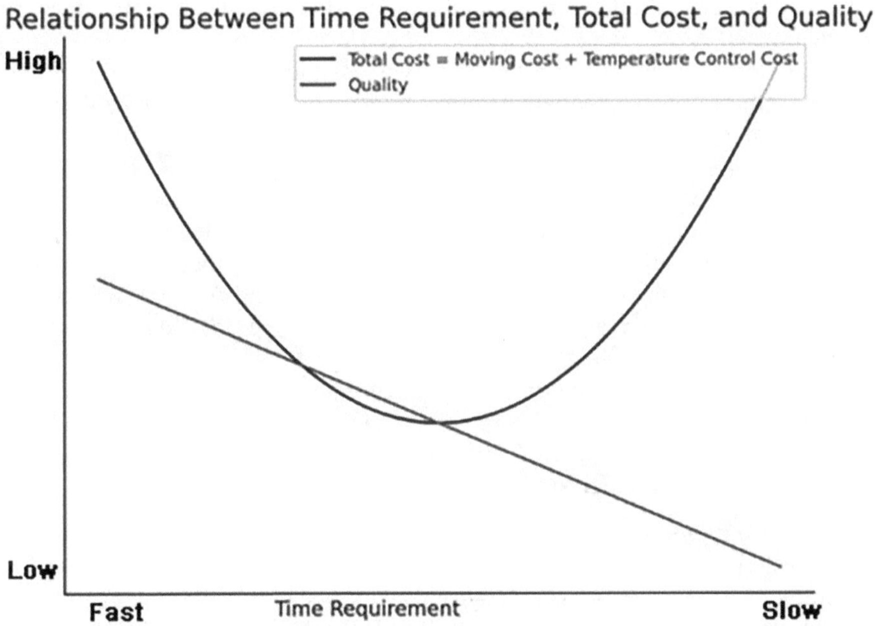

Fig. 1 The relationship between time requirement and total transportation cost for low-temperature logistics

means of subsistence, speedier and more efficient means of transportation are essential not only to deliver mass quantities of food but also to preserve the quality and overall integrity of the products conveyed."

Before 1840, most British urban residents obtained milk directly from cows kept in town or in nearby rural areas. However, the advent of railways allowed milk to be transported from more distant rural areas, where production costs were lower and economies of scale were realized. Rioux describes this as "the spatial restructuring of production," as milk supplies increasingly came from areas aligned with railway lines.

In the early stages of the milk trade, low-temperature logistics began to emerge. Some dairy firms required suppliers to cool the milk to slow the souring process. Rioux writes, "The cooling of the milk was generally done by standing the full churns in water or by pouring the milk over metal tubes through which water circulated." From the late 1870s onward, wholesalers aiming to reduce milk wastage during transit set up depots at country stations. These depots not only provided cooling facilities but also enabled bulk transportation, which helped reduce the time milk spent in transit (Whetham, 1964). However, the technology for low-temperature logistics was quite rudimentary at that time, and despite these efforts, the quality of milk upon arrival was often questionable. To prevent souring, firms added chemicals such as sodium carbonate, formaldehyde, and boric acid along the route. Even with these measures, bacteriological examinations suggested that large quantities of milk were unsafe to drink, with unsound milk causing diseases like tuberculosis in children.

Today, low-temperature logistics has evolved into a high-tech industry. For example, Omaha Steaks, the largest direct shipper of gourmet foods in the USA, ships several million refrigerated and frozen packages annually with United Parcel Service, Inc. In modern logistics, all stages—from production and processing to transportation and retail—are carefully controlled in low-temperature environments. Starting at the processing stage, steaks are rapidly cooled to a temperature that halts decomposition, maintaining this temperature until they reach individual consumers. While low-temperature logistics is more expensive than standard logistics, it offers overall savings by reducing value loss due to product degradation.

Low-temperature logistics can be divided into four main processes: low-temperature processing, low-temperature storage, low-temperature transportation, and low-temperature selling. Coordination and information technology play critical roles throughout these processes.

- *Low-temperature processing* refers to the processing of food under low temperatures and pre-cooling before storage. This includes tasks such as cleaning and cutting meat and seafood, cooling fruits and vegetables, quick-freezing cooked food, and processing dairy products in a low-temperature environment. This stage is vital as it lays the foundation for all subsequent processes. For instance, in the case of Omaha Steaks, pre-cooling involves "rapidly reducing products from the temperature at which they are picked, produced, or processed to their appropriate storage and transportation temperature." "Every hour of delayed pre-cooling equals a day of lost shelf life" (Smith, 2005).
- *Low-temperature storage* includes refrigeration and freezing, as well as air-conditioned storage, which extends the shelf life of food by controlling the composition and proportions of gases, temperature, and humidity in the environment. This process relies on refrigerators, freezers, and airtight warehouses.
- *Low-temperature transportation* involves medium- to long-distance transportation from the factory to wholesale stations, and short-distance transport from wholesale stations to retail stores. The instability of the gas environment, temperature, and humidity is the primary cause of food spoilage, wilting of horticultural products, or the death of live aquatic products. Vehicles must maintain a narrow temperature range over extended periods. This process is carried out using refrigerated railway cars, freezer trucks, freezer ships, and freezer containers. In recent years, freezer containers have become a promising technology, as self-cooling containers increase flexibility and reduce the need for costly upgrades to transportation infrastructure.
- *Low-temperature selling* includes low-temperature storage and display during wholesale and retail stages. Supermarkets like Carrefour and Tesco, as well as smaller grocery stores, now feature refrigerated counters and freezers. This stage can be a weak link in the low-temperature logistics chain, as both the equipment and the staff involved are generally smaller-scale and less robust.

- *Coordination* across these four processes is crucial in low-temperature logistics. Because the system is interconnected, failure in any process can lead to the failure of the entire system and irretrievable loss of goods. Problems often arise during transfers between different environments (e.g., from warehouse to vehicle, vehicle to warehouse, or vehicle to retail counter freezer).

The modernization of low-temperature logistics has been marked by the deep integration of information technology. To coordinate the allocation of logistics equipment and vehicles, managers rely on computer databases that collect, analyze, transmit, and publish information. These databases not only facilitate equipment allocation but also help logistics providers and users track shipments, settle payments, and ensure quality. For example, the database can track the origin and destination of Taiwanese fruit, providing this information to consumers as a quality guarantee. Fruit traders can integrate their stock management systems with the database to track turnover. This leads to greater market transparency and efficiency. Moreover, the database enables rapid detection of problems in the market.

Modern low-temperature logistics depend on both advanced technology and skilled human capital. "Improved training and education programs are strengthening and spreading professionalism at every link in the cold chain." Industrial services, such as equipment maintenance, quality inspection, database maintenance, material supply, and professional training, have also developed around this core business.

3 Theoretical Significance

An examination of the material flow of agricultural products from Taiwan to mainland China provides insight into various forms of regional economic integration, specifically the trade of tangible goods, services, and ideas. This analysis highlights the impact of technology on the spatial patterns of food production and consumption, illustrating the concept of "time-space compression" introduced by David Harvey. As Rioux (2014) notes, "Transport geography can contribute both theoretically and empirically to an evaluation of the intimate relationship existing between the sphere of spatial circulation of commodities and the preservation of their overall quality and material integrity." This perspective is central to understanding how logistics technologies influence not only the movement of goods but also the maintenance of quality and integrity throughout the supply chain.

Additionally, this study addresses the theoretical question of how the movement of physical goods fosters the dissemination of ideas, echoing the research of (Xu & Chiang, 2005). Through the three stages of cross-strait trade—each involving low-temperature logistics—this paper demonstrates that the trade of tangible goods generates a need for the trade of related services, which in turn drives knowledge transfer. Trade between two regions often progresses from lower stages (tangible goods) to higher stages (services and ideas), yet each advanced stage expands the scope of new business opportunities beyond the preceding one. This suggests that maximizing the benefits of trade requires advancing to higher stages of exchange (Alvarez et al., 2013).

Continued observation of the low-temperature logistics sector is important to understand its evolution. The composition of participating companies, the competitive landscape, and the technological advancements driving efficiency improvements are all subject to change. As firms enter and exit the market, shifts in industry dominance can alter supply chain dynamics, necessitating ongoing research to capture these trends. Additionally, policy environments at both national and regional levels impact the sector's trajectory, particularly as governments introduce new regulations aimed at improving food safety, reducing carbon emissions, and promoting supply chain resilience. These external factors shape the strategies adopted by logistics firms, influencing investment decisions and technological innovation.

Besides supply side changes, the low-temperature logistics sector is also affected by shifts in demand. The increasing prevalence of e-commerce and direct-to-consumer food delivery services has transformed logistics requirements, particularly in the transportation of perishable goods. These unceasing changes make continuous observation necessary.

4 Methods

This study utilizes a combination of historical analysis and qualitative case study to examine the evolution of cross-strait trade, with a specific focus on low-temperature logistics.

Primary and secondary sources, including government reports, trade documents, and industry publications, were gathered from various archives and databases. Historical analysis was applied to trace the milestones and transitions from the initial phase of tangible goods exchange to more advanced trade in services and ideas. This also includes reviewing significant trade agreements, such as the Economic Cooperation Framework Agreement (ECFA), and exploring their influence on Taiwan's logistics industry and the broader economic landscape.

A qualitative case study on Tianjin was also conducted to better understand the challenges and opportunities faced by the low-temperature logistics sector.

The combination of the two methods offers a comprehensive approach to understanding the complexities of Taiwan-China trade and the role of low-temperature logistics in shaping cross-strait economic exchanges.

5 Findings

Trade across the Taiwan Strait related to low-temperature logistics can be viewed as a history unfolding in three stages.

5.1 *Stage 1: Trade of Tangible Goods (Agricultural Products)*

Agriculture in Taiwan is primarily dominated by small family farms. Due to the high labor costs in Taiwan, the market prices of many agricultural products are significantly higher than those on the international market. To ensure food security and protect the interests of farmers, the Taiwanese government subsidizes the agricultural sector heavily each year. However, this policy places a substantial financial burden on the public budget, particularly as Taiwan's economy has stagnated in recent years. Additionally, it encourages a "grow for subsidy" mentality, leading to opportunistic production rather than long-term improvements in productivity. As a result, agricultural productivity in Taiwan has not significantly improved, and the sector's share of GDP continues to decline annually. According to the CIA World Factbook, agriculture accounted for just 1.9% of Taiwan's GDP in 2014.

Certain agricultural products, such as peaches, mangoes, grapefruits, and oranges, have suffered from overproduction and low prices in recent years. Farmers face losses both in good years due to low prices and in bad years due to low output.

While agriculture contributes only a small portion to Taiwan's GDP, the sector and its related industries—such as agro-chemicals, food processing, storage, and marketing—still employ millions of people. Thus, agriculture cannot be entirely abandoned. Taiwan possesses advanced agricultural expertise, but its domestic market is small and insular, making it ill-equipped to compete in a globalized economy. To enhance sector-wide competitiveness, Taiwan's agricultural industry requires access to a larger market. Mainland China, with its proximity, consumer habits, resources, and market size, represents an ideal partner for Taiwan in this regard.

One key aspect of this cooperation is the export of Taiwan's agricultural products to mainland China. As a tropical island, Taiwan enjoys natural advantages in producing various agricultural products (Table 1 (Ye, 2014)). Under the Economic Cooperation Framework Agreement (ECFA) between Taiwan and mainland China, many Taiwanese agricultural products can enter the mainland duty-free. The Council of Agriculture of Taiwan views the expansion into the mainland market as a critical

Table 1 Regionally advantageous agricultural products from Taiwan (Ye, 2014)

County in Taiwan	Advantageous products
Taipei, Taoyuan, Miaoli, Hsinchu, Yilan, Hualien	Tea
Changhua	Flammulina velutipes, dragon fruit, cuttle fish, and turtle egg
Nantou	Banana, orange, dragon fruit, and tea
Yunlin	Orange, hami melon, dragon fruit, grouper, and milkfish
Chiayi	Oncidium, banana, orange, hami melon, tea, grouper, and milkfish
Tainan	Oncidium, orange, hami melon, grouper, and milkfish
Kaohsiung	Lemon, dragon fruit, pacific saury, tea, grouper, cuttlefish, banana, milkfish, and turtle fish
Pingdong	Banana, lemon, dragon fruit, grouper, and turtle egg

priority. To support this effort, the Council conducts market research in Mainland China on consumer habits and industry standards. It also organizes agricultural companies to participate in exhibitions in mainland China to help build the brand recognition of Taiwanese food products.

The import of Taiwanese agricultural products has increased rapidly, particularly after the facilitation of transportation. In 2008, an agreement between mainland China and Taiwan enabled direct sea and air shipping, opening up more transportation routes. Under the agreement, Taiwan opened 6 ports, and mainland China opened 63 ports for sea shipping. Mainland China also opened 21 cities for direct air shipping and allowed more frequent flights per week. This has significantly accelerated the transportation of high-value fruits and seafood to the northern and western regions of mainland China. For example, transportation and customs clearance time for Taiwanese fruits exported to Shanghai has been reduced from 8 days to 4 days. Additionally, transportation costs have decreased by 15%, spoilage during transit has fallen from 15% to 5%, and the freshness of the products has been better preserved, extending their shelf life by 4 days.

Live aquatic products are even more time- and environment-sensitive than fruits. Their transit time is measured in hours, not days. Taiwan produces a large number of ornamental fish, which are highly favored by Chinese consumers. However, longer transportation and customs clearance times require packing the fish with more water to ensure a high survival rate, which increases the cost of air shipping. Taiwan also produces 15,000 metric tons of live grouper annually, with 12,000 metric tons being sold to mainland China through interlining via Hong Kong due to transportation capacity limitations. If all grouper could be directly shipped to mainland cities, consumers would benefit from fresher and cheaper fish, while fishermen could lower their costs.

Today, most Taiwanese fruits are transported to mainland China through the Xiamen Taiwan Fruit Wholesale and Distribution Center, which was originally established by the Xiamen municipal government and is now operated by a state-owned company. The center is located next to the Xiamen International Airport and the national expressway G319, and is just 2 kilometers from the Xiamen Dongdu Deepwater Wharfs. As of June 2013, according to the Taiwan Affairs Office of Fujian Province, over 100 mainland fruit trading firms and 262 Taiwanese fruit trading firms and farmers' associations conduct business at the center.

Based on Shi's (2012) study of the Xiamen Taiwan Fruit Wholesale and Distribution Center, Taiwanese fruits are exported to mainland China along such routes (Table 2 (Shi, 2012)): ships carrying freezer containers depart from Keelung, Taichung, and Kaohsiung ports in Taiwan, and then in two main ways these fruits reach mainland China:

- The "Little Three Direct Links" (Xiao San Tong): Large ships first arrive at Kinmen Island, a small island controlled by the Taiwanese government near Xiamen, where the cargo is unloaded onto smaller ships and transported to Xiamen Port.

Table 2 Cross-strait transportation route comparison

Ports	Distance (nautical mile)	Shipping time		
		"Big three direct links"	"Little three direct links"	Go through Hong Kong or Japan
Keelung-Xiamen	222	19 h	1 day	5–7 days
Taichung-Xiamen	135	15 h	1 day	5–7 days
Kaohsiung-Xiamen	165	17 h	1 day	5–7 days

- The "Big Three Direct Links" (Da San Tong): After 2008, large ships can directly sail to Xiamen Port. This route, taking about 1 day, is 4–6 days faster than routing via Hong Kong or Ishigaki-jima Island in Japan, and the shipping cost is significantly lower.

Once the freezer containers arrive at Xiamen Port, they undergo inspection, with fruits being scanned by X-ray either at the port or at the Wholesale Center. Mainland China has exempted certain varieties of fruits from this inspection process, and 22 types of Taiwanese fruit are duty-free.

Finally, when the freezer containers reach the Wholesale and Distribution Center, they are either directly hooked up to trailer trucks, or the fruits are unpacked and loaded onto freezer trucks or regular trucks for further transportation to their destination cities.

5.2 *Stage 2: Trade of Services (Low-Temperature Logistic Services)*

Once Taiwanese fruits arrive in Xiamen, they require local low-temperature logistics services to ensure quality, but mainland China lacks the adequate service capacity to handle such large volumes. Generally speaking, mainland China has a significant deficit in modern low-temperature logistics infrastructure. Taiwanese logistics providers view this situation as a profitable opportunity to enter the mainland market, marking the second stage of cross-strait trade: the trade of services.

Taiwanese logistics providers first identified opportunities when transporting goods to the Xiamen Wholesale Center. According to Shi's (Shi, 2012) study, most Taiwanese fruits are shipped to Xiamen in freezer containers. However, once the fruits are loaded, most trucks used for transportation lack the necessary cooling equipment. The facilities at the Wholesale Center remain rudimentary, consisting primarily of warehouses and offices, with inadequate cargo handling equipment and high-efficiency packing facilities. Shi's survey of trading firms reveals that many companies struggle to find freezer trucks when needed. Meanwhile, the limited capacity of the Wholesale Center is not being optimized. The use of refrigeration warehouses and market space is subsidized by the Xiamen municipal government, and the pricing does not reflect the true market value of the services, leading to inefficient use, such as wasted space in cold storage. Additionally, the Wholesale Center lacks market entry regulations, resulting in a fragmented industry. Many logistics companies only operate a small fleet, typically owning just dozens of trucks, which prevents economies of scale from being realized. This results in low profits, limiting their ability to expand their fleets or invest in advanced low-temperature logistics equipment to offer services beyond simple goods transportation. In contrast, logistics providers in developed countries are typically large corporations, either independent transportation specialists or divisions within large food producers or retail chains, employing hundreds or thousands of skilled workers and owning extensive fleets.

Beyond the Wholesale Center, the inadequacy of low-temperature logistics becomes even more apparent in the downstream distribution of fruits to consumers. Most fruits are sold to cities that are hundreds or even thousands of miles away, making freezer trucks essential for transport. However, the fleet of freezer trucks is small, and many fruits are transported in standard trucks, leading to spoilage. The rise of B2C (business-to-consumer) e-commerce in mainland China has further increased the demand for small-lot, long-distance low-temperature logistics, but there are not enough low-temperature vehicles to transport fruits from the Wholesale Center to consumers dispersed across the country.

Additionally, the Taiwan fruit supply chain in mainland China involves numerous fragmented players, with little vertical integration. Taiwanese fruit trading firms purchase fruits from Taiwan and ship them to Xiamen but must then seek out local, small, semi-professional low-temperature logistics providers. These firms play no role in the supply chain beyond the port, despite having rich marketing experience and innovative ideas from Taiwan. When Taiwanese fruit trading firms attempt to establish their own low-temperature logistics and retail networks in mainland China, they encounter challenges due to unfamiliarity with local business procedures, industrial standards, and retailer connections. Their headquarters in Taiwan lack timely access to critical market intelligence in mainland China. Furthermore, large supermarket chains in mainland China do not operate their own professional low-temperature logistics teams, making it difficult for them to seamlessly integrate with upstream Taiwanese fruit suppliers.

When Taiwanese low-temperature logistics providers interact with their mainland counterparts, they immediately recognize that the industry in mainland China is underdeveloped, especially outside major cities (Ye, 2014). In the United States and European countries, 90% of suitable goods are transported using low-temperature logistics, but the percentage in mainland China is much lower (Table 3 (Ye, 2014)). The total capacity of low-temperature warehouses in the USA is three times that of mainland China, and the per capita capacity in the USA is 14 times greater. Many warehouses in mainland China are outdated, relying on natural cooling rather than modern, mechanically cooled facilities. The total number of freezer trucks in mainland China is between 40,000 and 50,000. In the USA, on average there is one freezer truck for every 500 people, compared to one for every 30,000 people in mainland China.

Table 3 Transportation quality within in China, 2012 to 2015. ("Agricultural products low-temperature logistics development plan", as cited in (Ye, 2014))

	Low-temperature transportation rate		Loss rate	
Goods category	2012 level	Goal of 2015	2012 level	Goal of 2015
Fruits and vegetables	15%	30%	20%–30%	15%
Meat and poultry	30%	50%	12%	8%
Aquatic products	40%	65%	15%	10%

The underdeveloped low-temperature logistics industry in mainland China presents a significant opportunity for Taiwanese logistics providers. Taiwan has been developing its low-temperature logistics sector for over 20 years, acquiring extensive expertise and experience. Today, the utilization rate of low-temperature logistics for suitable goods in Taiwan reaches 80% to 90%, and the country has developed a comprehensive management system for the industry.

On June 21, 2013, Taiwan and mainland China signed the "Cross-strait Service Trade Agreement." This agreement opens numerous service industries, including distribution and transportation services, to Taiwanese companies. Both sides agreed to extend national treatment and the most-favored-nation treatment to each other, allowing capital related to these sectors to move freely between them. This agreement facilitates Taiwanese low-temperature logistics providers' access to mainland China's vast market. Once established in mainland China, these providers can transport Taiwanese agricultural products, but it is likely that they will also handle other goods. Furthermore, this presents a valuable opportunity for mainland China to receive much-needed low-temperature logistics services.

Taiwan's low-temperature logistics providers are distinguished by their technical advantages. These include more than 150 patents in equipment and software, highly skilled labor, and the ability to coordinate the four essential processes required for a connected logistics system.

Taiwanese logistics providers have pioneered automated low-temperature distribution centers, which save 48% of land space, reduce labor costs by 50%, and cut energy consumption by 30% to 71%. These centers also enable real-time stock management, improving efficiency and reducing errors.

Furthermore, Taiwanese providers offer customized low-temperature logistics services using adjustable freezer containers, allowing them to deliver goods that require different storage environments to multiple customers at the same time. In addition to transportation, they offer related services such as packing, distribution, and online tracking, creating a one-stop logistics solution. The industry trend emphasizes small volumes, large varieties, fresh products, high frequency, and cost efficiency.

Finally, full-process location and temperature monitoring is critical for ensuring product quality. Taiwanese logistics companies use electronic sensors, wireless communication, and Geographic Information Systems (GIS) to track the identity, temperature, time, and location of goods in real-time, ensuring precise quality control throughout the logistics process.

With these technical advantages, Taiwanese low-temperature logistics providers are well-positioned to meet the growing demand for such services in mainland China's market.

5.3 Stage 3: Dissemination of Ideas (Technology and Management Enabling Low-Temperature Logistics)

The dissemination of science and technology across the Taiwan Strait occurs through various channels. One such example is the development of standards for low-temperature logistics (Industrial Technology Research Institute, 2014). To establish an orderly competitive market and elevate public attention to quality, it is essential to create standards that regulate and assess the performance of low-temperature logistics providers. Taiwan can assist mainland China in developing standards in three key areas:

- Hardware standards: This includes standards for low-temperature warehouses, vehicles, and containers.
- Logistics practice standards: These cover the processes involved in low-temperature logistics, such as handling, storage, transportation, selling, and inspection.
- Management standards: These standards would regulate the overall operations of logistics companies, ensuring consistent service quality.

In addition to creating standards, Taiwan can help mainland China develop an evaluation system for logistics providers. This evaluation could be carried out by industry associations or the government to certify companies that perform well. The recognition of high-performing companies would create competitive advantages and incentivize the industry to focus on continuous quality improvement.

Beyond policymaking, Taiwan can also play a pivotal role in training professionals in low-temperature logistics (Industrial Technology Research Institute, 2014). As modern low-temperature logistics is a high-tech industry that requires specialized labor, there is a significant need for skilled workers in mainland China. Taiwan's training programs could target three groups:

- Current practitioners in the logistics field.
- Students in higher education and vocational schools.
- Socially recruited workers who may seek entry into the logistics profession.

The training could take several forms, such as full-time programs in Taiwan, work-study initiatives, full-time training in mainland China with Taiwanese instructors and materials, or on-site training by Taiwanese professionals stationed at mainland companies. Taiwan's unparalleled advantage in sharing knowledge and expertise with mainland China lies in their shared language and culture, which enables smoother communication and better understanding of local needs compared to other developed countries.

6 Case Study: Tianjin as Gateways for Taiwan Agricultural Products

The Taiwan government has identified low-temperature logistics as one of three pilot industries in the "Cross-strait Bridge-Building Project," aiming to set an example for broader economic cooperation. The project's overall objective is to leverage Taiwan's expertise in low-temperature logistics to establish two key cities—Tianjin and Xiamen—as gateways for Taiwan agricultural products entering mainland China, while also assisting in the industrial upgrade of mainland China's low-temperature logistics sector.

Tianjin is chosen as the case due to its unique position as the largest port in northern China and its critical role in facilitating Taiwan's low-temperature logistics expansion into the mainland. As the second-largest city in northern China, Tianjin serves as a key logistics hub for the entire region. It provides direct access to Beijing and extends its influence to inland provinces in the north and northwest. Unlike coastal provinces in the south, which have long absorbed foreign technology and capital, northern China has relatively limited engagement with international trade and investment. The economic disparity between northern and southern China has resulted in an uneven distribution of logistics infrastructure, particularly in advanced cold-chain systems. While low-temperature logistics networks in cities like Shanghai, Shenzhen, and Guangzhou have benefited from foreign direct investment and international trade, northern China has lagged in these developments. Taiwanese investment in Tianjin's logistics sector, therefore, represents a crucial effort to bridge this gap by introducing advanced low-temperature logistics technologies to a region that has historically been underserved.

Another reason for studying Tianjin is the disparity in infrastructure maturity between northern and southern China. Low-temperature logistics relies heavily on specialized infrastructure. In China, transportation infrastructure has been more developed in the southern coastal regions, where wealthier consumer markets and higher levels of foreign investment have driven demand for high-quality logistics services. Northern China has larger vacancy in the market.

Additionally, the cooperation between Tianjin and Taiwan in the logistics sector is worth notice, as it highlights the potential for cross-strait collaboration in such a city that has traditionally had limited economic ties with Taiwan and relatively less exposure to know-how from developed countries or regions, compared with Southeast coastal cities.

Tianjin, traditionally known as a major seaport city, has long been a significant market for aquatic products. In 2013, Tianjin's GDP per capita reached $16,262 US dollars, which classifies it as a high-income city by global standards. The demand for fresh and quality food has surged, driven by increased awareness of health and food quality. Consumers in Tianjin are willing to pay more for exotic, fresh tropical fruits and live aquatic products, necessitating modern logistics solutions to meet these demands.

Through an efficient network of railways, airports, and highways, Tianjin port is accessible within 12 h from the Beijing-Tianjin-Hebei area, within 1 day from Northern China, and within 2 days from Northwestern China. Tianjin also has direct connections with more than 500 ports in 180 countries, positioning it as an important international shipping center in Northern China, particularly with its expansion through the Tianjin Dongjiang Bonded Port Zone.

In addition to its role as a seaport, Tianjin has implemented the "waterless port" service, which benefits 23 inland cities. Goods originating from these cities can be inspected and customs-cleared locally, sealed, and transported directly to Tianjin port within 2 days for shipment. This service is expected to generate 460,000 TEU of traffic for Tianjin port by 2017, streamlining the process for inland goods to be transported through Tianjin.

Tianjin's role in the Jing-jin-ji (Beijing-Tianjin-Hebei) region further enhances its logistics potential. The Jing-jin-ji area, with a population exceeding 100 million, represents a massive market for fresh products that require low-temperature logistics services. This regional integration provides Tianjin with an even larger demand for modern logistics solutions, particularly for goods such as Taiwan's agricultural products, which require reliable and efficient transportation to maintain freshness.

Through Taiwan's involvement in Tianjin's logistics infrastructure and the development of low-temperature supply chains, the city is poised to become an essential gateway for Taiwan agricultural exports and a model for enhancing mainland China's low-temperature logistics capacity (Table 4). This collaboration underscores the growing importance of integrating Taiwan's technological and logistical expertise with mainland China's vast market needs.

Table 4 SWOT analysis of Tianjin as a low-temperature logistics center

Strength:	Tianjin is the largest seaport in Northern China, offering multi-modal transportation to a vast area. It benefits from the Jing-jin-ji integration and has a large local market. Tianjin is a key pilot city for cross-strait cooperation with Taiwan
Weakness:	Traditional logistic mode dominates, and international/customized logistics are lacking. There is a shortage of skilled labor, modern equipment, and coordination, along with too many intermediaries and a lack of industrial standards
Opportunity:	China's growing market for fresh foods, rising personal incomes, and demand for modern logistics services create opportunities. ECFA cooperation with Taiwan and the trend toward "green logistics" also present prospects for growth
Threat:	Price wars within the industry, along with competition from Shanghai Free Trade Zone, Yokohama, and Pusan, pose threats to Tianjin's position in the logistics market

7 Discussion

This study highlights the importance of continued observation of the low-temperature logistics sector to understand how it evolves over time. The findings reveal that the trade between Taiwan and mainland China, particularly in the realm of low-temperature logistics, has created a mutually beneficial relationship. Taiwan has gained access to a large and growing market for its agricultural products, particularly tropical fruits and live aquatic products, while mainland China has benefited from a broader variety of fresh and high-quality produce. Low-temperature logistics have played a key role in this exchange by facilitating the efficient and cost-effective transport of perishable goods across the Taiwan Strait.

The role of low-temperature logistics in transforming food consumption patterns in mainland China has been significant. By reducing transportation time and costs, these logistics services have democratized access to fresh produce, enabling even people to enjoy a variety of goods that were once out of reach.

Moreover, Taiwan's involvement in the low-temperature logistics sector has spurred modernization within mainland China's logistics industry. Taiwanese companies have introduced advanced refrigeration technology and transportation systems, which have led to improvements in the efficiency and reliability of low-temperature logistics in mainland China. The growth of infrastructure such as cold storage facilities and the development of skilled labor have been key components of this transformation.

Looking forward, we are worried about the increasingly antagonistic political relationship between Taiwan and mainland China. Political tensions have resulted in the suspension of key trade negotiations, including the Cross-Strait Service Trade Agreement. Without formal agreements in place, businesses on both sides face regulatory barriers, preventing the low-temperature logistic industry from evolving into higher stages of cooperation. Resuming negotiations on trade agreements would provide the necessary institutional framework for companies to engage in long-term strategic planning. However, the resolution of these political obstacles is beyond the capacity of business practitioners.

Beyond political barriers, China's slowing economy and capital shortages (Rosen et al., 2024) in infrastructure projects have also affected logistics development. Large-scale logistics parks and cold-chain facilities require substantial investment, but financing constraints have delayed key projects.

Furthermore, both Taiwan and mainland China face growing regulatory pressures to reduce carbon emission. The future of low-temperature logistics will depend on the adoption of energy-efficient and environmentally sustainable solutions. Transition to energy-saving refrigeration methods, electric vehicles, and other green supply chain practices will be essential for the industry.

8 Further Research

Future research should focus on the impact of technological advancements in logistics, particularly the integration of big data analytics and 5G telecommunication technologies. The adoption of these technologies has the potential to transform logistics operations by improving efficiency, reducing costs, and enhancing flexibility. Big data enables logistics firms to optimize transportation routes, predict demand fluctuations, and allocate resources more effectively, thereby reducing waste and increasing operational efficiency. Meanwhile, 5G technology enhances connectivity, allowing for real-time monitoring of temperature-sensitive goods throughout the supply chain. This development is particularly relevant for low-temperature logistics, where precise environmental control is essential to maintaining product quality. Examining how companies leverage these technologies to streamline operations and improve service helps to understand the future trajectory of the industry.

Further competitiveness research can focus on the challenges that the rapid advancement of mainland Chinese firms presents to their Taiwanese counterparts. While Taiwan has historically maintained a competitive advantage in logistics technology, mainland companies are rapidly adopting new innovations and expanding their market share. Unlike earlier periods when Taiwanese firms dominated cross-strait logistics cooperation, mainland Chinese firms now possess greater local knowledge and operational scale, making them formidable competitors. Additionally, many Chinese logistic companies are born in the mobile Internet age, benefiting from an understanding of new customer demand. The increasing economies of scale achieved by large mainland firms may gradually erode Taiwan's competitive edge, raising questions about how Taiwanese companies can maintain their position in this evolving landscape. Further research should continuously observe the competitive dynamics between Taiwanese and mainland firms.

References

Alvarez, F. E., Buera, F. J., Robert E., & Lucas, J. (2013). Idea flows, economic growth, and trade. NBER working paper.

Dong, X. (2021, Sept 21). First pineapples, now sugar apples. *Taiwan threatens to take China to WTO over new fruit import ban*. Retrieved from ABC NEWS.

Haime, J. (2024, Marc 23). 10 years on, *Taiwan's Sunflower Movement has wilted but its legacy lingers on*. Retrieved from South China Morning Post.

Hsu, H.-C., Hsu, H.-L., & He, M.-Z. (2021). Research for Maintaining Cross-Strait Peace and Economic Development in the Post-Epidemic Era. *Proceedings of the 2021 6th International Conference on Social Sciences and Economic Development (ICSSED 2021)* (pp. 227–232). Atlantis Press.

Industrial Technology Research Institute. (2014). Tianjin food low-temperature logistics cross-strait industrial cooperation development plan. Taipei, Tianjin.

Rioux, S. (2014). Food quality and the circulation time of commodities: Lessons from the British milk trade 1845-1914. *Journal of Transport Geography, 38*, 114–121.

Rosen, D. H., Wright, L., Smith, J., Mingey, M., & Quinn, R. (2024, Dec 21). After the fall: China's economy in 2025. Retrieved from Rhodium Group.

Shi, Y. (2012). *Current situation analysis and HACCP strategy research of Taiwan fruit cold chain logistics at Xiamen port*. Jimei University.

Smith, J. (2005). Specialized logistics for a longer perishable supply chain. *World Trade, 18*(11), 46–47.

Whetham, E. H. (1964). The London Milk Trade, 1860-1900. *The Economic History Review, 17*(2), 369–380.

Xu, B., & Chiang, E. P. (2005). Trade, patents and international technology diffusion. *The Journal of International Trade & Economic Development, 1*, 115–135.

Ye, J.-M. (2014). Discussion on cross-strait low-temperature logistics (1) and (2).

Evaluating the Impact of Prakerja Program on Income and Employment: Evidence from Sakernas Data

Fauzan Ghazi Alauddin and Heni Wahyuni

Abstract In April 2020, the Indonesian government launched the Prakerja Program aimed at improving the skills and competitiveness of the workforce. This initiative offers financial support to individuals seeking to enroll in a variety of training courses. This research assesses the program's effectiveness by utilizing data from Sakernas and employing the instrumental variable approach to mitigate endogeneity issues. The results reveal that participation in the program leads to an increase in both income and the likelihood of employment. Furthermore, the program significantly boosts income and employability in Java and urban regions. Conversely, its impact appears to be limited in non-Java areas, where it primarily facilitates income growth with minimal influence on employment opportunities. In rural areas, the program does not exhibit a significant effect on income or employment prospects, regardless of whether they are in Java or outside Java.

Keywords Program evaluation · Prakerja program · Income · Employment probability

1 Introduction

At the beginning of 2020, the Indonesian Government issued a policy to increase the competency of workers in Indonesia, known as the Prakerja Program, where the program aims to increase the competency of the workforce in Indonesia with the hope that in the future it will create increased productivity and expanded employment opportunities. The Prakerja Program is a type of training subsidy assistance provided by the government to the workforce who need to increase their abilities. According to the theory put forward by Becker (1962), education and training are important investments for individuals to improve individual skills and abilities so

F. G. Alauddin (✉) · H. Wahyuni
Department of Economics and Business, University of Gadjah Mada, Yogyakarta, Indonesia
e-mail: fauzanghazialauddin2000@mail.ugm.ac.id; hwahyuni@ugm.ac.id

E. Lau et al. (eds.), *Economics and Finance Readings*,
https://doi.org/10.1007/978-981-96-6998-1_7

that individuals can survive in the labor market. This type of government intervention according to Betcherman et al. (1999) is an active labor market policy whose aim is to increase the productivity and abilities of the workforce through increasing understanding or ability in workers' abilities.

Active labor market policies have been implemented in many parts of the world, and many studies have been carried out in various parts of the world, both from developed countries (Caliendo and Schmidl, 2016; Card et al., 2010, 2015; Kluve, 2010; and Vooren et al., 2019) and developing countries (Escudero et al., 2019; McKenzie, 2017). There are differences in the impact of interventions in active labor market policy programs between developed and developing countries. The differences in impacts that occur between developed and developing countries are likely due to differences in the macroeconomic conditions of each country and the maturity of the labor market in developed countries.

In the Indonesian context, there are several studies that discuss the effectiveness of training participation in the Prakerja Card Program, such as Al-Ayyubi et al. (2023) which discusses the impact of Prakerja Program participation in the young age group. Panjaitan et al. (2021) and Dinar (2022) discuss the factors that influence individuals in registering for Prakerja programs. As well as research from Habsari et al. (2022), Rawie and Samputra (2020), Consuello (2020), Yana (2021), Rahman and Rahman (2021), and Ria and Febrilyanti (2023) which discusses the impact of participation in the program Prakerja to individual expenditure, program benefits, and capacity building is discussed qualitatively. In short, the Prakerja Program is useful as social assistance during the pandemic, increases expenses, and can increase individual abilities.

Although the studies above have discussed various aspects related to the effectiveness and impact of participation in Prakerja programs, several studies have not examined what factors encourage individuals to participate in Prakerja programs as well as the effectiveness of program participation which has just been measured in the young age group. This research wants to know what factors encourage individuals to participate in the program as well as the results obtained by individuals after participating in the program which are measured using income and the employment probability based on areas and island of residence.

This study aims to enhance the body of knowledge surrounding the evaluation of Prakerja programs. It posits that individual participation in such programs may introduce potential endogeneity issues. To address this concern, the research will employ an instrumental variable approach to mitigate the anticipated omitted variable bias. This study aims to offer new perspectives on the assessment of the Prakerja initiative implemented in various regions and islands inhabited by individuals. This is particularly significant given Indonesia's status as an archipelagic nation, where the islands exhibit diverse infrastructural conditions. Consequently, the findings are anticipated to furnish valuable insights for policymakers in the formulation and execution of analogous programs in the future.

2 Literature Review

2.1 *Theoretical Foundation*

To understand the relationship between participation in Prakerja programs and income and the likelihood of employment, it is important to examine the impact of human capital accumulation on both the employed and the unemployed. This research uses Human Capital theory from Becker (1962), which states that one way to increase human capital accumulation is through formal education and training. The impact of increasing human capital accumulation will give individuals better skills, be competitive in the labor market, and increase opportunities to get better or more stable jobs.

2.2 *Recent Empirical Studies*

Research related to the evaluation of active labor market policies has been carried out in various countries. This is reflected in meta-analyses conducted by researchers such as Caliendo and Schmidl (2016), Card et al. (2010, 2015), Escudero et al. (2019), Kluve (2010), McKenzie (2017), and Vooren et al. (2019). The differences in these studies lie in the year of policy evaluation, the program being evaluated, and the location (country) of the evaluation implementation. The next paragraph will discuss program evaluation based on the location of policy implementation, namely in developed and developing countries.

Developed Countries Evaluations carried out in developed countries have been carried out by Caliendo and Schmidl (2016), Card et al. (2010, 2015), Kluve (2010), and Vooren et al. (2019) where the results of these studies found that participation in a training program can increase your chances of finding a job and increasing your income. However, the positive effects of participation only became significant after 1 year of completing the program. In other words, training programs do not have a significant impact in the short term but can provide substantial benefits in the medium (>1 year after training) or long term (2–3 years after training). Meanwhile, research by Caliendo and Schmidl (2016) devoted to the analysis of programs aimed at young people shows that training programs aimed at young age groups have varying results on employment status, with some programs showing positive effects and others not showing significant effects. However, participation in training has a negative impact on participation in formal education, indicating that training is often used as a substitute for formal education.

Developing Countries According to Escudero et al. (2019), training programs in Latin America and the Caribbean generally increase individuals' chances of employment, especially in the formal sector. The effectiveness of this program is increasingly high among women and young people, especially when the economy is growing. Further research shows that intensive training programs that specifically target poor individuals produce better results. However, the results of McKenzie's (2017) research show that in some areas, especially urban areas, training programs do not always have a significant impact on employment levels or income. This may be due to the labor market mechanism which is already working quite well in the region.

2.3 *Existing Research on Prakerja Program*

Various studies have been conducted to examine the effectiveness and factors that encourage individuals to register for Prakerja programs. Research by Panjaitan et al. (2021) found that factors influencing program registration were working hours, income, age, training, formal work status, Internet use, new business preparation, changes in income and working hours, education level, and increased skills and incentives. In line with Panjaitan, Nuryartono, and Anggraini, Dinar (2022) shows that fresh graduates, individuals with work experience, individuals who are unemployed due to the pandemic, and who have been looking for work for a long time have a higher probability of registering for the program. The main reason for enrolling in the program is to improve skills and earn incentives. Research by Al-Ayyubi et al. (2023) shows that Prakerja Program's participation increases young workers' participation in the informal labor market, but does not show significant changes in income in the short term. On the other hand, research by Habsari et al. (2022), Rawie and Samputra (2020), Consuello (2020), Yana (2021), Rahman and Rahman (2021), and Ria and Febrilyanti (2023) using qualitative methods found that the Prakerja Program is useful as social assistance, increasing individual expenditure, and increasing individual ability to work through training subsidies.

2.4 *Impact of Training Participation*

Several previous studies have shown that the impact of participation in training specifically for several groups has almost the same impact on income and employment status, where participation in training has a positive impact on income and employment status, or in other words, when individuals participate in training, the individual will experience an increase in income and a change in status from unemployed to employed. Several studies have examined the impact of training participation on certain groups such as women (Doerr, 2022), new graduates (Gaulke, 2021; Oswald-Egg and Renold, 2021), entrepreneurs or self-employed workers (Bairagya, 2021), adults (Ruhose et al., 2019), young (Das, 2021; Fairlie and Bahr, 2018; Chakravarty et al., 2019; Brattil et al., 2022; Alfonsi et al., 2020), workers in certain sectors (Adhvaryu et al., 2023), disabled workers (Takasaki, 2024), and low-skilled workers (Dauth, 2020).

3 Research Method

3.1 Research Design

The research design consists of two main designs. The first design aims to identify the factors that motivate individuals to participate in the Prakerja Program, using a probit model for analysis. The second design focuses on evaluating the impact of training completed by Prakerja participants, specifically examining how skill enhancement after training influences income and employment prospects.

However, during the implementation of the second design, potential endogeneity issues were identified in the participation variable. This issue is common in studies on human capital investment, where participation variables may be endogenous due to omitted variable bias. This bias occurs when certain influential variables are not included in the model, yet they affect program participation.

To address this endogeneity concern, this study will employ an instrumental variable approach. The instrumental variables used are individual motivation for program registration (to improve personal skills) and acceptance status (interaction variable), as well as Internet usage in the workplace. Individual interaction motivation and acceptance status are considered relevant because they can influence the likelihood of completing the training without directly affecting income or employment status, except through training completion. Similarly, Internet usage in the workplace is assumed to have no direct impact on income or employment opportunities. Therefore, these two variables are deemed suitable instruments, as they can influence program participation while maintaining no direct relationship with the dependent variable.

3.2 Data Sources

This study uses secondary data from the National Labor Force Survey (Sakernas) conducted by the Central Statistics Agency (BPS). Sakernas provides comprehensive data regarding the condition of the workforce in Indonesia and is carried out routinely every year by BPS. In this study, researchers used Sakernas data from 2021 and 2022. This data was processed as a pooled cross-section to increase the sample size, resulting in more robust estimates.

The unit of observation in this study is all individuals in the survey. In the analysis of factors that influence individual participation in the Prakerja Program, it is not limited to whether the individual is unemployed or already working. However, to analyze the impact of participation in the Prakerja Program on income and the possibility of working, this study will only use individuals who enrolled in the Prakerja Program, where the treatment group is individuals who completed the training (participated) while the control group is individuals who did not complete the training (not participated).

3.3 Econometrics Models and Instruments

This study aims to identify the determinants that affect individuals' participation in Prakerja programs. An analytical phase will be employed to assess individual factors influencing participation, drawing on the framework established by Heckman and Smith (2003). The selection of these influencing factors is informed by the research conducted by Kumar et al. (2019) as well as Renaud et al. (2004). Consequently, the model to be utilized is outlined as follows:

$$p\left(\text{Reg} = 1|X\right) = \phi\left(\alpha + \psi \boldsymbol{E}_{it} + \eta \boldsymbol{U}_{it} + \xi \boldsymbol{J}_{it} + \boldsymbol{X}_{it} + \varepsilon_{it}\right) \quad (1)$$

$$p\left(\text{Train} = 1|\text{Reg} = 1, \text{Acc} = 1, X\right) = \phi\left(+\psi \mathbf{E}_{it} + \eta \boldsymbol{U}_{it} + \xi \boldsymbol{J}_{it} + \boldsymbol{X}_{it} + \varepsilon_{it}\right) \quad (2)$$

In this study, a probit model was used to analyze various equations related to participation in the Prakerja Program. The first equation evaluates the likelihood of an individual enrolling in the program, which is influenced by three key variables: **E** (work or business experience), **U** (residence in an urban area), and **J** (residence on Java Island). This equation explains how these three variables affect an individual's probability of enrolling in the Prakerja Program. Meanwhile, the second equation examines how these same variables influence the likelihood of completing the training, conditional on the individual being accepted into the program.

The second design will address potential endogeneity issues in the analysis, and this study will apply the Instrumental Variables (IV) method to measure the impact on the wage equation. The variable suspected of being endogenous is program participation (**P**), as an individual's participation may be influenced by unobserved (omitted) factors, such as personal motivation, the availability of supporting infrastructure for completing training, or individual circumstances. Therefore, suitable instrumental variables—both relevant and exogenous—are required to mitigate the endogeneity problem.

In this study, two instrumental variables will be used: an interaction variable representing an individual's motivation to register for the program and their status within the program, and Internet usage in the workplace. The interaction variable reflects an individual's reason for enrolling, which indicates their goal or objective for participating in the program and their acceptance status. Meanwhile, Internet usage in the workplace serves as a proxy for the availability of Internet infrastructure, based on the assumption that individuals working in Internet-equipped environments are more likely to be exposed to digital resources.

To account for the potential endogeneity issue, this study will employ an instrumental variable approach using the two-stage least squares (2SLS) method, as outlined below:

$$p(\text{Work} = 1|X) = \phi(\alpha + \psi \boldsymbol{P}_{it} + \eta \boldsymbol{X}_{it} + \varepsilon_{it}) \tag{3}$$

$$\text{LogWages} = \alpha + \psi \hat{\boldsymbol{P}}_{it} + \eta \boldsymbol{X}_{it} + \varepsilon_{it} \tag{4}$$

Where the first stage in the equation above is as follows:

$$\hat{\boldsymbol{P}} = \alpha + \zeta \boldsymbol{M}_{it} * \boldsymbol{S}_{it} + \xi \boldsymbol{I}_{it} + v_{it} \tag{5}$$

To produce unbiased estimation results, the two instrumental variables must satisfy two key assumptions: relevance, meaning they are strongly correlated with the endogenous variable, and exogeneity, meaning they are not correlated with the error term in the outcome equation (Angrist & Pischke, 2009).

4 Result and Discussion

4.1 Descriptive Statistics

Table 1 presents descriptive statistics of variables related to the Prakerja Program and individual characteristics. For the Prakerja Program, variables include registration, motivation factors like improving skills and incentives, and participation metrics. Individual characteristics cover demographics such as gender, age, marital status, education level, and geographic distribution across Indonesian islands. Observations and mean values are provided.

Prakerja Program Participation—Among the total sample, only 5.8% of individuals registered for the Prakerja Program. Among those who provided data on their motivation for enrolling (22,892 observations), the primary reasons were financial incentives (44.6%), followed by skill improvement (32.2%), and trying out the program (16.3%). A smaller proportion cited having spare time (4.5%), ease of registration (1.3%), or other reasons (0.9%).Regarding program acceptance, 30.6% of the sample was admitted into the Prakerja Program. However, the percentage of individuals who completed training and participated in the program was slightly lower, at 27.2%. This indicates that not all accepted participants proceeded to complete the training.

Individual Characteristics—The sample consists of 53.3% male respondents, with an average age of 32.2 years. Among them, 32.7% are heads of households, while 62.9% are married. The average years of schooling is 11.59 years, suggesting that most respondents have completed at least high school education. In terms of geographic distribution, respondents are spread across different island regions. The largest proportion resides in Sumatra (37.0%), followed by Java & Bali (30.2%),

Table 1 Descriptive statistics

Variable	Obs.	Mean
A. Prakerja program		
Register[d]	394.315	0.058
Motivation[d]	22.892	
Improve skill[1]	7.372	0.322
Incentive[0]	10.220	0.446
Spare time[0]	1.043	0.045
Trying[0]	3.746	0.163
Easy to register[0]	303	0.013
Other[0]	208	0.009
Accepted[d]	22.892	0.306
Training[d]	22.892	0.272
Participate[d]	22.892	0.272
B. Individual characteristics		
Male[d]	22.892	0.533
Age	22.892	32.20
Head of household[d]	22.892	0.327
Married	22.892	0.629
Years of schooling	22.892	11.591
Island[d]	22.892	
Sumatra[0]		0.37
Java & Bali[1]		0.302
Nusa Tenggara[0]		0.045
Kalimantan[0]		0.099
Sulawesi[0]		0.154
Maluku & Papua[0]		0.026
Urban[d]	22.892	0.582
Internet usage[d]	22.892	0.400

Source: Author's calculation from Sakernas 2021 & 2022. Note: Superscript [d] indicates a dummy variable, motivation and island were constructed as dummy variables based on categorical classifications, where a value of 1 indicates the main category and 0 otherwise

Sulawesi (15.4%), Kalimantan (9.9%), Nusa Tenggara (4.5%), and Maluku & Papua (2.6%). Additionally, 58.2% of respondents live in urban areas, which may influence their access to education, employment, and Internet facilities. One important factor in digital engagement is Internet usage in the workplace, which is reported by 40.0% of respondents. This could indicate the level of access to digital tools and infrastructure, which may affect participation in online-based programs like Prakerja. Overall, the statistics suggest that financial incentives and skill improvement are the key drivers of participation in the Prakerja Program. Additionally, demographic factors such as education, urban residency, and Internet access could play a role in determining an individual's likelihood of enrolling and completing training.

4.2 Participation Result

The Table 2 below presents the estimation results of a probit model analyzing the likelihood of an individual registering for the Prakerja Program and completing training, with the dependent variables being Register and Training, respectively. Although control variables were included in the models, they are not displayed in the table. The coefficients reported represent marginal effects, with standard errors in parentheses. Statistical significance is indicated by asterisks.

The probit model estimation results examine determinants of participation in the Prakerja Program, focusing on two binary outcomes: registration (Register) and training engagement (Training). Both models incorporate control variables, though these are not displayed. Coefficients represent marginal effects on the latent variable's z-score, with significance levels (***$p < 0.01$, **$p < 0.05$) indicating robust statistical associations. For the Register model, prior experience exhibits a positive and highly significant effect (0.026, $p < 0.01$), suggesting that individuals with greater experience are more likely to enroll in the program. This aligns with the premise that experienced workers may proactively seek skill development opportunities. Similarly, urban residence is associated with higher registration probabilities (0.019, $p < 0.01$), likely due to better access to program information, digital infrastructure, or administrative support in urban areas. Conversely, residing in Java shows a small but significant negative association (−0.008, $p < 0.01$), which may reflect regional saturation of similar initiatives or competition from alternative employment opportunities in Indonesia's most populous island.

For the Training model, which analyzes post-registration engagement, experience remains a positive and significant predictor (0.033, $p < 0.05$), reinforcing its role in sustained program participation. Urban residence also retains its positive influence (0.021, $p < 0.05$), underscoring the importance of urban advantages, such as reliable Internet access or logistical ease, in facilitating training completion.

Table 2 Impact of demographic and regional on program participation

	Dependent variable	
	Register	Training
Experience	0.026***	0.033**
	(0.000)	(0.009)
Urban	0.019***	0.021**
	(0.000)	(0.009)
Java	−0.008***	−0.013
	(0.000)	(0.013)
Obs.	257,141	5105
Pseudo—R^2	0.128	0.039

Note: Standard errors are given in parentheses. The results are presented using marginal effects for probability Register, Training, and Participation. **p* < *0.10*, ***p* < *0.05*, ****p* < *0.001*

However, the negative coefficient for Java (−0.013) achieves statistical significance at the 5% level ($p = 0.013$), implying that even among registrants, Java residents are less likely to proceed to training. This could signal regional disparities in program delivery, such as inconsistent outreach or competing time demands unique to Java.

The models differ notably in explanatory power. The Register model (Obs. = 257,141) demonstrates moderate fit (Pseudo-R^2 = 0.128), indicating that observed variables, including experience and urbanity, explain a reasonable proportion of registration behavior. In contrast, the Training model (Obs. = 5105) shows weak explanatory power (Pseudo-R^2 = 0.039), suggesting unobserved factors—such as socioeconomic constraints, training quality, or individual motivation—play a dominant role in determining whether registrants transition to active participation. The stark attrition in sample size between registration and training stages further highlights systemic barriers to sustained engagement.

These findings carry critical policy implications. The persistent influence of urban residence underscores the need to address rural–urban divides in digital access and program awareness. Similarly, the negative association with Java warrants investigation into regional targeting strategies and potential structural barriers. However, the limited explanatory power of the training model emphasizes the necessity of complementary qualitative research to uncover contextual factors, such as cultural perceptions of training or household responsibilities, that quantitative metrics may overlook. Future iterations of the Prakerja Program could benefit from enhanced rural outreach, tailored regional interventions, and integrated support systems to bridge gaps between registration and meaningful participation.

4.3 Evaluation Result

The Table 3 below presents the estimation results examining the impact of program participation on wages and employment probability. The wage equation is estimated using the instrumental variable (IV) approach, addressing potential endogeneity in program participation, while the employment probability equation is estimated using a probit model. Although control variables are included in the models, they are not displayed in the results. The table provides separate estimations for the full sample and subgroups based on geographic location, distinguishing between urban and rural areas within and outside Java & Bali.

For the full sample, participation in the Prakerja Program has a statistically significant positive effect on wages (0.044, $p < 0.05$), suggesting that individuals who complete the program experience higher earnings. This supports the argument that the program enhances human capital, leading to improved labor market outcomes. However, program participation does not have a statistically significant effect on employment probability (0.009, $p > 0.1$), implying that while the program may increase earnings, it does not necessarily enhance the likelihood of securing

Table 3 Impact of program participation on wages and employment probability

	Dependent variable	
	Wages	Employment probability
A. Full sample		
Program participation	0.044**	0.009
	(0.017)	(0.007)
Obs	11,070	22,849
R-sq	0.157	0.097
B. Java - Urban		
Program participation	0.065*	0.021
	(0.036)	(0.016)
Obs	2613	4609
R-sq	0.110	0.084
C. Java - Rural		
Program participation	0.102	0.016
	(0.072)	(0.030)
Obs	818	1699
R-sq	0.114	0.116
D. Outside Java - Urban		
Program participation	0.051**	0.009
	(0.025)	(0.011)
Obs	4310	8702
R-sq	0.118	0.081
E. Outside Java - Rural		
Program participation	0.018	−0.001
	(0.033)	(0.011)
Obs	3329	7839
R-sq	0.151	0.130

Note: Standard errors are given in parentheses. All covariates included in the regression, starting from gender, ages, education head of household, family size, experience, residential area, and residential island. Marginal effects are presented for the employment probability in IV and Probit regression. *$p < 0.10$, **$p < 0.05$, ***$p < 0.001$

employment. The R-squared values for the wage and employment models are 0.157 and 0.097, respectively, indicating a moderate explanatory power.

Java: Urban Versus Rural When disaggregating the sample within Java, a significant positive effect of program participation on wages is observed only in urban areas (0.065, $p < 0.1$). This suggests that individuals in urban Java benefit from the program in terms of higher wages, possibly due to greater access to better-paying job opportunities or higher returns to skills. In contrast, in rural Java, the estimated coefficient for wages is positive but statistically insignificant (0.102, $p > 0.1$), indicating that program participation does not have a robust effect on earnings in these areas.For employment probability, neither urban nor rural Java show statistically significant effects (0.021, $p > 0.1$ and 0.016, $p > 0.1$, respectively). This aligns with the full sample results, reinforcing the notion that program participation may enhance earnings but does not significantly improve job acquisition chances.

Outside Java Program participation has a significant positive effect on wages in urban areas (0.051, $p < 0.05$), similar to the urban regions of Java. This suggests that the program is effective in boosting wages in urban labor markets across Indonesia, where participants likely have greater access to employment opportunities that reward skill enhancement. However, the effect in rural areas outside Java is small and statistically insignificant (0.018, $p > 0.1$), indicating that individuals in these regions do not experience significant wage improvements after participating in the program. Regarding employment probability, the effects remain insignificant across both urban and rural areas outside Java (0.009, $p > 0.1$ and −0.001, $p > 0.1$, respectively). This suggests that geographic differences do not alter the overall conclusion that while the program may improve wages in certain regions, it does not necessarily increase employment opportunities.

The findings indicate that the Prakerja Program positively influences wages, particularly in urban areas, both within and outside Java. However, the program does not significantly impact employment probability, suggesting that while it enhances earnings potential for those already employed, it does not directly facilitate job entry. The stronger wage effects in urban areas may reflect better access to job markets that reward additional skills, whereas the weaker effects in rural areas suggest that structural barriers—such as limited job opportunities—may hinder the program's effectiveness in improving earnings.

4.4 Discussion

The findings of this study align with prior research on the economic impacts of training programs in developing economies. For instance, Escudero et al. (2019) demonstrate that such interventions can enhance income levels and labor market prospects, a conclusion corroborated by McKenzie (2017). However, a notable divergence emerges in the context of employment probability: unlike these earlier studies, participation in the Prakerja Program did not significantly increase individuals' likelihood of securing employment. This discrepancy may reflect structural labor market challenges exacerbated by the COVID-19 pandemic. As highlighted in the International Labour Organization's (ILO, 2022) report, the pandemic precipitated a sharp decline in micro, small, and medium enterprise (MSME) turnover, compelling firms to adopt cost-efficiency measures such as reducing working hours and workforce downsizing. Concurrently, global unemployment surged, creating a saturated labor market characterized by heightened competition. The ILO further notes that this environment disproportionately disadvantages low-skilled workers, as employers increasingly favor candidates with advanced competencies amid a surplus of highly qualified job seekers. Consequently, even if training programs enhance skills, systemic barriers—such as reduced hiring capacity among MSMEs and skill mismatches—may attenuate their ability to translate human capital gains into tangible employment outcomes.

In the Indonesian context, participation in the Prakerja Program demonstrates a positive association with income enhancement, a finding that diverges from prior studies examining similar interventions. For instance, Al-Ayyubi et al. (2023) report no statistically significant income effects from training participation, while qualitative investigations by Habsari et al. (2022), Rawie and Samputra (2020), Consuello (2020), Yana (2021), Rahman and Rahman (2021), and Ria and Febrilyanti (2023) corroborate that the program enhances individual competencies but fails to translate these gains into measurable income improvements. This discrepancy may stem from structural economic dynamics unique to the Prakerja framework. Notably, interview-based evidence reveals that observed increases in household consumption among participants are attributable to direct cash incentives provided post-training, rather than skill-based income growth. This suggests that the program's short-term welfare effects are driven by liquidity injections rather than sustained human capital development, highlighting a critical gap between competency acquisition and labor market returns.

Also, the findings of this study reveal a pronounced urban–rural disparity in the economic returns of training participation, with urban participants experiencing stronger income gains compared to their rural counterparts. This divergence aligns with McKenzie's (2017) assertion that urban economies, characterized by diversified labor markets and advanced infrastructure, are better positioned to absorb and capitalize on skill development initiatives. By contrast, rural economies—often dominated by agriculture—face structural constraints that limit the relevance and applicability of training programs. Data from the Prakerja Program's platform corroborates this imbalance: the most sought-after training modules predominantly cater to urban-centric sectors (e.g., digital marketing, finance), leaving rural participants with fewer opportunities to acquire skills pertinent to agricultural livelihoods.

This mismatch underscores the criticality of aligning training content with regional economic profiles, as emphasized by Kumar et al. (2019). Their analysis demonstrates that training interventions in rural settings yield higher income returns when tailored to agricultural sectors, whereas programs targeting manufacturing or services exhibit muted effects. The authors attribute this discrepancy to sector-specific dynamics: non-agricultural sectors in rural areas often undervalue formal training due to informal employment structures or mismatches between acquired skills and on-the-job requirements. Consequently, even when rural participants complete training, the lack of sectoral alignment may prevent productivity gains from translating into measurable income improvements. These insights highlight the need for policymakers to design spatially and sectorally adaptive training frameworks, ensuring that rural populations receive contextually relevant skill-building opportunities.

From a human capital perspective, the findings of this study provide evidence that individual engagement in training can enhance income levels and employment opportunities, albeit the effect is relatively modest. Notably, these findings align with previous research conducted within the framework of human capital theory (Becker, 1962), this study corroborates the proposition that training participation enhances income levels, complementing formal education as a critical mechanism for skill development. Becker posits that post-educational training augments individual productivity, which in turn translates into higher wages—a linkage empirically validated in this analysis. However, the relationship between training and employment probability is contingent on employer perceptions of skill relevance. Firms are more likely to hire trained individuals if acquired competencies align with organizational productivity objectives; conversely, training lacking sector-specific applicability may fail to improve job prospects, as employers prioritize direct returns on human capital investments.

These findings align with a robust body of literature (e.g., Doerr, 2022; Gaulke, 2021; Oswald-Egg & Renold, 2021; Bairagya, 2021) demonstrating consistent positive returns to training on income. Nevertheless, disparities persist in employment outcomes across studies. For instance, Ruhose et al. (2019) and Das (2021) attribute such variability to mismatches between training content and labor market demands, while Fairlie and Bahr (2018) emphasize structural barriers in informal economies. This divergence underscores the mediating role of contextual factors—such as sectoral dynamics and employer valuation of skills—in determining whether human capital gains translate into employment opportunities.

5 Policy Implication

The estimation results provide critical insights for policymakers regarding the effectiveness of the Prakerja Program in enhancing labor market outcomes. While the program demonstrates a positive impact on wages, particularly in urban areas, its lack of significant effect on employment probability raises important considerations for improving the program's design and implementation.

Enhancing Employment Linkages Since program participation does not significantly increase employment probability, policymakers should consider integrating job placement services, employer partnerships, and internship programs into the Prakerja framework. Collaborating with private sector companies, particularly in industries with high demand for skilled workers, could improve job-matching opportunities for program graduates. Additionally, providing career counseling and networking opportunities may help participants translate their skills into actual employment.

Addressing Regional Disparities The results indicate that the program's impact on wages is stronger in urban areas than in rural areas, both within and outside Java. This suggests that rural participants may face structural barriers, such as limited job availability or lower returns to skills. To address these disparities, the government could: expand digital job opportunities by promoting remote work and digital entrepreneurship, particularly for rural participants; strengthen vocational training tailored to regional labor market demands, ensuring that skills acquired through the program align with local industries; invest in rural infrastructure, such as Internet access and transportation, to improve access to training and employment opportunities.

Improving Wage Growth Through Lifelong Learning The significant wage effect observed in urban areas suggests that skill enhancement through training has a positive return. To sustain wage growth, the government could introduce continuous upskilling programs beyond the initial training. Encouraging lifelong learning through stackable credentials, micro-certifications, and employer-sponsored training could help workers remain competitive in an evolving labor market.

Strengthening Program Targeting and Outreach To maximize the program's impact, better targeting mechanisms should be implemented to prioritize individuals who would benefit the most from skill development. The findings suggest that the program might be more effective for those already employed, rather than those seeking jobs. Policymakers should evaluate whether alternative training models, such as apprenticeships or direct employer-sponsored training, would be more effective for unemployed individuals. Additionally, enhancing awareness and accessibility—especially in underprivileged and rural areas—could ensure that more disadvantaged individuals benefit from the program.

Evaluating and Refining the Instrumental Variable Approach Given that the wage equation in this study was estimated using an instrumental variable approach, future policy evaluations should continue using robust econometric techniques to assess program effectiveness. Further research could explore additional instrumental variables or experimental designs (e.g., randomized control trials) to verify causality and refine policy recommendations.

6 Conclusion

The findings highlight the importance of complementing training programs with employment-focused interventions to enhance labor market outcomes. While the Prakerja Program effectively increases wages, particularly in urban areas, additional policy measures—such as job-matching services, regional workforce development, and continuous upskilling initiatives—are needed to maximize its impact. By addressing these gaps, the government can ensure that skill development programs contribute more effectively to both wage growth and employment opportunities, fostering a more inclusive and resilient labor market.

References

Adhvaryu, A., Kala, N., & Nyshadham, A. (2023). Returns to on-the-job soft skills training. *Journal of Political Economy, 131*(8), 2165–2208.

Al Ayyubi, M. S., Pratomo, D. S., & Prasetyia, F. (2023). Does pre-employment card program improve Indonesian youth labor market performance in pandemic era? *Cogent Economics & Finance, 11*(2), 2267752.

Alfonsi, L., Bandiera, O., Bassi, V., Burgess, R., Rasul, I., Sulaiman, M., & Vitali, A. (2020). Tackling youth unemployment: Evidence from a labor market experiment in Uganda. *Econometrica, 88*(6), 2369–2414.

Angrist, J. D., & Pischke, J. S. (2009). *Mostly harmless econometrics: An empiricist's companion*. Princeton University Press.

Bairagya, I. (2021). Impact of formal vocational training on the earnings of self-employed individuals in rural India. *Journal of Business Venturing Insights, 16*, e00269.

Becker, G. S. (1962). Investment in human capital: A theoretical analysis. *Journal of Political Economy, 70*(5, Part 2), 9–49.

Betcherman, G., Dar, A., Luinstra, A., & Ogawa, M. (1999). Active labor market policies: Policy issues for East Asia. Second Draft, Social Protection Unit, World Bank, Washington DC.

Bratti, M., Ghirelli, C., Havari, E., & Santangelo, G. (2022). Vocational training for unemployed youth in Latvia. *Journal of Population Economics*, 1–41.

Caliendo, M., & Schmidl, R. (2016). Youth unemployment and active labor market policies in Europe. *IZA Journal of Labor Policy, 5*, 1–30.

Card, D., Kluve, J., & Weber, A. (2010). Active labour market policy evaluations: A meta-analysis. *The Economic Journal, 120*(548), F452–F477.

Card, D., Kluve, J., & Weber, A. (2015). What works? A meta analysis of recent active labor market program evaluations.

Chakravarty, S., Lundberg, M., Nikolov, P., & Zenker, J. (2019). Vocational training programs and youth labor market outcomes: Evidence from Nepal. *Journal of Development Economics, 136*, 71–110.

Consuello, Y. (2020). Analisis Efektifitas Kartu Pra-kerja di Tengah Pandemi Covid-19. *Adalah, 4*(1), 93–100.

Das, N. (2021). Training the disadvantaged youth and labor market outcomes: Evidence from Bangladesh. *Journal of Development Economics, 149*, 102585.

Dauth, C. (2020). Regional discontinuities and the effectiveness of further training subsidies for low-skilled employees. *ILR Review, 73*(5), 1147–1184.

Dinar, Y. B. K. L. (2022). Probability to apply for the pre-employment card program during the Covid-19 pandemic in NTB Province. *Jurnal Ekonomi dan Statistik Indonesia, 2*(1), 98–106.

Doerr, A. (2022). Vocational training for female job returners-effects on employment, earnings and job quality. *Labour Economics, 75*, 102139.

Escudero, V., Kluve, J., López Mourelo, E., & Pignatti, C. (2019). Active labour market programmes in Latin America and the Caribbean: Evidence from a meta-analysis. *The Journal of Development Studies, 55*(12), 2644–2661.

Fairlie, R. W., & Bahr, P. R. (2018). The effects of computers and acquired skills on earnings, employment and college enrollment: Evidence from a field experiment and California UI earnings records. *Economics of Education Review, 63*, 51–63.

Gaulke, A. P. (2021). Post-schooling off-the-job training and its benefits. *Labour Economics, 70*, 102007.

Habsari, T. N., Sahabuddin, Z. A., & Sundari, S. (2022). The effectiveness of the pre-employment card program as unemployment benefits due to the Covid-19 pandemic in Indonesia. *International Journal of Social Science and Human Research, 5*(01), 226–232.

Heckman, J. J., & Smith, J. A. (2003). The determinants of participation in a social program: Evidence from a prototypical job training program.

Kluve, J. (2010). The effectiveness of European active labor market programs. *Labour economics, 17*(6), 904–918.

Kumar, R., Mandava, S., & Gopanapalli, V. S. (2019). Vocational training in India: Determinants of participation and effect on wages. *Empirical Research in Vocational Education and Training, 11*(1), 1–17.

McKenzie, D. (2017). How effective are active labor market policies in developing countries? A critical review of recent evidence. *The World Bank Research Observer, 32*(2), 127–154.

Oswald-Egg, M. E., & Renold, U. (2021). No experience, no employment: The effect of vocational education and training work experience on labour market outcomes after higher education. *Economics of Education Review, 80*, 102065.

Panjaitan, D. V., Nuryartono, N., & Anggraeni, L. (2021). Faktor-Faktor yang Memengaruhi Partisipasi Tenaga Kerja dalam Program Kartu Prakerja. *Jurnal Ekonomi dan Kebijakan Pembangunan, 10*(1), 20–43.

Rahman, D., & Rahman, K. (2021). Efektivitas Kebijakan Pemerintah Tentang Pengembangan Kompetensi Kerja Melalui Program Kartu Prakerja Studi Program Kartu Prakerja Dalam Mengatasi Pengangguran Di Kabupaten Tebo Provinsi Jambi. *Jurnal Kajian Pemerintah: Journal of Government, Social and Politics, 7*(1), 39–53.

Rawie, Y., & Samputra, P. L. (2020). Analisis cost and effectivity program kartu prakerja di Indonesia. *GEMA PUBLICA, 5*(2), 118–139.

Renaud, S., Lakhdari, M., & Morin, L. (2004). The determinants of participation in non-mandatory training. *Relations industrielles/Industrial relations*, 724–743.

Ria, A. N., & Febrilyantri, C. (2023). Efektivitas Program Kartu Prakerja Dalam Meningkatkan Kesejahteraan Penerima Pada Kecamatan Sampung Ponorogo Ditinjau Perspektif Ekonomi Islam. *Niqosiya: Journal of Economics and Business Research, 3*(2), 419–430.

Ruhose, J., Thomsen, S. L., & Weilage, I. (2019). The benefits of adult learning: Work-related training, social capital, and earnings. *Economics of Education Review, 72*, 166–186.

ILO. (2022). *Socioeconomic impact of the COVID-19 pandemic in Indonesia*. ILO.

Takasaki, Y. (2024). Impacts of vocational training for persons with disabilities: Experimental evidence from Cambodia. *Journal of Development Economics, 169*, 103277.

Vooren, M., Haelermans, C., Groot, W., & Maassen van den Brink, H. (2019). The effectiveness of active labor market policies: A meta-analysis. *Journal of Economic Surveys, 33*(1), 125–149.

Yana, S. D. (2021). Efektivitas Program Kartu Prakerja dalam Membangun Sumberdaya Manusia. *Jurnal Investasi Islam, 6*(1), 12–21.

The Performance of Momentum Trading Strategies in the U.S. Natural Gas Futures

Ikhlaas Gurrib, Dalia Hamdan, and Olga Starkova

Abstract This study investigates if the Rate of Change (ROC), a common measure of the direction and magnitude of a trend, is reliable to predict U.S. Henry Hub Natural Gas futures prices. The methodology focuses on the ROC and/or Moving Average (MA) price crossover models within a trading system. Monthly futures prices of natural gas are collected for the period May 2004–July 2024. Performance is measured using both Sharpe and Sortino ratios to consider both total and downside risks. The model is evaluated against a naïve buy-and-hold strategy. Findings suggest that the ROC using a period of 10 months provides a superior return per unit of risk relative to the naïve buy-and-hold strategy. There was no downside risk due to the presence of solely positive returns under the ROC-10 model. Supplementing the ROC-based model with a price crossover MA strategy did not improve the performance of the model.

Keywords Energy · Natural gas · Futures markets · Rate of change · Technical analysis · Performance

1 Introduction

Decoupling among energy commodities is becoming more apparent, with the wide difference between the natural gas prices and petroleum products motivating energy entities to extract higher-value hydrocarbon gas liquids (HGLs) from the natural gas stream (EIA, 2024). For instance, EIA expects the U.S. sectors to consume 7% more of natural gas with an assumption that the fourth quarter of 2024 will be colder than last year's, thereby increasing demand for space heating. Specifically, the decoupling between natural gas and other petroleum goods is evidenced with terms such

I. Gurrib (✉) · D. Hamdan · O. Starkova
School of Management, Canadian University Dubai, Dubai, United Arab Emirates
e-mail: ikhlaas@cud.ac.ae; dalia.hamdan@cud.ac.ae; olga.starkova@cud.ac.ae; https://www.cud.ac.ae; https://www.cud.ac.ae; https://www.cud.ac.ae

E. Lau et al. (eds.), *Economics and Finance Readings*,
https://doi.org/10.1007/978-981-96-6998-1_8

as decoupling, decarbonization, and energy policy. For years, in the USA, the energy market has traditionally been coupled with GDP growth. However, in 2016, the International Energy Agency (IEA) found that despite GDP growth of 3% per annum, the world greenhouse gas emissions (GHG) remained flat in 2014 and 2015 (IEA, 2015, 2016). The decoupling of the GHG and global growth was seen as an encouraging revelation setting the path toward achieving the agreed objective of increasing the global mean surface temperature to less than 2 °C above preindustrial levels (UNFCCC, 2016; Chemnick, 2016). In the same vein, during the same 2014–2016 period, oil prices lost more than two-thirds of their value. With prices continuing to roam around 40–50% of their 2011–2014 values, various oil-revenue dependent economies have suffered a substantial drop in consumption, economic growth, and investments (World Bank, 2018). Fluctuations in oil price led to heightened volatility in economic output, which in turn led various economies to adopt more stringent fiscal and monetary policies, including reforms to reduce reliance on oil. This also resulted in investors becoming more risk averse when investment decisions related to energy commodities and energy stocks, led by the crude oil market, are made.

Cross-market interdependence has also increased as a repercussion of globalized markets. However, such linkages are not straightforward, especially with the advent of new alternative assets. For instance, Gurrib (2019) found that an energy commodity price index and energy block chain-based cryptocurrency price index are not robust forecasters in the energy commodity and energy cryptocurrency markets. Similarly, while Gurrib and Kamalov (2019) reported a change in the return per unit of risk in both the natural gas and crude oil markets when comparing the pre- and post-2008 crisis, Gurrib (2018a) found that an energy futures index based on leading fossil fuels like natural gas, crude oil, and heating oil was unable to predict leading stock market index movements during the 2000 bubble. Furthermore, Gupta et al. (2017) reported that volatility in futures markets increased over time and is not unavoidably linked to volatility in other financial markets.

The energy market dynamics are evolving. For instance, Contu et al. (2021) assessed energy views on energy sources and reported mixed views. EIA (2018) forecasted the electric power sector to consume more energy than any other sectors, with renewable energy consumption growth being the fastest among other fuels. Natural gas consumption is anticipated to surge due to growth in the industrial sector, particularly for industrial heat and power, and liquefied natural gas production. Natural gas production is expected to account for nearly 40% of the US energy production by 2050. Wind and solar power generation lead the growth among other renewables. Gradually, traditional centralized power plants run by fossil fuels are facing competition with distributed power generation like micro turbines and solar panels. With subsidies for clean energy from climate conscious governments and falling solar and wind power costs, renewable energy sources are expected to provide over 10% of global electricity supply over 2017–2022 (EIA, 2018).

Various trading strategies have shown evidence of success in traditional markets including cryptocurrencies, currencies markets, bond, and equity markets (Nadaraja & Chu, 2017; Neely et al., 2014; Shynkevich, 2012, 2016). However, uncertainty in financial markets complicates the choice between fundamental analysis and/or technical analysis techniques for investors and traders. In their seminal work, Malkiel and Fama (1970) and Ball (1978) asserted the efficient market hypothesis which states that the current market prices reflect all available information, and the reliance on such information would be unprofitable or result in a positive return that is accompanied by an unacceptable risk level. The studies found that market timing-based strategies result in negative returns after adjusting for transaction costs. Fama and Ball support that technical analysis trading rules were not profitable for U.S. based futures markets. In comparison, Pruitt and White (1988) found their technical based system, which includes variables such as volume, Relative Strength Index (RSI), and moving average, outperforms the market after adjusting for transactions costs. In the same line of thought, Menkhoff (2010) found most fund managers in five countries use technical analysis. In support of technical trading, Szakmary et al. (2010) found trend-following strategies to be profitable in commodity futures markets and found their trading-based system to outperform the traditional buy-and-hold strategy in the S&P500 stock index futures market. Wong et al. (2003) found the use of RSI and moving average to yield significant positive returns in the Singapore Stock Exchange. Neely et al. (2009) found that both market conditions and profitability change over time when applying technical analysis techniques. This is in line with Gurrib (2018b) who investigated the performance of the Average Directional Index as a market timing tool for the most actively traded US based currency pairs and found weekly trading horizons to be more profitable than monthly ones. Beyaz et al. (2018) analyzed various companies using both fundamental and technical analysis and found differences in the performance using either analytical tool was less pronounced for energy stocks and combining both techniques improved forecasts of stock prices performance. More recently, Kamalov (2021) was able to apply machine learning techniques to achieve market beating performance in predicting significant swings in stock price. Although there exists a plethora of research on technical analysis, few authors have applied the momentum strategies within a trading system in their studies. There is a lack of focus on the market under study and the use of momentum rules in the application of the ROC indicator.

For this study, we tap into the performance of the ROC as a trading model and compare the results with the naïve buy-and-hold strategy. While there exist studies that have applied the ROC, this is the first study to investigate the use of ROC as a trading strategy for Henry Hub Natural Gas futures market in the USA. Our analysis of the leading energy stocks is the first to provide insights into whether this technical analysis tool is useful in energy derivatives markets. This paper contributes to the existing literature by comparing the results from the ROC trading strategy with a buy-and-hold strategy. It helps to determine if the ROC is a more reliable technical analysis tool. The performance of the ROC is measured using both the Sharpe and Sortino performance measures and compared with the traditional buy-and-hold strategy. Our approach provides guidance to the differences in predicting energy equity prices using technical analysis and naïve buy-and-hold strategies. The use of both the Sharpe and Sortino measures allows the possibility of capturing both the total and downside risks of trading energy stocks with the help of the technical analysis tool. Last, but not least, we look at the ability of the technical indicator to provide trading signals, by complementing the analysis with the existence of trends and the strength of the trend in place. The policy implications of disruptions in commodity prices with respect to profit potentials are presented. The analysis is of importance to traders and speculators in energy markets.

Our paper is structured as follows. We provide a review of existing literature on key factors affecting the natural gas market, the relationship between spot and futures energy markets, and performance measures used in our study. Next, the descriptive statistics for the data in the study is presented. Then we provide the methodology applied to set the trading system together with the research findings. We rest our case with some conclusive remarks.

2 Literature Review

2.1 Factors Affecting the Natural Gas Futures Market

In the United States of America (USA) as of 2018, the share of electricity generation by fuel is as follows: natural gas is 35.4%, coal 27.9%, nuclear 19.0%, hydroelectric and renewables 16.8%, others 0.9%, according to BP Statistical Review of World Energy 2019, 68th edition. These statistics imply that natural gas is the main fuel for power generation. Moreover, since the cost of procuring natural gas is the marginal cost of power generation, the relationship between the wholesale electricity market and the natural gas market is of great academic and practical interest. The USA energy market, including natural gas futures market is significantly influenced by government policies and regulations. For example, The Energy Policy Act of 2005, intended to encourage energy independence and energy sources diversity through tax incentives for renewables and the expansion of nuclear power (EPAct, 2005). Moreover, the USA energy market operates in a competitive environment, Market deregulation, as seen in some states, has led to increased competition among energy providers, offering consumers more choices but also facing challenges in maintaining reliability and grid stability in natural gas futures (Bushnell, 2019). Market prices fluctuate due to supply–demand dynamics, regulatory changes, and geopolitical factors, impacting both producers and consumers (EIA, 2021). Taxation also is an important factor affecting natural gas futures. Pulhan et al. (2020) examined the relationship between the prices of natural gas, crude oil, and taxation among selected EU-12 countries over 2001–2012. They found out that not only crude oil prices but also taxation has significant influence on the prices of natural gas within the EU-12 countries.

2.2 *Relationship Between Futures and Spot Prices in Natural Gas Markets*

The relationship between futures and natural gas spot prices has been tackled in literature. For instance, Nick (2016) investigated price discovery between spot and futures natural gas markets in Europe. The study found out that price formation has generally taken place on the futures market. The presence of market participants in the future market could explain this because future contracts offer the opportunity to trade the contract many times before its maturity, and, therefore, enable to close out the trading position without taking physical delivery. This increased the use of hedging and speculation by participants not interested in physical delivery, who dominate the spot market. This different structure of both markets led the futures market to be substantially informational superior compared to the spot market. Nick concluded that an indexation on the futures market prices rather than on spot market prices, therefore, promises to provide more valid price signals. Interestingly it was claimed that short-run and medium/long-run price drivers change and vary over time. In the case of the spot market, the determinants of prices were renewable infeed and electricity demand, while in the futures market, the main drivers are natural gas, coal, and carbon prices. The U.S. energy market state can be described as a constant state of transformation, influenced by evolving demand patterns, technological changes, policy changes, and environmental concerns. The market transitioning stage to a sustainable, resilient, and diverse energy landscape remains a crucial challenge. Understanding U.S. energy market dynamics is important for policymakers, stakeholders, and researchers to develop effective strategies that promote economic growth while addressing environmental and societal needs (Grasu & Popp, 2023).

2.3 *Trend-Following Indicators*

To increase analysis efficiency, several advanced indicators have been developed by technical analysts in the past few years. Although there are hundreds of indicators with more being added daily, this study will discuss one of the most used, i.e. the rate of change (ROC), a momentum indicator. ROC is a momentum indicator that refers to the speed of the movement of the price (Karasu & Altan, 2022). It is usually used to compare the most recent closing price to the previous closing price. The movement of this indicator has been used by the practitioners to identify whether the price is in a certain trend, either in an upward or downward trend. One of the most important momentum indicators is ROC, because it looks at the speed at which a variable change over a specific period. Practically, practitioners monitor the speed at which one variable change relative to another. Moreover, ROC can clarify the momentum behind the movement of the price; it quantifies the change in the percentage. For most parts, current price and ROC should move together. When the current price and ROC diverge, the technician looks to ROC for a clearer indication of the underlying trend. For momentum, the Rate of Change (ROC) indicator simply measures the price change, in percentage, between the price n days ago and the current price.

2.4 Technical Analysis and Performance

An extensive amount of literature exists when it comes to the success or failure of techniques such as machine learning, technical analysis, and regressions in financial markets (see Kamalov et al., 2021, 2024; Gurrib & Kamalov, 2021; Gurrib et al., 2022a, 2022b; Kumar et al., 2022). For instance, Smith et al. (2016) reported that 20% of hedge funds used technical analysis; Gencay (1999) reported profits in foreign exchange markets with Olson (2004) adding further that risk-adjusted trading-rule profits declined over time; Brock et al. (1992) support that technical trading provided significant forecasting, over a 90-year period, for the Dow Jones Industrial Average (DJIA). The latter study is also backed by proponents of the adaptive market hypothesis like Lo (2017) and Urquhart et al. (2015) who support that investors and markets adapt, such that technical trading rules lose their predictive power over time.

While there is a vast literature regarding the use of technical analysis in various markets such as foreign currencies, technical trading applications regarding the energy market have been covered relatively more in recent decades due to the financialization of crude oil, which made it a product of interest for professional crude oil futures traders (Zhang, 2017; Creti & Nguyen, 2015). While there is scarce literature regarding energy stocks and technical analysis, the relationship between technical analysis and energy futures market serves as a reference point for potential relationships between technical analysis and energy equities. Marshall et al. (2008b) applied 7000 rules on major commodity futures and found only some strategies were profitable, after adjusting for data snooping. Comparatively, Szakmary et al. (2010) reported moving average strategies resulted in positive returns for most commodity futures markets. Narayan et al. (2014) applied momentum-based trading strategies in commodity futures, ranked the commodities, and took long positions in the top performing commodities and short positions in the worst performing ones, a strategy which led to significant profit opportunities. Similarly, Narayan et al. (2013) found that simple moving average breaks-based trading strategies reliably produce statistically significant returns in oil and gold markets. While the same authors found that commodity futures, including oil, can predict commodity spot returns, Gurrib (2018a) supported that an energy futures index based on crude oil and heating oil is not a reliable predictor of major stock market indices, particularly, due to structural breaks like the 2000 technology bubble. This is also supported by Aggarwal (1988) who found not only an increase in volatility following the introduction of futures markets, but also an increase in volatility over time, suggesting futures markets is not necessarily linked to volatility in other markets. This suggests other factors like uncertainty shocks can drive volatility as well in markets. Lately, using technical analysis as proxies for momentum trading, Czudaj (2019) analyzed crude oil futures prices and found that the reaction to uncertainty varies significantly across different frequencies. While high frequencies witness a very brief reaction to uncertainty, lower frequencies displayed a more persistent reaction to uncertainty shocks. Further, Marshall et al. (2008a) found investors to rely more on technical analysis for short-term forecasting and provide more emphasis to technical indicators for intraday horizons compared to yearly based ones.

To measure the performance of portfolios based on market timing techniques, performance measures such as Sharpe, M2, Treynor, and Jensen's alpha are used in the investment industry. In line with the development of performance measures, asset-pricing models were developed to explore which aspect of a portfolio should lead to lower or higher expected returns. For instance, the capital asset-pricing model (CAPM) proposed by Sharpe (1964) suggests that relying on such a model assumes the portfolio is exposed to market risk. While Jensen's alpha (Jensen, 1968) is based on the difference between actual returns and expected return, it does not control firm-specific risk which could be important for investors in the short term (Fama, 1972). Equally, Treynor's ratio proposed by Treynor (1965) looks only at the excess return per unit of systematic risk, which is similar to Jensen's alpha as discussed in Aragon and Ferson (2006). The Sharpe ratio introduced in Sharpe (1964) captures excess return per unit of total risk, where excess return is the difference between return and a risk-free rate, where the 3-month US Treasury bill rate is used as a proxy. Recent studies which applied the Sharpe performance measure in commodities markets include and Gurrib et al. (2020, 2022a, 2022b, 2023).

While various applications exist regarding the use of Sharpe (see Gurrib (2016) and Aragon and Ferson (2006) for a review), the Sharpe ratio does not differentiate between downside and upside risk. This is particularly important since various financial markets tend to display non-normal distributions. For instance, Leland (1999) suggests the need to look into higher moments of distributions to capture investors' utility functions. For positively (negatively) skewed distributions, a portfolio would have a higher (lower) mean than for a normally distributed function, resulting in a relatively lower (higher) risk and higher (lower) excess return per unit of total risk. To tackle the issues related to the Sharpe performance measure and distributions, Sortino and Van der Meer (1991) introduced the Sortino ratio which compared to the Sharpe measure, looks at downside risk, where downside risk relates to returns falling below a defined target rate. Harry Markowitz, the founder of Modern Portfolio Theory, also discussed the importance of downside risk in his seminal Markowitz paper, despite using standard deviation in his portfolio theory model. Various studies used the Sortino, including Sortino and Price (1994), Ziemba (2003), and Chaudhry and Johnson (2008) where the latter found the Sortino ratio to be superior to the Sharpe when distribution of excess returns is skewed.

3 Research Methodology

For the purpose of this study, we adopt the methodology used in Gurrib et al. (2024) to explain the framework around the Rate of Change (ROC) technical indicator. The benefit of ROC helps to detect momentum in security markets. The formula can be expressed as follows:

$$\text{ROC}=\left[(\text{Close} - \text{Close} \times \text{periodsago})/(\text{Close} \times \text{periodsago})\right]^{*}100 \quad (1)$$

While assets with a positive ROC suggest a security is outperforming, with an expectation that the security price is expected to increase, a low or negative ROC is similarly aligned with an expected price decline, ROC broadens into positive region when there is an accelerating asset price increase. Conversely, ROC goes deeper into negative region when there is an accelerating price decrease.

Although there are almost 250 trading days in a year, it can be decomposed as 125 days for 6 months, 63 days per one quarter, or 21 days per month. A trend reversal spreads on the shortest timeframe and progressively extends to encompass broader timeframes. When ROC for both 250-day and 125-day periods is positive caused by the long-term uptrend, this implies that current prices surpass those ones of 6 and 12 months prior. Therefore, long positions placed 6 and 12 months should remain profitable leaving an investor in a positive mood. Typically, when the price of an asset reaches new highs or lows, ROC does not mimic the same and it can be a signal of a weakening trend leading to a potential reversal. An extremely high (low) level of ROC can illustrate that a security is overbought (oversold). In addition, when traders see how ROC crosses above (sell) a zero-mark, they tend to buy (sell) securities. Besides, with the usage of ROC, traders can confirm the direction of a trend when it follows suit a price movement. In conclusion, ROC is a beneficial indicator to determine a price momentum and possible reversals on the security market. Conversely, taking into consideration limitations of ROC, traders should also actively apply other technical and fundamental methods to make correct decisions (Rate of Change, n.d.).

As far as the performance measures are concerned, the Sharpe and the Sortino risk-adjusted values are estimated. While the Sharpe ratio is the excess return per unit of total risk, and assumes both upside and downside risk, the Sortino ratio assumes only downside risk. In line with Sortino and Van der Meer (1991), the Sortino ratio is calculated as follows:

$$Sortino\ ratio = \frac{\overline{R_A} - MAR_A}{\sigma_A^d}, \quad (2)$$

where $\sigma_A^d = \sqrt{\frac{\Sigma\left(R_A - MAR_A\right)^2}{n}}$ and represents the target downside deviation. $\overline{R_A}$ represents the average return generated from buying and selling the energy stocks, n is the number of returns, and MAR_A represents the minimum acceptable return. If

$(R_A - MAR_A) > 0$, the resulting value is substituted to zero, otherwise, the value is set as $R_A - MAR_A$. This ensures that the model captures only downside risk. The risk-free rate is assumed as the minimum acceptable return.

4 Data

For this study, we focus on the U.S. natural gas futures prices. As per the largest derivatives marketplace—Chicago Mercantile Exchange, the Henry Hub natural gas futures contract is the third largest physical commodity futures contract, by volume, globally. The contract specifications for both energy commodity futures are summarized in Table 1. Data is sourced from FactSet and NYMEX.

Due to the impact of weather on energy prices, it is important to conduct a preliminary seasonality analysis of natural gas futures prices in the USA. Table 2 reports the seasonality impact on natural gas futures prices in the USA. A 10-year average is also estimated to capture trends over the years. As observed, the months of April tend to witness the most positive changes in natural gas, compared to the prior month. Comparatively, the months of November and December tend to witness drops in energy prices, with the effect more pronounced in the natural gas commodity. Although not reported here, compared to other energy commodities like crude oil, natural gas prices fluctuated more, on a month-to-month basis.

It is important to note that the S&P Composite 1500 Energy index has been relatively volatile compared to the general S&P500 market index and the S&P GSCI Natural Gas Index. The performance of the three market indices can be observed in Fig. 1. We observe that the natural gas market and crude oil market (represented by the S&P 1500 Energy index) decoupled starting from late 2008. The demand for oil to produce electricity has plunged tremendously due to retirement of aged petroleum assets, lower natural gas prices, more efficient gas fired turbines, and more consciousness on the environmental impact of the relatively high sulfur content of oil. Despite the growth in natural gas production in the USA, which is a leading

Table 1 Asset specification details

Energy futures markets	Henry Hub Natural Gas (NYM $/ mmbtu)
Trading symbol	NG00
Sector	Energy
Contract unit	10,000 mmBTUs
Currency	U.S. dollar
Tick size	$10 per contract
Contract months	Jan, Feb, Mar, Apr, May, Jun, Jul, Aug, Sep, Oct, Nov, Dec
Settlement	Physical
Exchange	NYMEX

Source: FactSet, New York Mercantile Exchange (NYMEX)

Table 2 Natural gas price change (%). *Source:* authors

	Month-on-month % change in price											
	Jan	Feb	Mar	Apr	May	Jun	Jul	Aug	Sep	Oct	Nov	Dec
10 Year Avg	−1.8	−5.4	1.3	10.4	−1.3	3.0	2.2	9.6	1.0	7.5	−1.9	−15.1
2023	−34.6	6.7	−22.6	16.3	−12.1	22.4	−5.0	5.1	5.8	30.2	−26.5	−17.0
2022	37.0	−9.3	27.6	30.4	10.7	−33.8	52.6	11.7	−26.4	−2.3	4.9	−40.8
2021	1.5	9.6	−7.2	12.4	1.9	22.2	7.2	11.8	34.0	−5.8	−17.4	−22.1
2020	−15.9	−8.5	−2.6	18.8	−5.1	−5.3	2.7	46.2	−3.9	37.3	−16.9	−12.4
2019	−1.3	−0.1	−5.3	−3.3	−4.7	−5.9	−3.2	2.3	2.0	13.0	−13.4	−4.0
2018	1.4	−11.0	2.5	1.1	6.8	−0.9	−4.9	4.8	3.2	8.4	41.4	−38.2
2017	−15.4	−11.0	15.0	2.7	−6.3	−1.2	−7.9	8.8	−1.1	−3.7	4.5	−2.4
2016	−1.7	−25.5	14.5	11.2	5.1	27.8	−1.6	0.4	0.7	9.9	4.9	9.9
2015	−7.1	1.6	−3.4	4.2	−4.0	7.2	−4.1	−1.0	−6.1	−8.0	−3.7	4.6
2014	17.9	−6.8	−5.2	10.2	−5.7	−2.2	−13.5	5.8	1.4	−3.9	3.3	−29.2

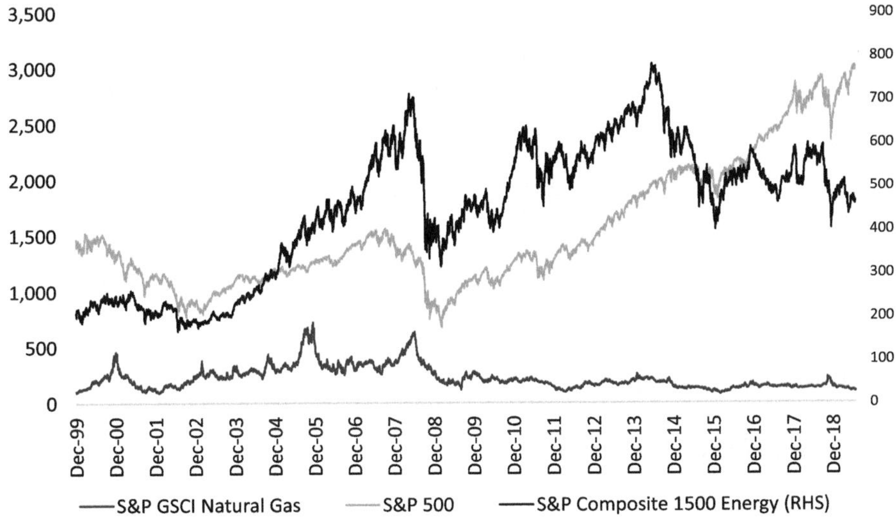

Fig. 1 Performance of S&P 1500 Energy, S&P500, and Natural Gas. Note: Figure shows the performance of the S&P 500 market index, S&P Composite1500 Energy index, and the S&P GSCI natural gas, which is displayed on the right-hand side vertical axis. Source: FactSet, S&P500 Dow Jones Indices

producer in the world, strong supply from shale players such as Marcellus/Utica has reduced the effect of the associated gas growth on natural gas prices (Mchich, 2018). Beginning in 2009, the S&P 500 general index had a relatively better performance compared to the S&P 1500 Composite Energy Index. The trend observed in the S&P Composite 1500 Energy Index makes the ROC a good candidate to be used as a technical indicator.

The study is conducted, using end of month prices, over the period 28th May 2004–31st July 2024. The risk-free rate is estimated using the 3-month US Treasury bill rate, which ranged from a minimum of −0.05% to 5.36% from May 2004 to July 2024, with an average of 1.48% over the period under study. The negative yield was in early 2020, where the financial players were concerned about the potential adverse impact of the coronavirus and related policy measures taken to address the flight from risky assets such as stocks to short-term treasuries. With growing uncertainty, this led to a shift into short-term government-issued securities, where the prices rose and the yield fell, creating an inverted yield curve. The risk-free rate is sourced from the St. Louis Federal Reserve (FRED) database. Energy futures prices are sourced from FactSet.

Table 3 Descriptive statistics of Henry Hub Natural Gas futures price. *Source*: authors

Mean	4.4988
Median	3.8160
Standard deviation	2.3933
Kurtosis	4.9650
Skewness	1.4329
Jarque-Bera	121.2640
p-Value	0.0000
ADF	−2.8192
p-Value	0.0571
Observations	241

5 Research Findings

5.1 Descriptive Statistics

As reported in Table 3, the average price of natural gas futures monthly was nearly \$4.50/mmbtu over the 241 months under study with a median price of \$3.81/mmbtu. The standard deviation was \$2.3933/mmbtu, resulting with an average price to risk value of 1.88. The kurtosis value of 4.96 suggests a leptokurtic distribution for natural gas futures. Similarly, the distribution was positive skewed with a skew of 1.43. The *p*-value of the Jarque-Bera test supports a normal distribution at 1% level. The Augmented Dickey–Fuller (ADF) stationarity test supports stationary series at the 10% level. The Henry Hub natural gas price series was stationary after first-order differencing. The period under study was May 2004–July 2024.

5.2 ROC

For an investment analyst on the trading floor, the long-term horizon is entirely different from that of an institutional investor. For instance, while for a trader, long-term can mean several days, for an investor, it can mean 12–18 months. While it is beyond the scope of this study to tackle all possible x periods, due to the use of monthly data, we position our analysis to a long-term investment horizon. Nonetheless, to allow the study to provide sufficient insights, we initially estimate the ROC using 9, 10, 11, 12, 13, and 14 months as x periods. Figure 2 displays the ROC values under each of the six scenarios. As observed, the rate of change under the 14 months scenario tends to dominate in terms of more negative and more positive values during the period of 2004–2024. Noticeably, the ROC dropped significantly in values in the later part of 2005, 2008, and 2022, consistent in price drops in the U.S. natural gas price during these specific periods. While the ROC drops fluctuated between −71% (12-months ROC) and −76% (10-months ROC), ROC spikes fluctuated between 135% (10-months ROC) and 183% (14-months ROC).

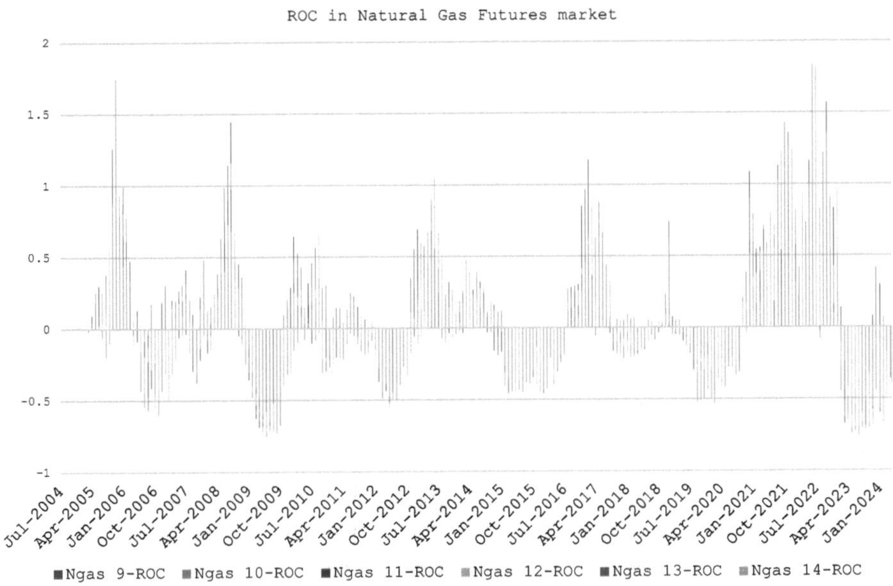

Fig. 2 ROC in the Henry Hub Natural Gas futures market. *Source*: authors

Table 4 Relationships between ROCs and natural gas futures prices. *Source*: authors

	Ngas	9-ROC	10-ROC	11-ROC	12-ROC	13-ROC	14-ROC
Ngas	1.000						
9-ROC	0.474	1.000					
10-ROC	0.483	0.918	1.000				
11-ROC	0.478	0.838	0.917	1.000			
12-ROC	0.470	0.773	0.843	0.915	1.000		
13-ROC	0.476	0.740	0.794	0.850	0.924	1.000	
14-ROC	0.477	0.718	0.768	0.809	0.868	0.937	1.000

This result is important as it portrays the importance of selecting the ROC model, particularly for those investors who want to benefit from price increases, since the ROC models under study do not significantly differ during price drops.

Although a graphical representation in Fig. 2 shows a relatively dominant ROC model based on 14 periods, statistical analysis is warranted. As observed in Table 4, a Pearson correlation analysis supports that end of month natural gas prices is positively correlated with all ROCs, ranging from 0.470 (ROC-12) to 0.483 (ROC-10). Further, the ROC model based on 10 months is strongly positively correlated with all other ROC periods. Resultingly, we select an ROC model based on 10 periods for further analysis.

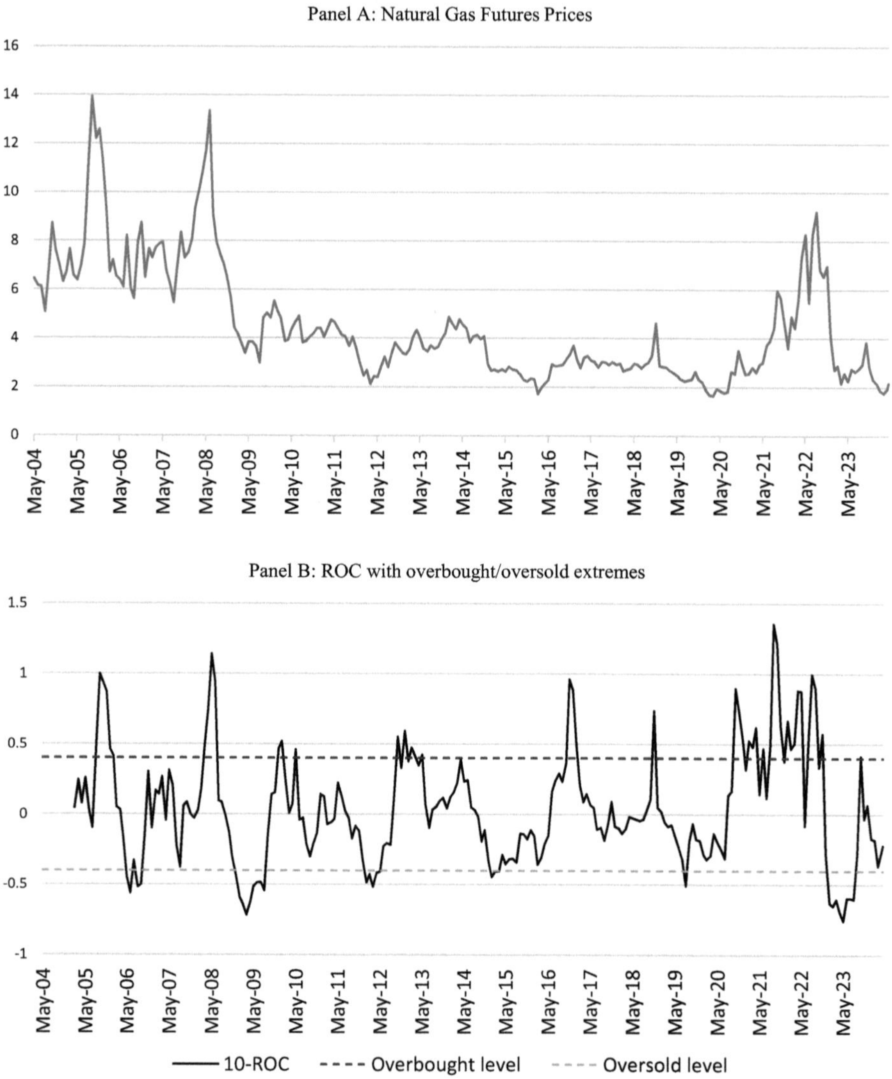

Fig. 3 Natural gas prices and ROC level. *Source:* authors

5.3 *Trading System Based on ROC*

To determine overbought and oversold extremes, it is vital to consider the volatility of the asset's rate of change under study. With a standard deviation of the ROC-10 model of 40% and an average of the standard deviation of all other ROCs from Table 4 at 42%, we assume an overbought/oversold level at +40%/−40%. Figure 3 Panels A and B displays the natural gas futures prices and the rate of change technical indicator over the monthly periods of May 2004 to July 2024. Panel A shows that natural gas prices have fallen drastically from nearly $6/mmbtu to $2/mmtbu over the two decades, with prices fluctuating significantly to reach highs of nearly $14/mmbtu. For most of the years during 2009–2020, the natural gas futures prices roamed around $2/mmbtu. Panel B includes the overbought and oversold levels as mentioned above. As observed in Panel B, the ROC tends to turn close to the overbought and oversold levels. This suggests that the overbought and oversold are relatively correctly specified to determine selling (overbought) and buying (oversold) signals. Alternatively stated, a selling (buying) signal from the technical indicator is captured when the previous period (say month) is lower (higher) than current period's ROC. It is important to note that while we used a 40% overbought and −40% oversold level, these levels differ across different financial assets. Narrowing (widening) the band would result in more (less) trading signals. Since any transaction results in transaction costs, it is vital to select proper overbought and oversold levels. To test the performance of the ROC-10 model, we constructed a trading system and report the total return, average return, average risk, and Sharpe performance measure.

Figure 4 reports the returns achieved upon implementing the ROC-10 model in the natural gas market. To calculate a return, an open position needs to be closed, i.e. a buy matched against the next sell, or a sale matched against the next purchase. In the event(s) of a buying signal, followed by another buying signal, or a selling signal followed by another selling signal, a return is calculated by offsetting a buy with the next available selling signal, and vice versa. Last, but not least, in the event of any

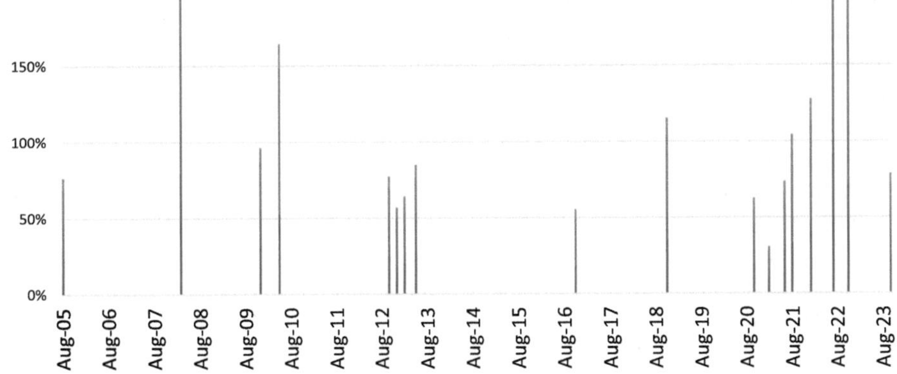

Fig. 4 Trading system based on ROC. *Source*: authors

open position at the end of the July 2024 period, the position is closed with the last price in the study sample. As observed in Fig. 4, the returns generated from the technical analysis indicator were all positive, fluctuating between 30% and 284%. Further, most returns were observed from 2020–2024 period, including the highest returns observed in July 2022. During 2013–2016, a period where natural gas prices dropped or did not fluctuate significantly, no return was generated. This supports that the momentum indicator, as it names posits, works better during period of fluctuating prices. The total returns achieved were 2019%, with an average return of 112% over the 18 trades. The average risk was 71%, resulting in an excess return per unit of risk of 1.548. Compared with a naïve buy-and-hold strategy which generated a negative return of 67% during the whole period, the momentum indicator performance was superior. Since all returns were positive, this meant that the Sortino ratio had little value as the latter captures downside risk.

5.4 ROC with a Moving Average Filter

To robust test the existing trading model, we include a moving average price crossover strategy as a confirmation filter to the existing system which is based on momentum. Explicitly, a buy (sell) signal is generated if the energy futures price crossover (cross under) the moving average indicator together with the momentum indicator crossing under (crossing over) the oversold (overbought) level. Results show that the combined use of the ROC-10 with the MA-10 yielded no trading signal. To ensure this is not due to model specification or the lagged impact of moving averages-based indicators, we also test for different MA periods ranging from MA (5) to MA (9). Only a MA (5) combined with an ROC-10 resulted in a positive return of 57% based on one trading signal. This suggests that the MA did not enhance the existing trading model, but rather reduced the possibility of positive returns from the natural gas futures market. Finally, but not least, we evaluate the use of a trading model based on the conditions meeting either a price/moving average crossover strategy or a ROC-10 model strategy. Consistent with the above, we compare the distinct ROC and MA models, which are based on 10 months. Alternatively stated, we constructed a model where trading signals are derived as long as either the ROC overbought/oversold or MA crossover/cross-under threshold levels are violated.

The waterfall in Fig. 5 reports the findings. With 27 (23) selling (buying) signals, the trading system yields a total return of 1125% over the 2004–2024 period over an average yearly return of nearly 13.35%, and an average return per closed position of 29.61%. The fluctuation in the natural gas futures prices, post 2021, contributed positively to the cumulative returns as observed in Fig. 5. Trading returns ranged from −59% in December 2018 to 204% in October 2022. This resulted in a relatively high average risk value of 53%, and a Sharpe of 0.528. Compared to the naïve buy-and-hold strategy which yielded −67% return, the trading system which considers either ROC or MA price crossover strategies outperformed significantly. All

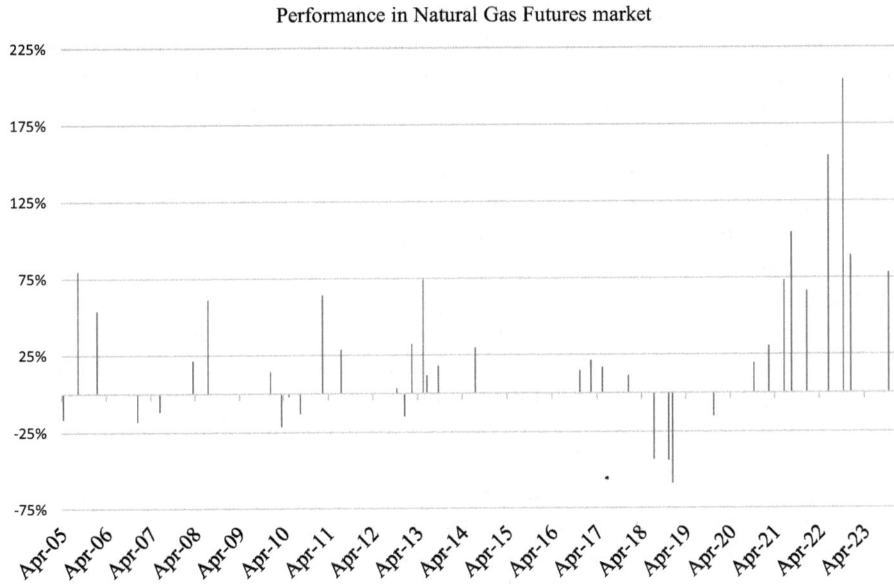

Fig. 5 Trading system based on ROC or moving average strategies. *Source*: authors

in, the first model which relies only on ROC model yielded a higher cumulative return of 2019%, with a Sharpe performance value of 1.672. Therefore, the use of ROC-10 model without MA is recommended for the natural gas futures market.

6 Conclusive Remarks

Energy commodities such as natural gas affect not only other commodities but also a range of alternative assets such as equities. The challenges of decoupling energy commodities, increased competitiveness of renewables, and other critical factors affecting demand and supply of natural gas have kept energy policy makers rigorously at work. Macroeconomic activity, economic sanctions, and technology have also affected energy markets. The drop in energy stock prices during the July 2014–December 2015 period caused by the corresponding drop in oil prices provides a good reference point. Investors and traders often use fundamental and technical analytical tools to gain profits through a set of strategies. This paper focuses on the rate of change as a technical analysis tool. It has not been documented sufficiently in the existing literature, especially in the energy derivatives market. Our analysis looks at its performance during May 2004–July 2024 for the U.S. Henry Hub Natural Gas futures market.

Our findings support that a rate of change model based on a period of 10 months provided a superior model performance compared to the naïve buy-and-hold strategy. An overbought (oversold) threshold level of 40% (−40%) captured most of the turning point in the technical analysis indicator for natural gas futures prices. The inclusion of a price crossover moving average strategy with the rate of change-based model did not improve the excess return per unit of risk. Although a model built on trading conditions, where buying (selling) signals are generated based on either oversold (overbought) scenarios from a ROC model or crossover (cross under) scenario from a price crossover moving average strategy, resulted in positive returns, the trading system which relied solely on the rate of change indicator outperformed all other models under analysis.

The policy implications concern principally the role of speculators in financial markets and, more specifically, energy equity and commodity markets. Our findings indicate that the use of the rate of change indicator can provide a profitable trading strategy despite the fact the natural gas futures prices ranged between $6/mmbtu and $2/mmtbu over the two decades, with prices fluctuating significantly to reach highs of nearly $14/mmbtu. Even though for most of the years (2009–2020) the natural gas futures prices roamed around $2/mmbtu, significant positive returns can be achieved using the rate of change technical analysis indicator. Our findings provide useful insights to regulatory bodies such as the Securities Exchange Commission (SEC) and the Commodity Futures Trading Commission (CFTC) to better comprehend the profitability of energy traders during the declining markets, as experienced in natural gas over the last two decades.

Two noticeable limitations of the study relate to the seasonality in the data and the combined impact of ROC with other indicators. Firstly, as observed earlier, the natural gas price is subject to seasonality in specific months of the year where the energy commodity is more/less consumed. This leads to a natural increase/decrease in the price which is not considered in the overbought/oversold indicator. Secondly, the paper only assesses the impact of combining a price moving average crossover model with the ROC, with the aim of improving returns. While a price moving average crossover model has its own merits in terms of bullish and bearish crossovers, the price moving average crossover is a lagging indicator and can result in less reliability during volatile markets.

To this end, future research avenues can include a seasonality adjusted component to the overbought/oversold threshold levels to take into account seasonality during specific months of the year. Last, but not least, evaluating the use of rate of change indicator with a broader range of indicators such as Fibonacci retracements and the Relative Strength Index (RSI) can provide more insights into whether such commodity markets are predominately driven by fundamentals or technicals.

References

Aggarwal, R. (1988). Stock index futures and cash market volatility. *Review of Futures Markets, 7*, 290–299.

Aragon, G. O., & Ferson, W. E. (2006). Portfolio performance evaluation. *Foundations and Trends in Finance, 2*(2), 83–190. https://doi.org/10.1561/0500000015
Ball, R. (1978, November 1–7). Filter rules: Interpretation of market efficiency, experimental problem and Australian experience. *Accounting Education.*
Beyaz, E., Tekiner, F., Zeng, X., & Keane, J. (2018). Comparing technical and fundamental indicators in stock price forecasting. https://doi.org/10.1109/hpcc/smartcity/dss.2018.00262
Brock, W., Lakonishok, J., & LeBARON, B. (1992). Simple technical trading rules and the stochastic properties of stock returns. *Journal of Finance, 47*(5), 1731–1764. https://doi.org/10.1111/j.1540-6261.1992.tb04681.x
Bushnell, J. (2019). Energy markets in the United States: The rules, the players, and the future. *The Energy Journal, 40*(2), 143–168.
Chaudhry, A., & Johnson, H. L. (2008). The efficacy of the Sortino ratio and other benchmarked performance measures under skewed return distributions. *Australian Journal of Management, 32*(3), 485–502. https://doi.org/10.1177/031289620803200306
Chemnick, J. (2016, September 6). U.S. and China formally commit to Paris Climate Accord. *Scientific American.* https://www.scientificamerican.com/article/u-s-and-china-formally-commit-to-paris-climate-accord/
Chicago Mercantile Exchange. (n.d.-b). *Henry Hub Natural Gas futures and options.* https://www.cmegroup.com/markets/energy/natural-gas/natural-gas.html
Contu, D., Elshareif, E. E., & Gurrib, I. (2021). Assessing views towards energy sources with social media data: The case of nuclear energy in the UAE. *Processes, 9*(11), 1945. https://doi.org/10.3390/pr9111945
Creti, A., & Nguyen, D. K. (2015). Energy markets' financialization, risk spillovers, and pricing models. *Energy Policy, 82*, 260–263. https://doi.org/10.1016/j.enpol.2015.02.007
Czudaj, R. L. (2019). Crude oil futures trading and uncertainty. *Energy Economics, 80*, 793–811. https://doi.org/10.1016/j.eneco.2019.01.002
EIA (2018). Annual Energy Outlook 2018, U.S. Energy Information Administration. https://www.eia.gov/pressroom/presentations/Capuano_02052018.pdf
EIA. (2021). *U.S. electricity industry overview.* https://www.eia.gov/electricity/monthly/epm_table_grapher.php?t=epmt_2_01
EIA (2024). Analysis & Projections, U.S. Energy Information Administration. https://www.eia.gov/analysis/
Energy Policy Act of 2005. (2005). In 109th Congress. https://www.congress.gov/109/plaws/publ58/PLAW-109publ58.pdf
Fama, E. F. (1970). Efficient Capital Markets: A review of theory and Empirical work. *Journal of Finance, 25*(2), 383. https://doi.org/10.2307/2325486
Fama, E. F. (1972). Components of investment performance. *Journal of Finance, 27*(3), 551. https://doi.org/10.2307/2978261
Gençay, R. (1999). Linear, non-linear and essential foreign exchange rate prediction with simple technical trading rules. *Journal of International Economics, 47*(1), 91–107. https://doi.org/10.1016/s0022-1996(98)00017-8
Grasu, S., & Popp, R. M. (2023). An overview of the USA energy market. *Revista De Management Comparat International, 24*(4), 499–512. https://doi.org/10.24818/RMCI.2023.4.499
Gupta, S., Choudhary, H., & Agarwal. (2017). Hedging efficiency of Indian commodity futures. *Paradigm, 21*(1), 1–20. https://doi.org/10.1177/0971890717700529
Gurrib, I. (2016). Optimization of the double crossover strategy for the S&P500 Market Index. *Global Review of Accounting and Finance, 7*(1), 92–107. https://doi.org/10.21102/graf.2016.03.71.07
Gurrib, I. (2018a). Can an Energy Futures Index predict US Stock Market Index movements? *International Journal of Energy Economics and Policy, 8*(5), 230–240. https://www.econjournals.com/index.php/ijeep/article/view/6622

Gurrib, I. (2018b). Performance of the Average Directional Index as a market timing tool for the most actively traded USD based currency pairs. *Banks and Bank Systems, 13*(3), 58–70. https://doi.org/10.21511/bbs.13(3).2018.06

Gurrib, I. (2019). Can energy commodities affect energy blockchain-based cryptos? *Studies in Economics and Finance, 36*(4), 682–699. https://doi.org/10.1108/sef-10-2018-0313

Gurrib, I. (2023). Momentum in low carbon and fossil fuel free equity investing. *International Journal of Energy Economics and Policy, 13*(5), 461–471. https://doi.org/10.32479/ijeep.14342

Gurrib, I., & Kamalov, F. (2019). The implementation of an adjusted relative strength index model in foreign currency and energy markets of emerging and developed economies. *Macroeconomics and Finance in Emerging Market Economies, 12*(2), 105–123. https://doi.org/10.1080/17520843.2019.1574852

Gurrib, I., & Kamalov, F. (2021). Predicting bitcoin price movements using sentiment analysis: A machine learning approach. *Studies in Economics and Finance, 39*(3), 347–364. https://doi.org/10.1108/sef-07-2021-0293

Gurrib, I., Elsharief, E., & Kamalov, F. (2020). The effect of energy cryptos on efficient portfolios of key energy listed companies in the S&P Composite 1500 Energy Index. *International Journal of Energy Economics and Policy, 10*(2), 179–193. https://doi.org/10.32479/ijeep.8676

Gurrib, I., Kamalov, F., Starkova, O., Makki, A., Mirchandani, A., & Gupta, N. (2023). Performance of equity investments in sustainable environmental markets. *Sustainability, 15*(9), 7453. https://doi.org/10.3390/su15097453

Gurrib, I., Kweh, Q. L., Ting, I. W. K., & Nourani, M. (2022a). The impact of COVID-19 on the performances and risks of the U.S. energy ETF and equity portfolios. *International Journal of Business Excellence, 1*(1), 1. https://doi.org/10.1504/ijbex.2021.10043522

Gurrib, I., Nourani, M., & Bhaskaran, R. K. (2022b). Energy crypto currencies and leading U.S. energy stock prices: are Fibonacci retracements profitable? *Financial Innovation, 8*(1). https://doi.org/10.1186/s40854-021-00311-8

Gurrib, I., Starkova, O., & Hamdan, D. (2024). Trading momentum in the US crude oil futures market. *International Journal of Energy Economics and Policy, 14*(5), 593–604.

International Energy Agency. (2015). *Global emissions of carbon dioxide from the energy sector.*

International Energy Agency. (2016). *Decoupling of global emissions and economic growth confirmed.* https://www.iea.org/news/decoupling-of-global-emissions-and-economic-growth-confirmed

Jensen, M. C. (1968). The performance of mutual funds in the period 1945-1964. *Journal of Finance, 23*(2), 389–416. https://doi.org/10.1111/j.1540-6261.1968.tb00815.x

Kamalov, F., Elnaffar, S., Gurrib, I., & Cherukuri, A. (2024). Comprehensive hybrid regression model for financial forecasting in neutrosophic logic. *International Journal of Neutrosophic Science, 23*(3), 245–261. https://doi.org/10.54216/ijns.230321

Kamalov, F., Gurrib, I., & Rajab, K. (2021). Financial forecasting with machine learning: Price vs return. *Journal of Computer Sciences/Journal of Computer Science, 17*(3), 251–264. https://doi.org/10.3844/jcssp.2021.251.264

Karasu, S., & Altan, A. (2022). Crude oil time series prediction model based on LSTM network with chaotic Henry gas solubility optimization. *Energy 242*, 122964.

Kumar, R. B., Sujit, K., & Gurrib, I. (2022). Environmental initiatives: Impact on firm wealth creation. *International Journal of Green Economics, 16*(2), 130–147. https://doi.org/10.1504/ijge.2022.127906

Leland, H. E. (1999). Beyond mean–variance: Performance measurement in a nonsymmetrical world. *Financial Analysts Journal, 55*(1), 27–36. https://doi.org/10.2469/faj.v55.n1.2239

Lo, A. W. (2017). *Adaptive markets: Financial evolution at the speed of thought.* Press Princeton. https://assets.press.princeton.edu/chapters/i10932.pdf

Marshall, B. R., Cahan, R. H., & Cahan, J. M. (2008a). Can commodity futures be profitably traded with quantitative market timing strategies? *Journal of Banking & Finance, 32*(9), 1810–1819. https://doi.org/10.1016/j.jbankfin.2007.12.011

Marshall, B. R., Cahan, R. H., & Cahan, J. M. (2008b). Does intraday technical analysis in the U.S. equity market have value? *Journal of Empirical Finance, 15*(2), 199–210. https://doi.org/10.1016/j.jempfin.2006.05.003

Mchich, A. (2018). *Are crude oil and natural gas prices linked?* Chicago Mercantile Exchange. Accessed September 20, 2018, from www.cmegroup.com/education/articles-and-reports/are-crude-oil-natural-gasprices-linked.html

Menkhoff, L. (2010). The use of technical analysis by fund managers: International evidence. *Journal of Banking & Finance, 34*(11), 2573–2586. https://doi.org/10.1016/j.jbankfin.2010.04.014

Nadarajah, S., & Chu, J. (2017). On the inefficiency of Bitcoin. *Economics Letters, 150*, 6–9. https://doi.org/10.1016/j.econlet.2016.10.033

Narayan, P. K., Ahmed, H. A., & Narayan, S. (2014). Do Momentum-Based trading strategies work in the commodity futures markets? *Journal of Futures Markets, 35*(9), 868–891. https://doi.org/10.1002/fut.21685

Narayan, P. K., Narayan, S., & Sharma, S. S. (2013). An analysis of commodity markets: What gain for investors? *Journal of Banking & Finance, 37*(10), 3878–3889. https://doi.org/10.1016/j.jbankfin.2013.07.009

Neely, C. J., Rapach, D. E., Tu, J., & Zhou, G. (2014). Forecasting the equity risk premium: The role of technical indicators. *Management Science, 60*(7), 1772–1791. https://doi.org/10.1287/mnsc.2013.1838

Neely, C. J., Weller, P. A., & Ulrich, J. M. (2009). The adaptive markets hypothesis: Evidence from the Foreign Exchange Market. *Journal of Financial and Quantitative Analysis, 44*(2), 467–488. https://doi.org/10.1017/s0022109009090103

Nick, S. (2016). The informational efficiency of European natural gas hubs: Price formation and intertemporal arbitrage. *The Energy Journal, 37*(2), 1–30. https://doi.org/10.5547/01956574.37.2.snic

Olson, D. (2004). Have trading rule profits in the currency markets declined over time? *Journal of Banking & Finance, 28*(1), 85–105. https://doi.org/10.1016/s0378-4266(02)00399-0

Pruitt, S. W., & White, R. E. (1988). The CRISMA trading system. *Journal of Portfolio Management, 14*(3), 55–58. https://doi.org/10.3905/jpm.1988.409149

Pulhan, A., Yorucu, V., & Evcan, N. S. (2020). Global energy market dynamics and natural gas development in the Eastern Mediterranean region. *Utilities Policy, 64*, 101040. https://doi.org/10.1016/j.jup.2020.101040

Rate of Change (ROC). (n.d.). *Stockcharts*. https://school.stockcharts.com/doku.php?id=technical_indicators:rate_of_change_roc_and_momentum

Sharpe, W. F. (1964). Capital asset prices: A theory of market equilibrium under conditions of risk. *Journal of Finance, 19*(3), 425–442. https://doi.org/10.2307/2977928

Shynkevich, A. (2012). Performance of technical analysis in growth and small cap segments of the US equity market. *Journal of Banking & Finance, 36*(1), 193–208. https://doi.org/10.1016/j.jbankfin.2011.07.001

Shynkevich, A. (2016). Predictability in bond returns using technical trading rules. *Journal of Banking & Finance, 70*, 55–69. https://doi.org/10.1016/j.jbankfin.2016.06.010

Smith, D. M., Wang, N., Wang, Y., & Zychowicz, E. J. (2016). Sentiment and the effectiveness of technical analysis: Evidence from the Hedge Fund Industry. *Journal of Financial and Quantitative Analysis, 51*(6), 1991–2013. https://doi.org/10.1017/s0022109016000843

Sortino, F. A., & Price, L. N. (1994). Performance measurement in a downside risk framework. *the Journal of Investing, 3*(3), 59–64.

Sortino, F. A., & Van Der Meer, R. (1991). Downside risk. *Journal of Portfolio Management, 17*(4), 27–31. https://doi.org/10.3905/jpm.1991.409343

Szakmary, A. C., Shen, Q., & Sharma, S. C. (2010). Trend-following trading strategies in commodity futures: A re-examination. *Journal of Banking & Finance, 34*(2), 409–426. https://doi.org/10.1016/j.jbankfin.2009.08.004

Treynor, J. L. (1965). How to rate management of investment funds? *Harvard Business Review, 43*(1), 63–75.

UFCCC. (2016). *United Nations framework convention on climate change, Paris Agreement.* http://unfccc.int/paris_agreement/items/9485.php
Urquhart, A., Gebka, B., & Hudson, R. (2015). How exactly do markets adapt? Evidence from the moving average rule in three developed markets. *Journal of International Financial Markets, Institutions & Money, 38*, 127–147. https://doi.org/10.1016/j.intfin.2015.05.019
Wong, W., Manzur, M., & Chew, B. (2003). How rewarding is technical analysis? Evidence from Singapore stock market. *Applied Financial Economics, 13*(7), 543–551. https://doi.org/10.1080/09603100220000020906
World Bank. (2018). *Oil exporters: Policies and challenges. Commodities market outlook.*. https://thedocs.worldbank.org/en/doc/734451528311174935-0050022018/original/CMOApril2018SpecialFocusOilExporters.pdf
Zhang, D. (2017). Oil shocks and stock markets revisited: Measuring connectedness from a global perspective. *Energy Economics, 62*, 323–333. https://doi.org/10.1016/j.eneco.2017.01.009
Ziemba, W. T. (2003). *The stochastic programming approach to asset, liability, and wealth management.* The CFA Institute Research Foundation.. https://www.cfainstitute.org/-/media/documents/book/rf-publication/2003/rf-v2003-n3-3924-pdf.pdf

Health Care, International Trade, and Sectoral Transition: Theory and Evidence from BRICS

Tonmoy Chatterjee and Sharmi Sen

Abstract This study investigates the relationship between foreign direct investment (FDI) and health indicators—life expectancy (LE) and infant mortality rate—using both linear and non-linear Granger causality tests. Our findings reveal that there exist significant bidirectional causality between FDI and health metrics in India and China. Improvements in health metrics attract FDI, while an increase in FDI positively influences life expectancy. In contrast, Brazil and South Africa exhibit unidirectional causality from FDI to LE in the linear framework but bidirectional causality in the non-linear model, indicating the presence of complex interdependencies. However, for the Russian Federation, no significant causal relationship is observed, implying that FDI and health metrics do not influence each other in a linear or non-linear sense. To further explore these dynamics, we develop a three-sector general equilibrium model where two sectors produce final traded goods, and a third non-traded sector provides health services. Our model demonstrates that transitioning from a regime of international health capital immobility to mobility can lead to the expansion of the health sector. In a variant of the model, we show that health sector output increases under international health capital mobility. However, under full international capital mobility, one sector—either Agriculture or Manufacturing—may contract and ultimately vanish. These findings provide a theoretical foundation for understanding the impact of trade and FDI on the health sector and its sectoral implications for developing economies. Our results highlight the necessity of strategic policy frameworks to balance trade, health investment, and sectoral development.

Keywords Health sector · International health capital mobility · Vanishing sector · General equilibrium

T. Chatterjee
Department of Economics, Bhairab Ganguly College, Kolkata, India
e-mail: tchatterjee@bhairabgangulycollege.ac.in; https://bhairabgangulycollege.ac.in/

S. Sen (✉)
Department of Economics, Monash University, Melbourne, Australia
e-mail: khigurashi4@gmail.com; https://www.monash.edu/

E. Lau et al. (eds.), *Economics and Finance Readings*,
https://doi.org/10.1007/978-981-96-6998-1_9

1 Introduction

The BRICS nations—Brazil, Russia, India, China, and South Africa—represent some of the world's largest emerging economies, collectively accounting for over 40% of the global population and nearly a quarter of global GDP. With an average annual GDP growth rate of 6–8%, these countries have become key drivers of international economic development (Nayyar, 2019; Chatterjee & Chatterjee, 2024). However, despite their rapid economic expansion, BRICS nations continue to face significant challenges in social infrastructure, particularly in the healthcare sector. Strengthening healthcare systems is essential for ensuring sustainable economic growth, improving public well-being, and enhancing global competitiveness.

Healthcare has emerged as a vital sector within BRICS, with each nation investing in medical infrastructure, pharmaceutical research, and digital health solutions. However, healthcare expenditure as a percentage of GDP varies significantly across these nations. India allocates approximately 5–6% of its GDP to healthcare, while China spends 4.7%, Brazil 9.2%, Russia 5.3%, and South Africa 8.1%. Despite these investments, public health infrastructure in many BRICS countries remains underdeveloped, leading to increased reliance on private sector participation and foreign direct investment (FDI).

Global economic uncertainties, such as the 2008 financial crisis, the Eurozone slowdown, and the COVID-19 pandemic, have further highlighted the need for resilient healthcare systems in BRICS nations. The COVID-19 crisis, in particular, exposed critical gaps in public health preparedness and supply chain dependencies, reinforcing the urgency of healthcare sector reforms (Chatterjee & Chatterjee, 2023). However, BRICS countries have also demonstrated their potential as global healthcare leaders. India and China have emerged as major pharmaceutical hubs, Brazil has made significant strides in universal healthcare through its *Sistema Único de Saúde (SUS)*, Russia has invested in medical technology and biotechnology, and South Africa has played a crucial role in vaccine development and infectious disease research (Pinto & de Albuquerque, 2018).

Foreign Direct Investment (FDI) has played an instrumental role in the modernization of healthcare services across BRICS nations. Investments in hospital infrastructure, medical technology, pharmaceuticals, and telemedicine have led to significant improvements in healthcare accessibility and quality. India, for example, allows 100% FDI in healthcare, attracting multinational investments in hospitals, medical devices, and biotech research. China's healthcare sector has also witnessed rapid FDI growth, particularly in digital health and biotechnology. Similarly, Brazil has encouraged foreign investments to strengthen its healthcare system, particularly in response to the COVID-19 pandemic (Khilji et al., 2021). However, concerns remain about the potential downsides of increased foreign involvement, including higher treatment costs, privatization pressures, and reduced accessibility of essential medicines.

Governments across BRICS are actively reviewing their FDI policies to balance investment incentives with national healthcare priorities. India and Brazil, for instance, have raised concerns over foreign acquisitions of domestic pharmaceutical firms, fearing that such takeovers may increase drug prices and undermine access to affordable generic medicines. South Africa has faced challenges in ensuring equitable healthcare access amid rising private sector dominance, while Russia has been focusing on strengthening its domestic pharmaceutical industry to reduce import dependency. Meanwhile, China has been promoting a dual approach—encouraging foreign investments while simultaneously bolstering state-controlled enterprises in the healthcare sector (Chanda, 2001; López et al., 2021).

Public health expenditure across BRICS nations remains lower than in developed economies. For example, in India, government spending on healthcare as a share of GDP increased only marginally from 0.96% in 2004–2005 to 1.01% in 2008–2009, while in Russia, it remains at about 3% (Chatterjee, 2024). The gap between demand and available healthcare services has led to increased private sector participation, further driving FDI into the sector. While foreign investments have played a crucial role in enhancing healthcare infrastructure and innovation, BRICS nations must carefully manage their healthcare policies to ensure that economic growth translates into equitable and affordable healthcare for all.

As BRICS nations continue to emerge as global economic powerhouses, the role of healthcare in sustaining long-term growth cannot be overlooked. The interplay between economic development, FDI, and public health policies will determine how these nations navigate future challenges and opportunities in the global healthcare landscape. Examining the impact of FDI on healthcare systems within BRICS is essential for understanding how foreign investments can be leveraged to strengthen public health outcomes while maintaining national interests and ensuring healthcare equity (Outreville, 2007).

In this chapter, we have structured a theoretical model based on general equilibrium trade models with special emphasis to the health sector. From that model we are going to examine the impact of FDI in the healthcare. In a general equilibrium trade models, there exists two different ways through which one can show the effect of FDI on the output levels of different sectors. One is through infinitesimal change in foreign capital (change in exogenous foreign capital) and other is finite change in foreign capital (change in endogenous foreign capital). In this chapter, we want to show how the behaviour of health sector changes due to the presence of endogenous foreign health capital (or, endogenous foreign capital). Here we want to correlate the issues of international health capital mobility (or, international capital mobility), health sector, and vanishing sector.

The main motivation behind the present chapter follows from the fact that existing literature on theoretical works related to any specific problem in a developing economy attempts to examine the impact of exogenous changes (may be in the form of exogenous change in capital stock) on variables like factor prices, output levels of various sectors, and national income rather than on the implications of endogenous changes in capital on the above-mentioned variables. Contrary to the conventional works, here we discuss the implication of regime switch from no capital mobility to full capital mobility (in the form of both usual capital and health capital), thus discussing the impact of finite changes in policies. This is more in line with contemporary literature on trade and capital flows such as Marjit and Kar (2005), etc.

In this chapter, we consider that total foreign health capital stock consists of both domestic health capital and foreign health capital. Similarly, total capital stock of the economy consists of both domestic capital and foreign capital. We have considered two regimes here. One is the regime of international health capital immobility (or, international capital immobility) and the second one is the regime of international health capital mobility (or, international capital mobility). In the context of first regime, we have considered both foreign capital and foreign health capital as exogenous implying the existence of international capital immobility and foreign health capital immobility. In the second regime, we have considered endogenous foreign health capital and foreign capital.

The chapter is organized in the following manner. Section 2 reviews a brief literature and Sect. 3 describes facts and figures about BRICS nations' health status. Section 4 describes and discusses empirical model and its results. Section 5 considers the basic model. Finally, the concluding remarks are made in Sect. 6.

2 Brief Literature Review

The relationship between healthcare and international trade in BRICS nations has been widely studied, particularly in the context of economic growth, foreign direct investment (FDI), and public health policy. Several studies emphasize the role of BRICS countries as emerging global healthcare hubs, with a growing presence in pharmaceutical exports, medical tourism, and biotechnology innovation. The expansion of healthcare markets within BRICS has been driven by increasing urbanization, demographic shifts, and rising income levels, leading to greater demand for quality healthcare services.

Research suggests that healthcare investment is closely linked to economic development in BRICS. Bloom and Canning (2000) argue that improved healthcare outcomes contribute to higher labour productivity and economic growth. In BRICS, variations in healthcare expenditure and infrastructure development have influenced economic disparities within and between these nations. For example, Brazil's *Sistema Único de Saúde (SUS)* has played a significant role in expanding healthcare coverage, while India's reliance on private-sector-led growth has resulted in uneven healthcare access (Pinto & de Albuquerque, 2018).

The role of FDI in the BRICS healthcare sector has been a focal point of academic discourse. According to UNCTAD (2020), BRICS countries have increasingly attracted FDI in pharmaceuticals, hospital infrastructure, and telemedicine. India and China, in particular, have emerged as major players in the global pharmaceutical trade, supplying affordable generic medicines to developing nations (López et al., 2021). However, scholars caution that increased foreign ownership of domestic pharmaceutical firms may lead to higher drug prices and reduced accessibility to essential medicines (Nayyar, 2019). BRICS nations have made significant contributions to global health by supplying low-cost medicines and vaccines. India, known as the "pharmacy of the world," exports affordable generic drugs, while China is a leading producer of active pharmaceutical ingredients (APIs) (Kaplan & Laing, 2005). Brazil and South Africa have been instrumental in HIV/AIDS treatment through domestic pharmaceutical production and trade agreements. However, trade policies, intellectual property rights (IPR), and WTO regulations continue to shape the global competitiveness of BRICS pharmaceutical industries (Correa, 2012).

Despite rapid advancements, challenges such as healthcare inequality, regulatory barriers, and geopolitical tensions impact the BRICS healthcare sector. Studies highlight the need for stronger regulatory frameworks to balance foreign investment benefits with national healthcare priorities (Peng et al., 2018). Additionally, concerns about over-reliance on foreign medical supplies, particularly highlighted during the COVID-19 pandemic, have reinforced the need for greater self-sufficiency in pharmaceutical production and healthcare infrastructure across BRICS (Khilji et al., 2021).

In conclusion, existing literature underscores the importance of healthcare investment, trade policies, and foreign direct investment in shaping the healthcare landscape of BRICS nations. As these countries continue to integrate into the global healthcare economy, strategic policies will be essential to ensure that economic growth translates into equitable and sustainable healthcare systems (Table 1).

Table 1 Summary of literature on healthcare in BRICS and international trade

Theme	Key findings	Relevant studies
Healthcare Systems and Economic Growth	Improved healthcare outcomes contribute to economic productivity and long-term growth. Variations in BRICS healthcare expenditure impact economic disparities.	Bloom and Canning (2000), Pinto and de Albuquerque (2018)
Foreign Direct Investment (FDI) in Healthcare	BRICS countries attract FDI in pharmaceuticals, hospitals, and telemedicine. Concerns exist over rising drug prices due to foreign acquisitions.	UNCTAD (2020), Nayyar (2019)
Pharmaceutical Trade and Global Health Contributions	India and China lead global pharmaceutical trade, exporting generic medicines and APIs. Brazil and South Africa play key roles in HIV/AIDS treatment. Trade policies and WTO regulations influence market competitiveness.	Kaplan and Laing (2005), Correa (2012), López et al. (2021)
Challenges in Healthcare Trade and Policy	Healthcare inequality, regulatory barriers, and geopolitical tensions affect BRICS health sectors. COVID-19 highlighted the need for self-sufficiency in pharmaceuticals.	Peng et al. (2018), Khilji et al. (2021)

3 Facts and Figures on Health status and FDI from BRICS Nations

Here, to showcase the association between health and international trade among BRICS group, we consider Life Expectancy at birth (LE) and Infant Mortality Rate (IMR) to represent health status and foreign direct investment inflow (FDI) to represent international trade activities[1] (Chatterjee & Dinda, 2022). Figures 1 and 2 illustrate Life Expectancy (LE) among BRICS nations from 1990 to 2022, and reveal an overall upward trend, indicating improvements in public health, socioeconomic conditions, and medical advancements. In 1990, life expectancy was lower in countries like South Africa and India, reflecting challenges such as infectious diseases, economic disparities, and limited healthcare infrastructure. However, by 2014 and continuing through to 2022, significant progress was evident, particularly in China and Brazil, where life expectancy increased substantially due to strengthened healthcare systems, economic growth, and public health initiatives. South Africa experienced fluctuations, particularly due to the HIV/AIDS epidemic in the 1990s and early 2000s, which suppressed LE growth; however, advancements in treatment and healthcare access have improved outcomes in recent years. Overall, while all BRICS nations have shown gains in life expectancy, disparities remain, with some countries achieving higher LE than others, emphasizing the importance of continued efforts in addressing health inequalities and enhancing the quality of life across all socioeconomic groups.

Figures 3 and 4 depicting the Infant Mortality Rate (IMR) among BRICS nations from 1990 to 2022 show a significant downward trend, indicating improvements in child health and overall healthcare systems. In 1990, IMR levels were notably high in countries like India and South Africa, reflecting socioeconomic challenges and

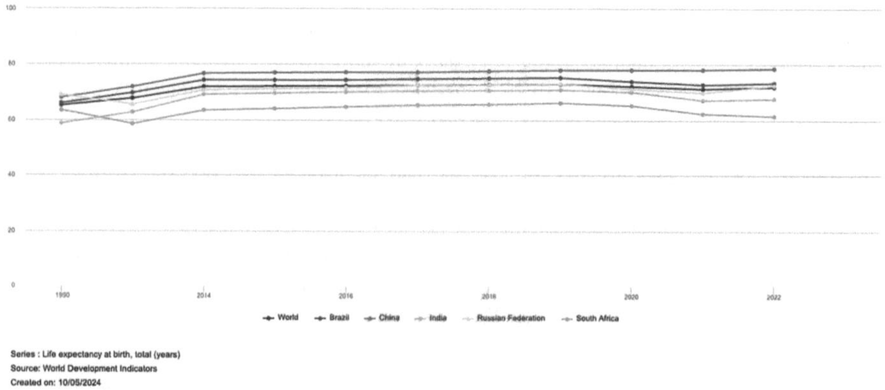

Fig. 1 Life expectancy (LE) at birth among BRICS during (1990–2022). Source WDI

[1]All the data are collected from the World Bank (WDI) database from 1990 to 2022. The data are available at—https://databank.worldbank.org/source/world-development-indicators

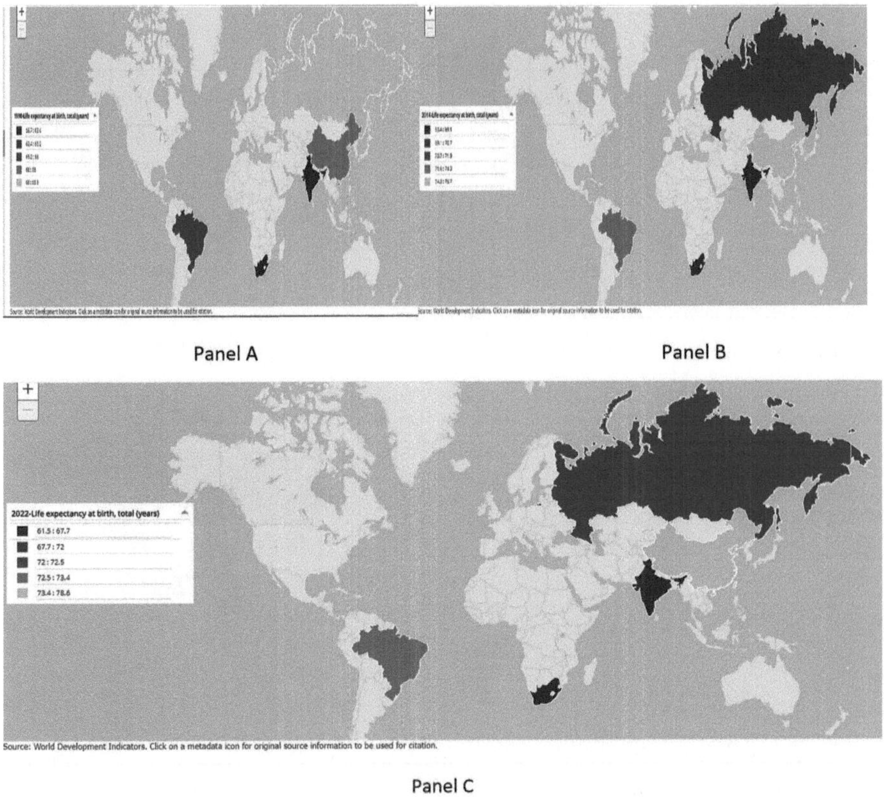

Fig. 2 Panel (**a**): LE within BRICS during 1990; Panel (**b**): LE within BRICS during 2014; Panel (**c**): LE within BRICS during 2022. Source WDI

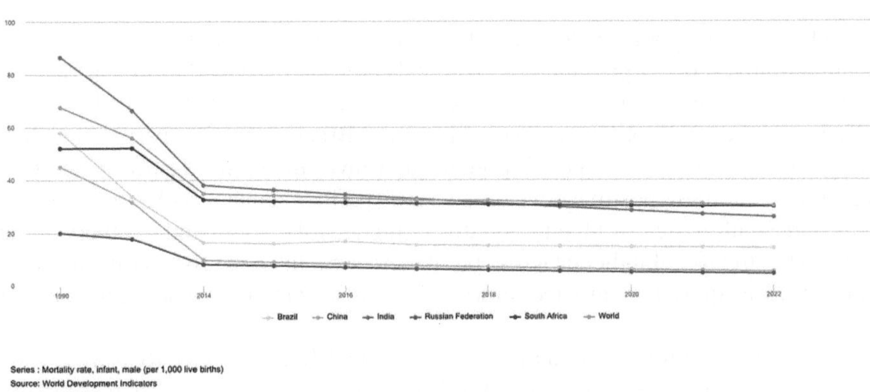

Fig. 3 Infant mortality rate (IMR) among BRICS during (1990–2022). Source WDI

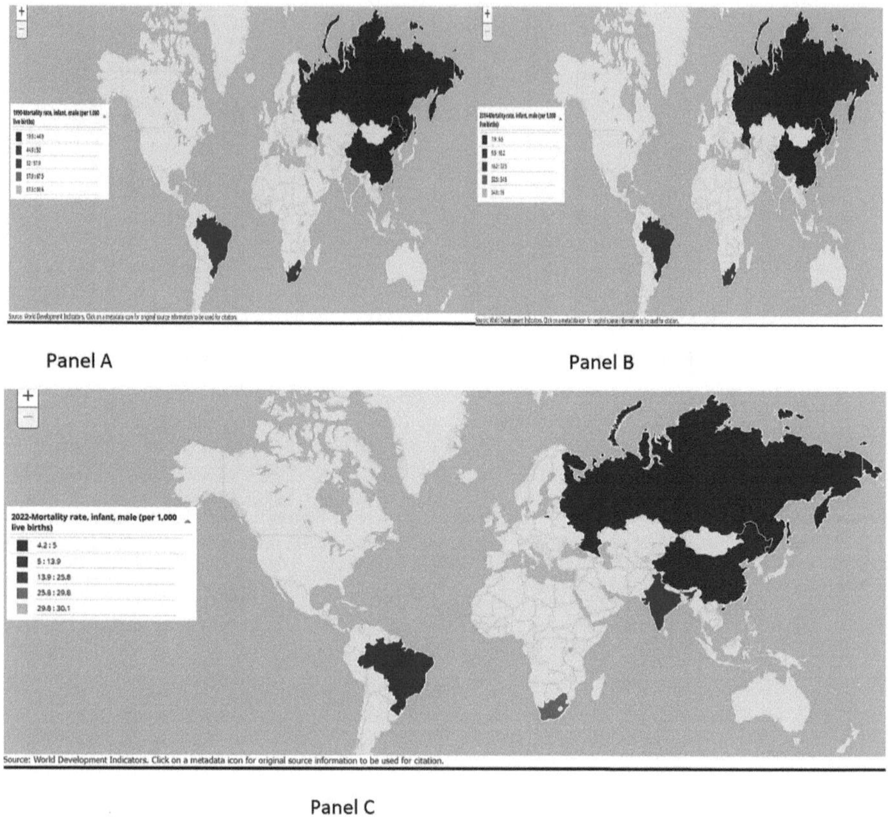

Fig. 4 Panel (**a**): IMR within BRICS during 1990; Panel (**b**): IMR within BRICS during 2014; Panel (**c**): IMR within BRICS during 2022. Source WDI

limited access to quality healthcare. Over the years, concerted efforts in public health initiatives, better prenatal and postnatal care, and expanded healthcare access contributed to marked reductions in IMR. By 2022, all BRICS nations had successfully lowered their IMR figures, with China and Brazil achieving particularly low rates, showcasing effective health policies and investments in maternal and child health. Despite these positive developments, disparities remain, with countries like India and South Africa still having relatively higher IMR compared to others in the group. This trend highlights progress but underscores the need for continued focus on healthcare equity and targeted interventions to sustain and further reduce infant mortality.

In the context of life expectancy (LE) among the BRICS nations, Russia presents a unique trend compared to its peers. While there has been an overall increase in life expectancy from 1990 to 2022, Russia's progress has been more volatile. In 1990, Russia had relatively high life expectancy compared to some other BRICS countries, but it experienced significant declines in the 1990s due to socioeconomic turmoil following the dissolution of the Soviet Union. This period saw increased mortality rates due to factors such as economic instability, poor healthcare infrastructure, and a rise in non-communicable diseases and alcoholism.

Figure 5 depicts FDI data for BRICS nations (Brazil, Russia, India, China, and South Africa) over the years 1990, 2014, and 2022, it is evident that there has been significant growth and shifts in the distribution of FDI among these countries. In 1990, China stood out as the dominant recipient of FDI among BRICS nations, reflecting its rapid economic reforms and opening to foreign investment. By 2014, while China continued to lead, other nations such as Brazil and India showed marked increases, indicating their growing roles as attractive investment destinations due to economic expansion and policy improvements. The 2022 figures highlight further diversification, with India and Brazil solidifying their positions as key FDI players, even as geopolitical tensions and global economic conditions have influenced investment flows. Russia and South Africa, while part of the group, have experienced varied FDI trends, impacted by factors such as political and economic stability. Overall, the trend demonstrates (using Fig. 6) a gradual increase in FDI

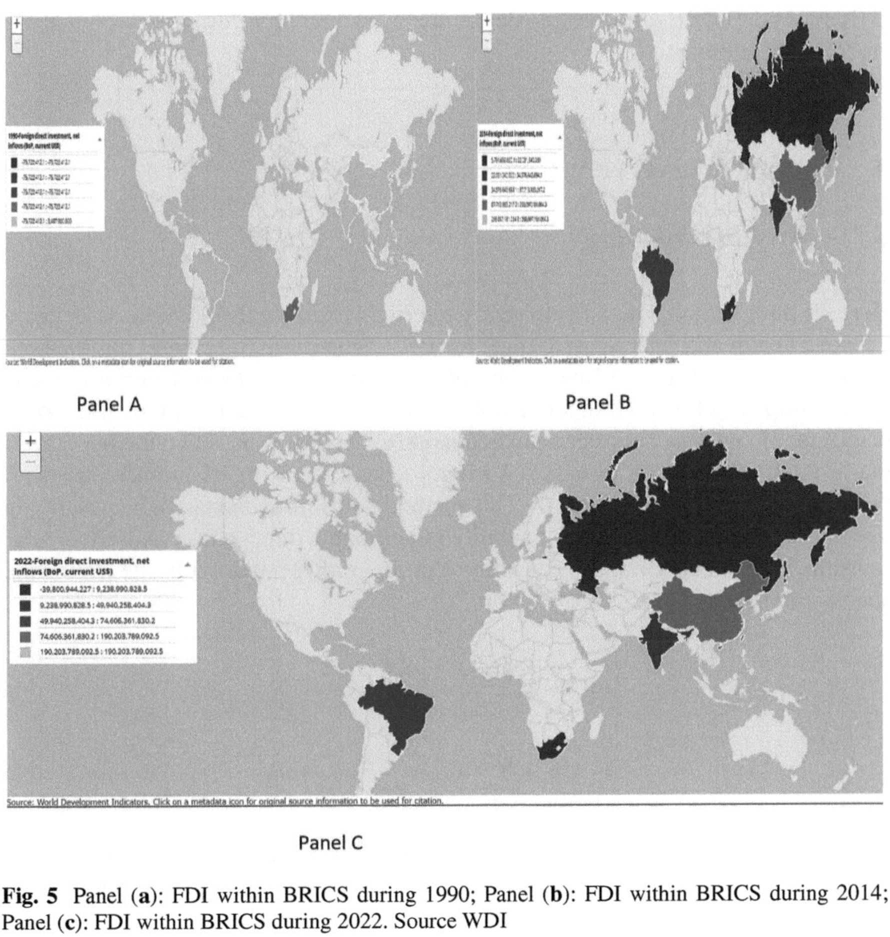

Fig. 5 Panel (**a**): FDI within BRICS during 1990; Panel (**b**): FDI within BRICS during 2014; Panel (**c**): FDI within BRICS during 2022. Source WDI

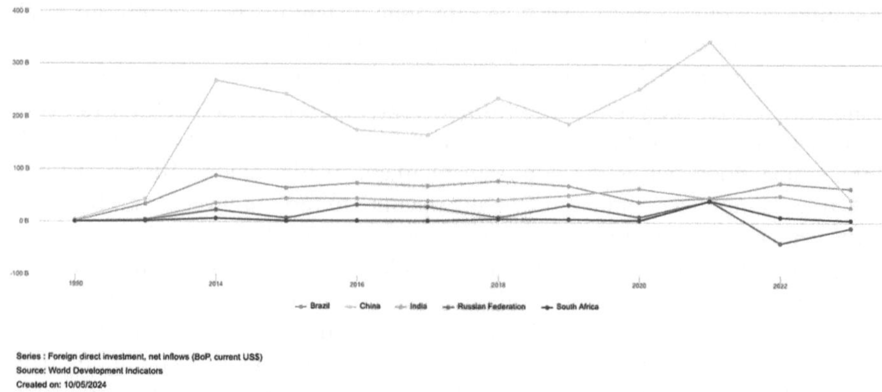

Fig. 6 FDI inflow in BRICS from 1990–2022. Source WDI

inflows across the BRICS, with China maintaining leadership but with notable rises in India and Brazil, showcasing the dynamic nature of investment within these emerging economies.

4 Empirical Overview

4.1 Brief Methodology

Here we have started with an empirical exercise to examine the possible association between health and international trade for BRICS nations. To perform this we consider both linear and non-linear causality tests for better understanding the said relationship. The linear Granger causality test is a widely used econometric tool to determine if one time series can predict another. The test is based on the hypothesis that if the past values of a variable X improve the forecasting of another variable$Y$, then X is said to Granger-cause Y. This method helps in understanding causality in a temporal sense, implying predictability rather than a direct cause-and-effect relationship.The linear Granger causality can be represented with the following specifications:

$$Y_t = \alpha_0 + \sum_{i=1}^{p} \alpha_i Y_{t-i} + \sum_{j=1}^{q} \beta_j X_{t-j} + \varepsilon_t \tag{1}$$

$$X_t = \gamma_0 + \sum_{i=1}^{r} \gamma_i X_{t-i} + \sum_{j=1}^{s} \theta_j Y_{t-j} + u_t \tag{2}$$

Where, α_i, β_j, γ_i and θ_j are the coefficients; ε_t and u_t are error terms assumed to be white noise; p, q, r and s denote the lag lengths, often determined by information criteria like the Akaike Information Criterion (AIC) or Bayesian Information Criterion (BIC). Again, the non-linear Granger causality test extends the linear test to account for complex relationships that linear models may not capture. Real-world economic interactions often involve non-linear dynamics due to structural breaks, thresholds, and non-linear dependencies. The non-linear test is therefore more robust for analysing complex economic relationships. It can be expressed in terms of the following expression:

$$Y_t = f\left(Y_{t-1},\ldots\ldots,Y_{t-p},X_{t-1},\ldots\ldots\ldots,X_{t-q}\right) + \in_t \tag{3}$$

where *f* represents non-linear function.

4.2 Empirical Outcomes

The unit root test results in Table 2 reveal the stationarity properties of life expectancy (LE), infant mortality rate (IMR), and foreign direct investment (FDI) across BRICS nations using three different tests: Augmented Dickey–Fuller (ADF), Im, Pesaran, and Shin (IPS), and Harris and Tzavalis (HT). For India and China, LE and IMR are stationary at levels (I(0)) in all tests, while FDI is stationary at first difference (I(1)), indicating that the data needs to be differenced once to achieve stationarity. In contrast, Brazil shows non-stationarity at levels for all three variables across all tests, requiring differencing for stationarity (I(1)). South Africa presents a similar trend to India and China with stationary LE and IMR at levels but FDI at first difference. The Russian Federation differs by showing FDI stationarity at levels in the ADF test but mixed results in IPS and HT, where FDI shows non-stationarity at levels in some cases.

Table 3 shows linear Granger causality results with p-values indicating the significance of causality between FDI and health metrics (LE and IMR). India and China exhibit significant bidirectional causality (Health⇄Trade). This suggests that health improvements contribute to attracting FDI, and increased FDI positively influences life expectancy. However, Brazil and South Africa show a similar unidirectional causality running from FDI to LE, with the exception that LE does not

Table 2 Results of unit root tests

	Augmented Dickey–Fuller			Im, Pesaran, and Shin			Harris and Tzavalis		
Country	LE	IMR	FDI	LE	IMR	FDI	LE	IMR	FDI
India	I(0)	I(0)	I(1)	I(0)	I(0)	I(1)	I(0)	I(0)	I(1)
China	I(0)	I(0)	I(1)	I(0)	I(0)	I(1)	I(0)	I(0)	I(1)
Brazil	I(1)	I(1)	I(1)	I(1)	I(1)	I(1)	I(1)	I(1)	I(1)
South Africa	I(0)	I(0)	I(1)	I(0)	I(0)	I(1)	I(0)	I(0)	I(1)
Russian Federation	I(0)	I(0)	I(0)	I(0)	I(0)	I(1)	I(0)	I(1)	I(1)

Note: Results are obtained by considering intercept and trend

Table 3 Results of linear Granger causality

Country	FDI to LE	LE to FDI	FDI to IMR	IMR to FDI	Remarks
India	0.13 (0.01)	0.08 (0.08)	−1.08 (0.04)	−0.19 (0.07)	Health⇔Trade
China	0.22 (0.00)	1.01 (0.07)	−1.05 (0.03)	−0.58 (0.05)	Health⇔Trade
Brazil	0.28 (0.03)	2.35 (0.32)	−0.23 (0.06)	−0.37 (0.09)	Health⇔Trade (LE does not cause FDI)
South Africa	0.09 (0.04)	2.21 (0.37)	−0.71 (0.06)	1.19 (0.32)	Trade ⇨ Health
Russian Federation	−0.41 (0.23)	1.19 (0.31)	1.21 (0.19)	0.72 (0.12)	No Causation between Health & Trade

Note: Based on author(s)' calculation. Values in parenthesis represent p-value

Table 4 Results of non-linear Granger causality

Country	FDI to LE	LE to FDI	FDI to IMR	IMR to FDI	Remarks
India	0.19 (0.03)	0.05 (0.06)	−1.01 (0.01)	−0.25 (0.08)	Health⇔Trade
China	0.31 (0.02)	0.92 (0.07)	−1.01 (0.02)	−0.28 (0.03)	Health⇔Trade
Brazil	0.18 (0.03)	1.05 (0.08)	−0.13 (0.07)	−0.35 (0.09)	Health⇔Trade
South Africa	0.11 (0.03)	0.21 (0.07)	−0.37 (0.06)	−0.19 (0.02)	Health⇔Trade
Russian Federation	−0.55 (0.13)	2.19 (0.15)	−0.21 (0.19)	−0.33 (0.12)	No Causation between Health & Trade

Note: Based on author(s)' calculation. Values in parenthesis represent p-value

cause FDI. This suggests that while FDI improves life expectancy, the reverse relationship is not evident in the linear analysis. Interestingly, no significant causation between FDI and health indicators is found in case of Russian Federation, indicating that FDI flows and health metrics do not influence each other in a linear sense.

Table 4 reflects non-linear Granger causality between FDI and health indicators. Similar to the earlier scenario, that is, in case of nations like India and China, we find consistent evidence of bidirectional causality (Health⇄Trade), as shown by significant p-values in both directions for FDI to LE and LE to FDI. This reinforces the findings in the linear test but suggests more complex relationships. Interestingly, non-linear tests show bidirectional causality for both Brazil and South Africa (Health⇄Trade). Unlike the linear results, the non-linear tests show that LE may influence FDI, capturing non-linear dynamics or external factors not captured by linear models. However, similar to the linear results, no significant causality is detected in case of Russian Federation, suggesting that even under non-linear considerations, FDI and health metrics do not show interdependence.

From our empirical prelims, we find the following theoretically examinable hypothesis. One, economic intuition behind the both-way causation between health and international trade in case of developing economies. Two, why for some developing economies causation runs only from international trade to health? Three, does such causation, that is, international trade affects health, affect the autarky sectoral distribution of any representative developing economy? Following are formed to examine these queries in a more calibrated manner by employing a General equilibrium arguments.

5 The General Equilibrium

5.1 *International Health Capital Immobility*

We consider a small open economy where international health capital is immobile[2] and it consists of three sectors in a Heckscher–Ohlin–Samuelson framework. One of the three sectors is the agricultural sector(A), which produces its output using labour (L) and capital (K). Another sector is the manufacturing sector (M), which produces output by using labour and capital. This is the import competing sector while sector A is a sector that produces exportable products. The third sector is the health sector (H) which uses labour as well as health capital (N) which is specific to this sector. The health sector produces a non-traded final commodity.[3] Sector M is protected by tariff (t). Here K consists of domestic capital (K_D) and foreign capital (K_F) and we assume that K_D and K_F are perfect substitutes. All these three sectors[4] use labour which is perfectly mobile among these three sectors. Health capital is specific to sector H while K is completely mobile between sectors A and M. It is to be noted that health capital consists of both domestic health capital (N_D) and foreign health capital (N_F), and we assume that N_D and N_F are perfect substitutes.

In our model, sector A produces its output X_A, sectors M and H produce output X_M and X_H, respectively. Here we assume that the agricultural sector is more labour intensive compared to the manufacturing sector. The agricultural product is considered as the numeraire and its price is set equal to unity. We assume that both foreign capital income and foreign health capital income are completely repatriated. Production functions exhibit constant returns to scale with diminishing marginal productivity for each factor.

[2] International health capital immobility is a situation where domestic rate of return on foreign health capital (R) is greater than the rate of return on foreign health capital in the international market (R^*) and there is restriction on the entry of foreign health capital to the domestic economy.

[3] In a developing economy, most of the health commodities are non-traded final commodities such as different types of hospital facilities as well as health facilities like availability of medicines, health check-up facilities, etc. (Chatterjee, 2024).

[4] All the three sectors produce final commodities in this model but one of them produces non-traded final commodity.

The notations used in the model are stated as follows:

X_i = product produced by the ith sector, i = A,M,H; P^*_A = world price of commodity A; P_A = domestic price of commodity A, we assume $P_A = P^*_A = 1$; P^*_M = world price of good M; $P_M = P^*_M(1+t)$ = domestic price of good M; P_H = domestically determined price of good H; L = fixed number of workers in the economy; N_D = domestic health capital stock of the economy; N_F = foreign health capital stock of the economy; N = economy's aggregate health capital stock; K_F = foreign capital stock; K_D = domestic capital stock; K = economy's aggregate capital stock; a_{ji} = quantity of the jth factor for producing one unit of output in the ith sector, j=L,K,N and i =A,M,H; θ_{ji} = distributive share of the jth input in the ith sector; λ_{ji} = proportion of the jth factor used in the production of the ith sector; t = *ad valorem* rate of tariff on the import of commodity M; W = competitive wage rate; r = rate of return to capital; R = rate of return to health capital; D_i = consumption demand for the ith final commodity, i = A,M,H; E^H_{PH} =own price elasticity of demand for commodity H; E^H_Y = income elasticity of demand for commodity H; Y = national income at domestic price; I = import demand for commodity M; σ_i = elasticity of factor substitution in sector i, i = A, M, H.

The equational structure of the model is as follows:

The competitive equilibrium condition in the product market for the three sectors gives us the following equations:

$$a_{LA}W + a_{KA}r = 1 \quad (4)$$

$$a_{LM}W + a_{KM}r = P_M^*(1+t) \quad (5)$$

$$a_{LH}W + a_{NH}R = P_H \quad (6)$$

Sector specificity of health capital is given by the following equation

$$a_{NH}X_H = N_D + N_F = N \quad (7)$$

We assume for simplicity that a_{LH} is fixed.[5]

Perfect mobility of capital between sectors A and M can be expressed as

$$a_{KA}X_A + a_{KM}X_M = K_D + K_F = K \quad (8)$$

Full employment of labour implies the following equation:

$$a_{LA}X_A + a_{LM}X_M + a_{LH}X_H = L \quad (9)$$

The demand for the non-traded final commodity is given by

$$D_H = D_H(P_H, P_M, Y) \quad (10)$$

[5] In this paper, we have assumed a_{LH} as fixed coefficient.

We assume that commodity H is a normal good with negative and positive own price elasticity and income elasticities of demand, respectively, that is, $E^{H}_{PH}<0$ and $E^{H}_{Y}>0$.

The cross price elasticity is positive, that is, $E^{H}_{PM}>0$.

The demand–supply equality condition for commodity H is

$$D_H(P_H, P_M, Y) = X_H \tag{11}$$

The demand for commodity M and the volume of import are, respectively, given by the following equations:

$$D_M = D_M(P_H, P_M, Y) \tag{12}$$

$$I = D_M(P_H, P_M, Y) - X_M \tag{13}$$

The national income of the economy at domestic prices is given by

$$Y = X_A + P_M X_M + P_H X_H - rK_F - RN_F + tP_M{}^*I \tag{14.1}$$

or

$$Y = WL + RN_D + rK_D + tP_M{}^*I. \tag{14.2}$$

The working of the model is as follows. There are 11 endogenous variables in the system: W, r, R, P_H, X_A, X_M, X_H, D_M, D_H, I and Y. Here we have 11 independent equations (Eqs. 4–14.6) to solve for 11 unknowns.

5.2 International Health Capital Mobility

Here we assume that in the presence of international health capital immobility we have $R > R^*$, where R^* is the given return on foreign health capital in the international market. In such a situation we have no foreign health capital inflow. If R falls to $\tilde{R}$, where, $R>\tilde{R}> R^*$, we find that there is some amount of inflow of foreign health capital (N_F) and at last we will reach at the equilibrium level[6] of N_F where, $R = R^*$.

Here, we assume that N_D is exogenous, whereas N_F is assumed to be an endogenous variable and we use $R = R^*$ in our basic model. By using Eqs. (4) and (5), we can solve for W and r. Once W and R are known a_{NH} is also known. Using $R = R^*$ in our basic model, we find that Eq. (6) gives us the value of P_H. Hence, from Eq. (7), we can express X_H as a function of N_F and, hence by using Eqs. (8) and (9), we can express X_A and X_M in terms of N_F. From Eq. (12), D_M can be expressed as a function of Y only, since P_H and P_M are given. Thus, I can be expressed in terms of Y and

[6] At $R=R^*$, we have the equilibrium level of foreign health capital inflow due to equilibrium in the international health capital market.

N_F. Using this fact in Eq. (14.2), we can express Y as a function of N_F. Thus, from Eq. (10), one can express D_H in terms of N_F and hence N_F can be determined from Eq. (11). Once N_F is known, then X_A, X_M, X_H, D_H, D_M, I are also known. In order to examine the impact of an increase in N_F on R we need to explore the relationship between P_H and R on one hand and X_H and N_F on the other hand. To find out the relationship between P_H and R, we establish the following lemma.

Lemma 1 *A fall in R leads to a fall in P_H iff $\sigma_H<1$.*

Proof of Lemma 1 Differentiating Eq. (3) and by using $da_{LH} = dW= 0$, we get,

$$\theta_{NH}\left(\hat{R}+\hat{a}_{NH}\right)=\hat{P}_H$$

By definition $\sigma_H = (\hat{a}_{NH} - \hat{a}_{LH})/(\hat{W} - \hat{R})$

Using the envelope result $Wda_{LH} + Rda_{NH} = 0$ and by inserting $\hat{a}_{LH}=\hat{W}= 0$ in the expression ofσ_H one obtain

$$\hat{a}_{NH} = -\hat{R}\sigma_H$$

Using the value of $\hat{a}_{NH}$ in the expression of $\hat{P}_H$ we can write

or, $\hat{R}=\left[1/\theta_{NH}\left(1-\sigma_H\right)\right]\hat{P}_H$,

or, $\hat{P}_H=\theta_{NH}\left(1-\sigma_H\right)\hat{R}$

Hence, $\hat{R}< 0$ implies $\hat{P}_H< 0$, iff $\sigma_H< 1$.

We thus find that the lemma holds if the production function for the health sector is non-Cobb–Douglas.

Similarly, the relationship between N_F and X_H can be established by the following lemma:

Lemma 2 *Under the assumption that $-\frac{\mu}{\sigma_H}\hat{N}_F<\hat{R}< 0$, where $\mu = (N_F/N)$; an increase in N_F leads to an increase in X_H.*

Proof of Lemma 2 To prove this lemma, we have to first of all show that $\hat{X}_H> 0$, when$\hat{N}_F> 0$. Differentiation of Eq. (7) gives us

$$\hat{a}_{NH}+\hat{X}_H=\mu\hat{N}_F$$

By definition $\sigma_H = (\hat{a}_{NH} - \hat{a}_{LH})/(\hat{W} - \hat{R})$

By using the envelope result $Wda_{LH} + Rda_{NH} = 0$ and by inserting $\hat{a}_{LH}=\hat{W}= 0$ in the expression of σ_H one obtain

$$\hat{a}_{NH} = -\hat{R}\sigma_H$$

Thus, $\hat{X}_H$ can be written as $\hat{X}_H= \mu\,\hat{N}_F + \hat{R}\sigma_H$

Hence, we can say that $\hat{X}_H> 0$, when $\hat{N}_F> 0$ iff $\hat{R}> -\frac{\mu}{\sigma_H}\hat{N}_F$.

In fact when $\hat{N}_F > 0$, we have $\hat{R} < 0$.

Thus, $\hat{X}_H > 0$, iff $-\frac{\mu}{\sigma_H}\hat{N}_F < \hat{R} < 0$.

An increase in N_F implies a fall in R. A fall in R implies an increase in a_{NH}. Given a_{LH}, from Eq. (6), we can say that P_H will also fall due to fall in R.[7] Again from Eq. (7), we can argue that there will be an increase in X_H due to an inflow of N_F.[8] An increase in X_H implies an increase in $a_{LH}X_H$ and hence a fall in $(L - a_{LH}X_H)$ as a_{LH} is fixed, that is, a reduction in the labour availability to sectors A and M. A fall in the labour endowment available to sectors A and M causes a Rybczynski effect as a result of which X_M increases and X_A falls, given that sector A is more labour intensive than sector M. Using Eqs. (14.2), (13) and after some manipulation, we can say that an increase in N_F leads to a fall in Y, due to the factor price effects and tariff revenue effect.[9]

Proposition 1 *A shift from international health capital immobility regime to an international health capital mobility regime leads to under some reasonable conditions: (i) a decrease in the rate of return to health capital and a decrease in the price of the output of the health sector; (ii) increase in the levels of output of both health and manufacturing sector and a reduction in the level of output of the agricultural sector and (iii) a fall in national income.*

5.3 *Extension 1*

5.3.1 Immobility of International Health Capital

The model is similar to that of the basic model but the only difference is that here we assume that the wage rate of the health sector is fixed at a higher level ($\bar{W}$) compared to the competitive wage rate(W). Thus, we have $\bar{W} > W$. In this version of the model Eq. (6) changes to

$$a_{LH}\bar{W} + a_{NH}R = P_H \tag{6.1}$$

Equation (14.2) can be rewritten as

[7] See Lemma 1.

[8] For details, see Lemma 2.

[9] An increase in N_F leads to a fall in R. Thus, fall in R implies a fall in Y. We call it factor price effect. From Eq. (14.2), we can express Y as a function of P_H and I. Using this fact in Eq. (13), we can express I in terms of P_H and hence we can express Y in terms of P_H only. Thus, D_M is expressed in terms of P_H. An increase in N_F leads to a fall in P_H and an increase in X_M. Here a fall in P_H leads to a fall in D_M. Thus, increase in X_M and decrease in D_M lead to a reduction in I. Hence, reduction in I leads to a fall in Y. We call it tariff revenue effect.

$$Y=\left(\bar{W}-W\right)a_{LH}X_H+WL+RN_D+rK_D+tP_M^*I \tag{14.3}$$

Equations (6.1) and (14.3) are added to our basic model.[10] The other equations and the equilibrium conditions of the other markets remain the same. Determination of the general equilibrium is possible, since we have 11 independent equations to solve for 11 unknowns.

5.3.2 International Mobility

This version of the basic model is almost similar to that of earlier version, that is, the model is used in the Sect. 5.1. Here we assume that R falls to $\tilde{R}$, where, R>$\tilde{R}$> R*, and we find an inflow of N_F so that ultimately R will reach to R*.

By assuming N_D as an exogenous variable and N_F as an endogenous variable and after using R=R* we can determine the general equilibrium. An increase in N_F implies a fall in R. Given a_{LH}, from Eq. (6.1), we can say that P_H will also fall due to fall in R (see Lemma 1). On the other hand, from Eq. (7), we can argue that there will be an increase in X_H due to an inflow of N_F.[11] An increase in X_H implies an increase in $a_{LH}X_H$, as a_{LH} is fixed and hence a fall in $(L - a_{LH}X_H)$, that is, a reduction in the labour availability to sectors A and M. A fall in the labour endowment available to sectors A and M causes a Rybczynski effect as a result of which X_M increases and X_A falls, given that sector A is more labour intensive than sector M.[12] Using Eqs. (14.3), (13) and after some manipulation, we can say that an increase in N_F leads to a fall in Y, due to the factor price effect and tariff revenue effect.[13] An increase in X_H leads to an increase in Y. This is known as labour reallocation effect.[14] Thus, the effects of an inflow of N_F on Y depend upon the net effect of factor price effect, tariff revenue effect, and labour reallocation effect. If the labour reallocation effect dominates the other effects, then Y is positively affected, and welfare increases. Thus, the following proposition can now be established.

Proposition 2 *A shift from international health capital immobility regime to an international health capital mobility regime leads to an increase in national income and hence an increase in social welfare under some reasonable conditions. The sectoral effects of such a regime change are similar to that of proposition 1.*

---

[10] Equation (14.3) is same as (14.2) if we assume W =$\bar{W}$.

[11] See footnote no. 9.

[12] We shall get opposite results if we assume that sector A is more capital intensive relative to sector M.

[13] This is already explained in footnote no. 10.

[14] The workers of health sector enjoy a wage rate ($\bar{W}$), which is higher compared to the competitive wage rate (W) that prevails in rest of the economy. Hence increase in employment in the health sector (because $\bar{W} > W$) is at the cost of reduction in employment in the other sectors of the economy. Thus, the wage differential ($\bar{W}$ - W) leads to the labour reallocation effect.

5.4 *Immobility of International Capital*

The model which we use in this section is similar to that of the model of Sect. 5.1 and hence the working of the general equilibrium[15] is similar to that of Sect. 5.1.

5.4.1 International Mobility

Here we use the model of the Sect. 5.1. We assume that K_D as an exogenous and K_F as an endogenous variables. Here we also assume that r falls to $\tilde{r}$, where $r>\tilde{r}>r^*$, and we find an inflow of K_F and ultimately r will reach to r*. By assuming K_F as an endogenous variables and after using $r=r^*$ in our variant of the basic model, we will face a problem of uniqueness[16] to solve the general equilibrium. Thus, determination of the general equilibrium is not possible. However, from here we can infer that an inflow of K_F leads to a fall in r. From Eqs. (4) and (5), we can argue that a reduction r leads to an increase in W in both of these equations. If W increases more in Eq. (5) than in Eq. (4), we find that sector A vanishes. On the other hand, if W increases more in Eq. (4) than in Eq. (5), we find that sector M vanishes. This leads to us the following proposition.

Proposition 3 *A shift from international capital immobility regime to an international capital mobility leads to (i) either only manufacturing sector survives and the agricultural sector vanishes, or (ii) only the agricultural sector survives and the manufacturing sector vanishes.*

Scenario 1: Extension 1 with Insignificant Sector A

The new equational structure can be written as

The competitive equilibrium condition in the product market are given by the following equations:

$$a_{LM}W + a_{KM}r = P_M^*(1+t) \tag{5}$$

$$a_{LH}\overline{W} + a_{NH}R = P_H \tag{6.1}$$

Sector specificity of health capital is given by the following equation:

$$a_{NH}X_H = N_D + N_F = N \tag{7}$$

Sector specificity of capital for sector M (when sector A vanishes) can be expressed as

$$a_{KM}X_M = K_D + K_F = K \tag{8.1}$$

Full employment of labour implies the following equation:

$$a_{LM}X_M + a_{LH}X_H = L \tag{9.1}$$

The demand for the non-traded final commodity is given by

[15] This is explained in footnote no. 11.

[16] Inserting $r=r^*$ in the variant, we can get two different values of W, one from Eq. (4) and other from Eq. (5).

$$D_H = D_H(P_H, P_M, Y) \tag{10}$$

The demand–supply equality condition for commodity H is

$$D_H(P_H, P_M, Y) = X_H \tag{11}$$

The demand for commodity M and the volume of import are, respectively, given by the following equations:

$$D_M = D_M(P_H, P_M, Y) \tag{12}$$

$$I = D_M(P_H, P_M, Y) - X_M \tag{13}$$

The national income of the economy at domestic prices is given by

$$Y = P_M X_M + P_H X_H - rK_F - RN_F + tP_M^{*} I \tag{14.4}$$

or

$$Y = (\bar{W} - W) a_{LH} X_H + WL + RN_D + rK_D + tP_M^{*} I \tag{14.3}$$

Given $r = r^*$ from Eq. (5), we can calculate the value of W. For given a_{LH}, from Eq. (6.1), we can express R as a function of P_H. Thus, it is an indecomposable structure. Hence, a_{NH} can be expressed as a function of P_H. For given N, X_H can be expressed as a function of P_H also. Similarly, from Eq. (8.1), we can express X_M in terms of K_F. For given a_{LH} and a_{LM}, from Eq. (9.1), we can express K_F as a function of P_H. Thus, X_M can be expressed as a function of P_H. From Eq. (14.3), we can express Y as a function of P_H and I. From Eq. (13), I can be expressed as a function of P_H since X_M is a function of P_H. Hence, Y can be expressed in terms of P_H only. So from Eq. (10), D_H can be expressed as a function of P_H. As a result of this, Eq. (11) helps us to determine the value of P_H. Once P_H is known K_F , X_M , Y, R and X_H are also known. Thus, Eqs. (10) and (12) help us to determine the values of D_H (since X_H is already known) and $D_{M,}$ respectively. Finally, using Eq. (13), we can get the value of I. To find out the relationship between X_M and $K_{F,}$ we establish the following lemma.

Lemma 3 *Under the assumption that* $-\frac{\gamma}{\sigma_M}\hat{K}_F < \hat{r} < 0$, *where* $\gamma = (K_F/K)$; *an increase in* K_F *leads to an increase in* X_M.

Proof of Lemma 3 To prove this lemma, we have to first of all show that $\hat{X}_M > 0$, when $\hat{K}_F > 0$. Differentiation of Eq. (8.1) gives us

$$\hat{a}_{KM} + \hat{X}_M = \gamma \hat{K}_F$$

By definition $\sigma_M = (\hat{a}_{KM} - \hat{a}_{LM})/(\hat{W} - \hat{r})$ and using the envelop result $Wda_{LM} + Rda_{KM} = 0$ we can write

$$\hat{a}_{KM} = \sigma_M \theta_{LM} (\hat{W} - \hat{r})$$

From Eq. (5), we get $\hat{W} = -(\theta_{KM} / \theta_{LM})\,\hat{r}$ and inserting it in the expression of $\hat{a}_{KM}$ we can write $\hat{a}_{KM} = -\sigma_M \hat{r}$

Thus, $\hat{X}_M$ can be written as $\hat{X}_M = \gamma \hat{K}_F + \hat{r}\,\sigma_M$

Hence, we can say that $\hat{X}_H > 0$, when $\hat{K}_F > 0$ iff $\hat{r} > -\frac{\gamma}{\sigma_M}\hat{K}_F$.

In fact when $\hat{K}_F > 0$, we have $\hat{r} < 0$.

Thus, $\hat{X}_M > 0$, iff $-\frac{\gamma}{\sigma_M}\hat{K}_F < \hat{r} < 0$.

An increase in K_F implies a fall in r. From Eq. (5), we can say that a fall in r implies an increase in W. From Eq. (8.1), we can argue that a fall in r implies an increase in a_{KM}. To maintain full employment condition of the capital market it follows that X_M must increase.[17] An increase in W has both positive and negative effects on Y. The positive effect is generated due to the wage income effect as reflected by the second term on the right-hand side of Eq. (14.3). The negative effect is generated due to the labour reallocation effect. It is reflected by the first term on the RHS of Eq. (14.3). A fall in r has a negative effect on Y as reflected by the fourth term on the RHS of Eq. (14.3). If the sum of labour reallocation effect and domestic capital income effect dominates over the wage income effect, we find that there is a fall in Y. For given P_H, a fall in Y implies a fall in D_M. Thus, a fall in D_M and an increase in X_M lead to fall in I. Again a fall in I leads to further fall in Y. From Eq. (10), we can say that for given P_H and for given X_H, a fall in Y leads to a downward shift of the demand curve of non-traded health commodity which implies a fall in P_H. From Eq. (6.1), we can say that fall in P_H implies a fall in R, because R and P_H are positively related. A fall in R implies an increase in a_{NH} and, hence from Eq. (4), we can argue that X_H must have to fall to maintain full employment condition of the health capital market.

Proposition 4 *A shift from a regime of international capital immobility to capital mobility causes (i) the agricultural sector to vanish and both health and manufacturing sectors to survive; (ii) a decrease in the rate of return to health capital, a decrease in price of the output of the health sector, and an increase in wage rate; (iii) an increase in the level of output of the manufacturing sector and a decrease in the level of output of the health sector and finally, (iv) a fall in national income, under some reasonable conditions.*

Scenario 2: Extension 1 with Insignificant Sector M

The modified equational structure can be written as follows. The competitive equilibrium conditions in the product market are given by the following equations:

$$a_{LA}W + a_{KA}r = 1 \tag{4}$$

$$a_{LH}\bar{W} + a_{NH}R = P_H \tag{6.1}$$

Sector specificity of health capital is given by the following equation:

$$a_{NH}X_H = N_D + N_F = N \tag{7}$$

Sector specificity of capital for sector A (when sector M vanishes) can be expressed as

$$a_{KA}X_A = K_D + K_F = K \tag{8.2}$$

[17] See Lemma 3.

Full employment of labour implies the following equation:

$$a_{LA}X_A + a_{LH}X_H = L \tag{9.2}$$

The demand for the non-traded final commodity is given by

$$D_H = D_H(P_H, Y) \tag{10.1}$$

The demand–supply equality condition for commodity H is

$$D_H(P_H, Y) = X_H \tag{11.1}$$

The national income of the economy at domestic prices is given by

$$Y = X_A + P_H X_H - rK_F - RN_F \tag{14.5}$$

or

$$Y = (\bar{W} - W)a_{LH}X_H + WL + RN_D + rK_D \tag{14.6}$$

Determination of the general equilibrium is possible, since we have eight independent equations to solve for eight unknowns. In order to examine the impact of inflow of K_F on X_A we have to establish the following lemma.

Lemma 4 *Under the assumption that* $-\frac{\gamma}{\sigma_A}\hat{K}_F < \hat{r} < 0$, *where* $\gamma = (K_F/K)$; *an increase in* K_F *leads to an increase in* X_A.

Proof of Lemma 4 The proof of Lemma 4 is similar to that of Lemma 3.

An increase in K_F implies a fall in r. From Eq. (4), we can say that a fall in r implies an increase in W. From Eq. (8.2), we can argue that a fall in r implies an increase in a_{KA}. To maintain full employment condition of the capital market, it follows that X_A must increase.[18] From Eq. (14.6), we can say that a fall in r and an increase in W lead to a fall in Y under some reasonable conditions.[19] From Eq. (10.1), we can say that for given P_H, a fall in Y leads to a downward shift of the demand curve of non-traded health commodity which implies a fall in P_H. A fall in R implies an increase in a_{NH} and, hence from Eq. (7), we can argue that X_H must have to fall to maintain full employment condition of the health capital market. This leads to the following proposition.

Proposition 5 *A shift from a regime of international capital immobility to capital mobility causes (i) the manufacturing sector to vanish and both health and agricultural sectors to survive;(ii) a decrease in the rate of return to health capital, a decrease in price of the output of the health sector, and an increase in wage rate; (iii) an increase in the level of output of the agricultural sector and a decrease in the level of output of the health sector and finally, (iv) a fall in national income, under some reasonable conditions.*

---

[18] This is explained in Lemma 4.

[19] The reason is similar to that of the earlier case (Case 1 where Sector A is the vanishing sector).

6 Concluding Remarks

6.1 Summary of the Results

This study examines the causal relationship between foreign direct investment (FDI) and health indicators—life expectancy (LE) and infant mortality rate (IMR)—through both linear and non-linear Granger causality analyses. Empirical findings indicate that India and China exhibit strong bidirectional causality, implying that improved health conditions attract FDI, while FDI positively impacts life expectancy. Brazil and South Africa display unidirectional causality from FDI to LE in the linear model, but the non-linear test reveals bidirectional causality, suggesting more complex interactions. In contrast, no significant causation is detected for Russia, indicating the absence of interdependence between FDI and health indicators. Theoretical findings based on a three-sector general equilibrium model further clarify the sectoral impacts of international health capital and general capital mobility. Under international health capital mobility, the health and manufacturing sectors expand while agriculture contracts, potentially leading to a decline in national income. When general capital mobility is introduced, one sector—either agriculture or manufacturing—disappears, altering the economic structure significantly. In certain scenarios, health and manufacturing sectors survive while agriculture vanishes, and in others, health and agriculture persist while manufacturing disappears. These results highlight critical trade-offs in capital mobility policies.

6.2 Policy Caveats and Recommendations

Given the observed bidirectional relationship between health and trade in India and China, policymakers should prioritize health sector investments to attract FDI, reinforcing economic growth. For Brazil and South Africa, where non-linear effects suggest that LE influences FDI, policies should focus on improving healthcare infrastructure to maximize foreign investment benefits. The absence of significant causality in Russia indicates that health sector improvements alone may not be sufficient to attract FDI; broader economic factors must be considered.

In terms of capital mobility, policymakers must be cautious in implementing unrestricted capital flows, as results suggest potential sectoral contractions. Expanding international health capital mobility may boost health sector output but could lead to wage rate fluctuations and income redistribution. Striking a balance between capital mobility and sectoral stability is crucial to preventing adverse economic shocks. Countries must adopt strategic trade and investment policies that safeguard critical sectors while leveraging the benefits of capital flows.

6.3 *Limitations and Future Research Agendas*

First, this study primarily relies on Granger causality tests, which capture correlation but do not establish definitive causation. Future research should incorporate panel structural models to identify deeper causal mechanisms. Additionally, while the general equilibrium model provides key theoretical insights, it assumes certain sectoral rigidities that may not hold across diverse economies. Empirical validation of these theoretical predictions through sectoral data analysis is necessary. Second, another limitation is the exclusion of institutional and governance factors that may mediate the health–FDI relationship. Future studies should explore how political stability, regulatory quality, and labour market dynamics influence these interactions. Lastly, research should extend to other developing and developed economies to assess the generalizability of our findings and explore how digital health investments and technological advancements reshape the FDI–health nexus in the modern era.

References

Bloom, D. E., & Canning, D. (2000). The health and wealth of nations. *Science, 287*(5456), 1207–1209. https://doi.org/10.1126/science.287.5456.1207

Chanda, R. (2001). *Trade in health services*. Working Paper, No 70. Indian Council for Research on International Economic Relations (ICRIER).

Chatterjee, N., & Chatterjee, T. (2023). COVID-19, online education and role of mentoring in developing economies—A theoretical build-up with an empirical overhaul. In R. Bhattacharyya, R. C. Das, & A. Ray (Eds.), *COVID-19 pandemic and global inequality*. Springer. https://doi.org/10.1007/978-981-99-4405-7_13

Chatterjee, N., & Chatterjee, T. (2024). Inquiring the nexus between international trade, economic growth, and environment for the BRICS economies. In R. Bhattacharyya & D. Mazumdar (Eds.), *Contemporary issues in international trade* (pp. 179–193). Emerald. https://doi.org/10.1108/978-1-83797-320-020241011

Chatterjee, T. (2024). *International trade, economic crisis and the sustainable development goals*. Emerald. https://doi.org/10.1108/978-1-83753-586-620241024

Chatterjee, T., & Dinda, S. (2022). What determines the health status in developing countries?-Evidence from a dynamic panel. *Journal of Economic Development, 47*(4).

Correa, C. M. (2012). Intellectual property rights and the use of compulsory licenses: Options for developing countries. *Trade and Development Review, 5*(1), 73–89.

Kaplan, W., & Laing, R. (2005). *Local production of pharmaceuticals: Industrial policy and access to medicines*. World Bank Policy Research Working Paper No. 2963.

Khilji, N., Mahmud, M., & Akbar, M. (2021). COVID-19 and the healthcare trade: Implications for BRICS nations. *International Journal of Health Policy and Management, 10*(3), 145–160. https://doi.org/10.34172/ijhpm.2021.42

López, R. A., He, G., & Liu, Y. (2021). The role of BRICS in global pharmaceutical trade: Challenges and opportunities. *Journal of International Trade & Economic Development, 30*(5), 723–742. https://doi.org/10.1080/09638199.2021.1876384

Marjit, S., & Beladi, H. (1997). Protection and the gainful effects of foreign capital. *Economics Letters, 53*, 311–326.

Marjit, S., & Kar, S. (2005). Emigration and wage inequality. *Economics Letters, 88*, 141–145.

Nayyar, D. (2019). The impact of foreign direct investment on domestic pharmaceutical firms in India: A policy perspective. *Economic and Political Weekly, 54*(12), 41–48.

Outreville, J. F. (2007). FDI in the health care sector and most favoured location in developing countries. *European Journal of Health Economics, 8*(4), 305–312.

Peng, B., Wang, X., & Zhang, Y. (2018). Regulatory frameworks and FDI in the healthcare sector: A comparative analysis of BRICS nations. *Global Health Governance, 12*(2), 55–72.

Pinto, A. C., & de Albuquerque, C. (2018). Brazil's health system reforms: Achievements and challenges. *Revista de Saúde Pública, 52*(1), 10–18. https://doi.org/10.1590/s1518-8787.201805200057

United Nations Conference on Trade and Development (UNCTAD). (2020). *World Investment Report 2020: International production beyond the pandemic*. United Nations.

India's Foreign Policy and China-India Economic and Strategic Competition in the Indo-Pacific Region: The Strategic Update

Robert Dygas

Abstract This chapter concentrated on (1) identifying the nature and channels of influence of China's economic statecraft in South Asia and (2) India's strategic competition both in terms of policies of competition with China in the Indo-Pacific Region but also policies towards smaller neighbours who might be considering deeper economic ties and strategic concessions to China. The relevant theories were discussed in this context and the opinion of the author. The theory of geoeconomics, Modelski's hegemonic cycles, and transition power theory introduced by Abramo Fimo Kenneth Organski and Jacek Kugler can highlight the key factors of the analysed topic India and China have their economic and political goals regarding the Indo-Pacific Region. The article also discussed how successful have India's efforts been and the trajectory for the future of Sino-Indian geoeconomics competition in South Asia, so the novelty work was undertaken it this case in the light of multiple studies in this subject. To become a leading power in the Indo-Pacific Region, India will need to establish multilateral affiliations, especially with Australia and New Zealand, the Quadrilateral Framework (QAUD), BRICS, the G20 and the UN Framework Convention on Climate Change to face China's power.

Keywords Geoeconomics · RCEP · BRICS · QUAD · SCO · SLOC · Indo-Pacific

1 Introduction

Indo-Pacific geostrategic concept replaced the Asia-Pacific one to define Asian regionalism (Saha, 2022). The competition between China and India in the Indo-Pacific Region has an impact on the global economy. China formed the Regional Comprehensive Economic Partnership (RCEP) in 2021 which is still the largest free

R. Dygas (✉)
Department of East Asian Economic Studies, SGH Warsaw School of Economics, Warsaw, Poland
e-mail: rdygas1@sgh.waw.pl; https://www.sgh.waw.pl

E. Lau et al. (eds.), *Economics and Finance Readings*,
https://doi.org/10.1007/978-981-96-6998-1_10

trade agreement (FTA) by GDP of the 14 countries (26 Tr USD) with an export value of 5.2 Tr USD of the Indo-Pacific Region (PwC, 2020). India withdrew from RCEP negotiations in November 2019 mainly due to the hegemonic position of China in this free trade agreement which can deepen the negative trade balance of India. On the contrary, India entered the FTA in the Indo-Pacific Economic Framework (IPEF) led by the USA (India's position in the global economy is improving but still, India is a rather import-oriented country compared to China). One of the Government of India's ambitions is to have a positive trade balance. Compared with 2022, the overall trade balance in 2023 has improved from −10.52 bn USD to −5.30 bn USD (Ministry of Commerce and Industry, 2023). Besides that India, according to rating agency S&P Global can be the third top global economy with a GDP value of 6.7 Tr USD by 2031 (S&P Global, 2023). China's GDP in 2023 reached already 13 Tr USD which is a challenge for India itself. To become a leading power in the Indo-Pacific Region, India will need to establish multilateral affiliations, such as the Quadrilateral Framework, BRICS, the G20 and the UN Framework Convention on Climate Change to face China's power.

The main difference between India and China is the political system and the goal of China to be the centre of the world. China is progressing with its economic expansion of The Belt and Road Initiative (BRI) involving more than 130 countries which can be treated as a threat to global economic security (Dygas, 2023). Chinese strategy has a long tradition and it comes from the ancient time's art of war tactics—Sun Tzu (Cleary, 2005). China built its economic strength based on the opportunities created by other countries in the Indo-Pacific region. China has different economic and political tools for approaching developed and less developed countries in the Indo-Pacific Region. One such tool is the Chinese Communist Party (CCP) cell inside the structure of each of the private Chinese companies. If any company from other parts of the world interacts with a Chinese private company, the potential risk of business data access by the Chinese Communist Party is quite possible (Livingstone, 2020). That is why the economic and strategic competition is complex and needs to be analysed with references to relevant theories in the long-term perspective. It is worth adding that India and China while competing in the Indo-Pacific Region have a real military conflict regarding the disputed border of the state of Sikkim (3440 km) in the Himalayan region. China is also active in The South China Sea (SCS) building artificial islands with military bases and having conflicts with ASEAN countries (Philippines, Taiwan, and Vietnam) regarding the Paracel and Spratly Islands. China in August 2023 published a new map of The South Chinese Sea known as "the 10-dash line claim map" with China's rights to the area between the eastern coast of Taiwan and the waters near the Island of Borneo, Malaysia. It creates a big concern about establishing China's "SCS Air Defence Identification Zone" in the future (MEMRI, 2024).

2 Literature Review

Since the issue of strategic competition between China and other countries like India in the Indo-Pacific region combines the fields of international economics, finance, economic policy, and social geography, it is worth using the concept known in the literature as geoeconomics. Its precursors are considered to be the authors of the concept of "geopolitics", which was first used by the Swedish scientist Rudolf Kjellen in 1899 (Davidsen, 2021), and the theory developed by Sir Halford Mackinder in 1904. A broader historical perspective on the transition from geopolitical theory to geoeconomics was presented in the publication of three Greek economists Deniozos et al., (2019). They point out that the distinction between geopolitics and geoeconomics was introduced in 2009 by Deborah Cowen and Neil Smith, and they believe that geopolitics should be treated as a means of acquiring territory to achieve the goal of accumulating wealth, while geoeconomics reverses the procedure and means striving directly to accumulate wealth through market control (Cowen & Smith, 2009).

The evolution of the idea of geoeconomics as one of the scientific trends in socio-economic geography was presented by Russian scientists Anokhin and Lachininskii (2015) from the University of Saint Petersburg. According to these authors, geoeconomics describes the formation and functioning of economies (economic agents) at the global level. Edward Luttwak, an economist and former advisor to USA President George H.W., also contributed to the development of this concept. Bush (he worked as a consultant in the United States Department of Defense and a senior consultant at the Center for Strategic and International Analysis in Washington). He gave this concept a geostrategic meaning, considering geoeconomics as an independent trend in science and a method of explaining the economic conflicts of Western countries. Pascal Lorot, on the other hand, believed that geoeconomics concerns economic strategies that are aimed at the protectionism of national corporations operating in selected sectors (Luttwak, 1999). These activities aim to control a given segment of the global economy, which proves the economic and social power of such strategies (Lorot, 2000).

This definition is based on the hypothesis that national policies influence market structures and states will attempt to reshape dominant trends to suit their interests. Also, the Azerbaijani economist Vusal Gasimli developed a unique concept of geoeconomics. He defines it as the study of the interdependence between economics, geopolitics, and geography, referring to the connections between the Earth and the universe (Gasimli, 2015). In Poland, the propagator of geoeconomics is Edward Haliżak, whose motivation to deepen this issue was new forms of international activity of states within the international order (Haliżak, 2012). It can therefore be said that the concept of geoeconomics also includes the analysis of the importance and position of a given country in the world economy (e.g. in the context of international competition between China and India in the Indo-Pacific Region). An example is the Arctic region, where economically strong countries such as Russia, the

USA, China, Germany, and France compete with each other to manage open fishing areas, extract natural resources, and ensure environmental protection (Karaś, 2020).

Another important aspect of an analysed topic related to geoeconomics is the impact of the economic power of India and China in the Indo-Pacific Region. Such power can be referred to as the theory of force transition by Abramo Fimo Kenneth Organski and Jacek Kugler, and power-economy and powerometry which allow to model and measure such powers (Kugler & Organski, 2011). Mirosław Sułek indicated different forms of the powers. He indicated that for India and China, the applicable form is a demographic and spatial power based primarily on population and territory (and to some extent on geographic location). By its nature, it is passive; a state based on such power can only play a certain role in the international arena at the highest quantitative levels (such as China or India) (Sułek, 2017). In the opinion of the author, it is not completely right in today's world economic situation and requires some modification. Sułek also proposed some measures (power metrics) of the country's power. The first type is economic power, which is determined by economic development indicators measured by labour productivity and the level of national income per capita. The second is the military power. The mixed forms for analysis can be adopted, e.g. economic and military power, and calculate the power of a given country based on the general power formula. The important elements of this method included variables such as gross domestic product, population, area of a given country, military expenditure, and the number of soldiers. (Sułek, 2017). Although Sułek's approach is interesting and simple in the opinion of the author, it is quite general and does not take into consideration more important geoeconomic factors, which can be understood together with Haliżak geoeconomics theory. Those factors should determine the position of the country in the world taking into consideration also the political economy and military aspects.

The econometric model for estimating the power of China, India, and other countries in the context of sustainability development was done by Robert Dygas, Tomasz Napiórkowski, and Waldemar Milewicz in 2021. They concluded that the most important geoeconomic factors which influence the power of the country are: (1) human capital index, (2) physical capital per employee, (3) openness to international trade, (4) openness to foreign direct investments (FDI), (5) military power, (6) foreign currency reserves, and (7) Sustainable Development Index (SDI) (Dygas et al., 2021). These theories should be considered together with the hegemonic cycles of economic development of the countries introduced by George Modelski in 1987 (Modelski, 1987) and the theory of hegemonic stability by Robert Gilpin in 1981 (Gilpin, 1981). The process of economic and strategic rivalry between China and India in the Indo-Pacific Region takes place in the context of the weakening position of the United States and China's simultaneous pursuit of a leadership role in the global economy. According to the power transition theory, the country defined as the hegemon (currently the USA) must lose its position to the country with the greatest economic potential after the hegemon (currently China). This happens as a result of the loss of distribution potential to stabilize and maintain the current order. According to this theory, an aspiring country (challenger) such as India could challenge the hegemon by achieving 80% of its potential (Ambrożek, 2018). Looking from the perspective of Modelski's hegemonic cycle theory each significant change in world power happens every 100 years (Modelski, 1987).

3 The Nature and Channels of Influence of China's Economic Statecraft in South Asia

The nature of China's influence comes from Confucianism as the codified ideology (Zhao, 2018). China wants to be "the centre of the world" where all the countries are influenced by China in economic, institutional, social, and political perspectives (Sinocentrism). The interesting fact is that China uses a multichannel strategy to be the biggest economy in the world by 2049. The most important aspects of the Chinese influence and the channels are presented in Table 1 below.

Xi Jinping has already announced that he wants China to be number one in the global economy by 2049, the 100th anniversary of the People's Republic of China (PRC) and the 100th anniversary of NATO establishment. From this perspective, China is using a step approach to reach this goal to dethrone the USA as the main

Table 1 The multichannel of China's world influence

The channel	Tools	Influence effects	The concerns for the future
Economic	Belt and Road Initiative (BRI)	+150 countries involved in infrastructure investment projects	The debt crises will materialize in heavily indebted countries
Institutional	Membership in WHO, IMF, BRICS, WTO, and SCO	Global regulations regarding trade, financial settlements, and health protection	Giving China a greater ability to project its power more widely
Social	China Towns in megacities across the world Chinese AI systems to support society	Chinese products are distributed in retail shops, and Chinese systems for face recognition are tested by other countries	Societies development pending on the AI system
Military	Military agreements with Russia, Iran, North Korea, and Solomon Islands "The new 10-dash line claim map"—China's claims concerning the territory of The South Chinese Sea	Acquisitions of the strategic seaports across the world (Hambantota and Gwadar Port) China's Militarization of The Paracel and Spratly Group of Islands	Chinese Sea Line of Communication (SLOC) "The String of Pearls" can encircle India and dominate the Indo-Pacific Region Improvement of China's Intelligence, Surveillance, and Reconnaissance (ISR) and other mission capabilities in the South China Sea and increase China's air force presence in the South China Sea

Source: Based on the author's research

competitor. One of those steps is the strategic influence and control of the Indo-Pacific Region. China uses its soft power and BRI to influence also international organizations in this region such as ASEAN. Some countries in the Indo-Pacific region are tempted by the Chinese BRI to have their economy move forward and develop paying the price of indebtedness or bankruptcy like in Sri Lanka's case where corruption and badly managed government governance caused problems for the whole country and were fostered or taken advantage of by China. Sri Lanka's Hambantota port was very important in the strategy of the BRI same as Djibouti not only from the business but also military perspective.

This was the strategic concept of building the Sea Line of Communication (SLOC) by China linking the most strategically positioned seaports across the globe. As a response, in 2014, India formed IO-5 (Indian Ocean Security Group) as the security provider in the Indo-Pacific Region together with Mauritius and the Ocean island states of Seychelles, but it could not compete with the Chinese SLOC named also "The String of Pearls" (Naval Forces, 2014). China invested 1 bn USD in Hambantota which can be considered an example of the Chinese debt trap experienced by Sri Lanka's government defaulted on foreign debt payments (Frayer, 2022). China managed to be involved in BRI 25 United Nations agencies including not only The World Bank Group, the International Monetary Fund (IMF), and The Food and Agriculture Organization (FAO). Besides these UN agencies, there are also Chinese banks involved as the main source of BRI's financing. The Chinese government through its involvement in international organizations in BRI managed to promote Chinese technology standards in international business (Paulson Institute, 2015).

The FDI in the Indo-Pacific Region helped China to access the latest technology projects and also the competitors' tender offers. It was possible mainly because as Chinese companies overtook foreign companies quite often the management board was not changed but it was influenced by the Chinese owners. Another good example of BRI's influence on international organizations is the China-IMF Capacity Development Center opened in 2018 to provide Indo-Pacific developing countries like Indonesia, Sri Lanka, Philippines, and Thailand with macroeconomic training as well as training on sovereign debt management, to help countries with assessing their sustainable external debt financing capacity.

Besides that China is the global producer of different goods which makes the companies in the world dependent on production in many sectors. The active involvement of China in the international trade blocks was also a good way for BRI implementation but BRI is not a trading bloc itself. It was even proved by *the Poisson model of bilateral trade* formulated by Santos Silva and Teneyro (2006) that China became the main beneficiary of BRI by linking the trade blocks such as NAFTA, UE, and ASEAN+1 along the BRI (OECD, 2018). That is very smart for China to influence the business globally through different sides and levels along the BRI. In this sense, the BRI becomes the platform for promoting international trade with the application of its technology for better control of the trading partners. An example can be the RCEP Agreement in the Indo-Pacific region where China is using the quick response codes (QRs) technology for trading goods among the

RCEP's members. It will boost the RCEP economy dominance where the main beneficiary is China (Lim, 2022).

Due to the overwhelming military presence of China in the Indo-Pacific Region, India developed its strategy based on the military alliances with Mauritius, Seychelles, and Maldives. India's main partners besides Mauritius, Seychelles, and Maldives in the Indo-Pacific Region are Singapore, Australia, Japan, and Vietnam. Besides that India signed a partnership agreement with ASEAN countries and the USA in 2015. An important reaction to China's dominant military and trade position in the Indo-Pacific Region was the last Quadrilateral Security Dialog (QUAD) Summit in 2022 with Australia, the USA, and Japan. All of these above multilateral activities from India's side are rather defensive even though India and China have not resolved the northern borderline conflict. China can also run its military activities using also current wars in Ukraine and Israel to partner with Russia's military. India is also looking for trade opportunities and can partner with Russia to buy cheaper oil. It is the effect of the perceptiveness of The Indo-Pacific Region by current PM Narendra Modi, who defined this region "from the shores of Africa to that of the Americas" (Ministry of External Affairs, 2018) and also India's membership in BRICS and Shanghai Cooperation Organisation (SCO) where Chinese and Russian influences are dominant. The involvement of India in the organizations where China and Russia are active and entering trade transactions with China and Russia could make it hard for India to be "self-reliant" (Atmanirbhar Bharat).

India's *Atma Nirbhar Bharat* concept of self-sufficiency is to be understood as the country's ability to take a central place in global supply chains. In turn, the mantra, defined as "Minimum government, maximum management", is to be the basis for the agenda of India's participation in creating a new economic order based on 3T (tourism, trade, and technology) (Reddy & Chenoy, 2021). India for years has been Russia's top arms customer, buying at least 1.6 bn USD worth in 2011, or 21% of all of Russia's defence exports (Grove, 2012). From the perspective of the Power theory described by Mirosław Sułek in 2017, the power of China can be classified as the aggressive military-economic and India as the moderate economic power (Sułek, 2017). India builds international relations with Indo-Pacific countries on mutual understanding with no imperialistic tactics. China uses its military and economic capabilities in investment initiatives such as BRI in the Indo-Pacific Region to force the countries in the region to follow Chinese aspirations to recognize Taiwan as an integral part of China.

The difference between India and China in their approach to initiatives undertaken in the development of the Indo-Pacific Region lies in the evolutionary strategy used by India. It starts with your own country but without the use of regime practices, as in China. India also aims to limit state interventionism, which is intended to reduce bureaucracy and stimulate trade and foreign direct investment. The latter retain their autonomy, unlike China, where every Western company investing in this country is subject not only to the government regime but also to surveillance and consent to the propaganda of the communist authorities. India tends to create a new balance of power based on several centres of power (polycentricity and multilateralism) on the principles of peace and harmony of cooperation within these several centres.

Despite their differences, India and China have also cooperated in bilateral, regional, and multi-nation forums in the past. As of now, India invests in different connectivity projects In Sri Lanka, Nepal, Bangladesh, and Maldives to counter China and retain its position in the Indo-Pacific region. India uses its SAGAR Mala (Security and Growth for All in the Region)/Naya Disha policy and Act East policy with the partner countries to establish a counterpart to China's presence in the Indo-Pacific region. Concerning Sri Lanka, it seemed that India did not react on time when China took over the investments in the main seaports of Sri Lanka (Hambantota). In 2021, India decided to invest in the western terminal of the Colombo Port. In that sense, China's actions forced India to take steps not to lose its relations and influence on Sri Lanka.

India is also cooperating with Bangladesh in regional and subregional platforms such as the South Asian Association for Regional Cooperation (SAARC), Bay of Bengal Initiative of Multisectoral Technical and Economic Cooperation (BIMSTEC), Bangladesh, China, India and Myanmar (BCIM), Indian Ocean Rim Association (IORA), ASEAN Regional Forum (ARF), and Bangladesh, Bhutan, India and Nepal (BBIN) grouping. With big turbulences in the past and an anti-India campaign in the Maldives "IndiaOut", from 2018, India managed to reestablish its presence in The Maldives and to sign a 1 bn USD Coast Guard Harbour in UthuruThilafalhu (UTF) project. India also opened its general consulate in the Maldives (Shivamurthy, 2022). Those examples show that China has a more effective strategy in the Indo-Pacific region than India which is not only the question of the policy and financial aid but also the abilities of India and China to compete globally.

4 India and China's Abilities for the Competition

India and China's abilities for the competition should be based on a result of a closer analysis of the seven geoeconomic factors which were selected to build the model of country empowerment (Dygas et al., 2021): (1) human capital index *HCI*, (2) physical capital per employee *PCE*, (3) openness to international trade *OpIT*, (4) openness to foreign direct investments *OpFDI* (FDI), (5) military power *Mpwr*, (6) foreign currency reserves *FCR*, and (7) sustainable development index *SDI*. The comparison of data for China and India is presented below in Table 2.

Table 2 China and India's geoeconomic factors comparison (2019–2023)

	HCI	PCE	OpIT	OpFDI	Mpwr	FCR	SDI
China	0.65	2.69	38.14%	2.2	3rd	3.17 Tr USD	72.01
India	0.49	2.19	49.37%	8.4	4th	623 bn USD	63.45

Source data 2019 2023: The World Bank (2020), PwC (2020), FRED (2019), GFP (2023), Ministry of Commerce and Industry (2023), SDIndex (2023), S&P Global (2023), Statista (2022), Trading Economies (2023), The Global Economy (2022), White&Case (2023)

Explanation of data presented in Table 2

HCI result for China is higher than the average in East Asia and the Pacific region (59%) and for India is lower (World Bank, 2020). China in 2019 had comparable PCE (FRED, 2019). India was more open in 2022 to international trade than China because China protects its market and is quite strict on the asymmetric law to the foreign partners, and the average result data from the World Bank for India in the period 1960–2022 was 24.39% and for China 26.81% (The Global Economy, 2022). The openness for FDI for China on a scale of 0–10 in 2022 was 2.2, which was less than the open economy average of 6.6. India was one of the top destinations of FDI in the Indo-Pacific Region and was ranked as the world's seventh FDI destination (Statista, 2022; White&Case, 2023). India tried to defend itself from China's investment expansion and in 2021–2023 rejected 58 FDI projects from China (Adhikari, 2023). According to Global Fire Index in 2022, China was the third strongest military country in the world, while India had the fourth position (GFP, 2023). China is also strengthening its military position in the Indo-Pacific region by building military bases in the South China Sea using BRI. In 2020, they spent USD252 billion on armaments, which is more than India, Japan, and Germany combined (Statista, 2021). The foreign currency reserves of China are much higher than India's at the end of 2023 (Tradingeconomics, 2023). India was ranked 112 regarding SDI in 2023 while China 65 for 195 UN countries (SDIndex, 2023). When implementing the Sustainable Development Goals, India is guided by the *One World* principle and international cooperation in implementing these goals (UN, 2017). The Indian government agency NITI Aayog in cooperation with the United Nations in India has developed its own SDG India Index. Its values have been calculated since 2018 and take into account the specificity of local government's activities in the implementation of sustainable development goals in individual 28 states and 8 union territories of India (SDG India, 2021). This indicator makes it possible to analyse the progress in the implementation of the SDGs, specified in the UN 2030 Agenda, in the social, economic, and environmental dimensions. The administrative division of India and the use of 115 national indicators are taken into account. Although this indicator is specific only to India and is difficult to compare to other countries, based on the data available on the (SDG India, 2021) website, it can be read that in 2020, 17 states recorded significant progress in the implementation of the Sustainable Development Goals, while in 2018 this progress was recorded only in three Indian states (Kerala, Himachal Pradesh, and Tamil Nadu).

Looking at the results in Table 2, there is an impression that China has a dominant position not only in the Indo-Pacific Region but in the global economy. It is the result of the different strategies of competition between India and China and also investment activities done by the developed countries in China with the expectations of high returns. A significant difference between India and China in their international activities is the lack of use of asymmetric trade contracts. China does not avoid them, for example, offering to increase the import of agricultural products from a given country in exchange for the purchase of Chinese vaccines produced by Sinopharm, which have not been approved by the European Medicines Commission (PAP, 2021).

5 Conclusion

China has a very strong position in this region and will obstruct India by all means. It should be emphasized that India did not join the Indo-Pacific CERP agreement in 2020 precisely because of its development strategy. India is also involved in organizations where China and Russia play important roles such as BRICS and SCO. Currently, China has the largest naval and military fleet in the world, strongly expanding the Indo-Pacific military region. Moreover, an important element of China's global strategy, declared by its leader Xi Jinping, is being the "centre of the world". It is understood as the so-called Great Renaissance, based on strong economic and military development, analogous to the glory days of the former Empire of China. To this end, China has launched the New Long March programme, which is intended to make China a country with strong internal development, based on a rich and innovative middle class, by 2049. This is the 100th anniversary of the People's Republic of China and also the 100th anniversary of the NATO establishment. This has reference to Modelski's hegemonic cycle theory which claimed that after 100 years there is a change in the world economy leadership. Therefore, China launched a BRI initiative: sea and land, allocating USD1 trillion for this purpose. It was much more than the American Marshall Plan to rebuild Europe in 1947 (Brands and Sullivan, 2020). China is also strengthening its military position in the Indo-Pacific region by building military bases in the South China Sea using BRI. In 2020, they spent USD252 billion on armaments, which is more than India, Japan, and Germany combined (Statista, 2021).

Despite the very strong economic position of China, which competes with the USA for global leadership, India is an alternative for the world economy for further development. Failure to take advantage of this opportunity that India currently offers may lead to a situation in which China will play a decisive role in the world economy.

In the end, it is worth noting that the official strategy of China could be misleading and very different to the hidden one, that is why the real economic and military strategy of China in the Indo-Pacific Region is hidden and analysing the same facts by the scientists, authors, governments' officials, and rivals can have different conclusions.

References

Adhikari, A. (2023). *India's FDI clampdown: Only 3 Chinese FDI applications made the cut in FY23*. Accessed January 07, 2024, from https://www.businesstoday.in/latest/in-focus/story/indias-fdi-clampdown-only-3-chinese-fdi-applications-made-the-cut-in-fy23-390946-2023-07-24

Ambrożek, M. (2018). Zmiana pozycji geopolitycznej Chin z perspektywy teorii cykli hegemonicznych oraz teorii tranzycji potęgi. *Przegląd Geopolityczny, 26*, 95–114.

Anokhin, A., & Lachininskii, S. (2015). Evolution of the ideas and contents of geoeconomic studies. *Regional Research of Russia, 5*(1), 82–87. https://doi.org/10.1134/S2079970515010037

Brands, H., & Sullivan, J. (2020). *China has two paths to global domination*. Accessed January 07, 2024, from https://foreignpolicy.com/2020/05/22/china-superpower-two-paths-global-domination-cold-war

Cleary, T. (2005). *The art of war, Sun Tzu* (pp. 1–170). Shambhala Publications.

Cowen, D., & Smith, N. (2009). After geopolitics? From the geopolitical social to geoeconomics. *Radical Journal of Geography, Antipode, 41*(1), 22–48. https://doi.org/10.1111/j.1467-8330.2008.00654.x

Davidsen, P. (2021). *The emancipation of political science: Contextualizing the state theory of Rudolf Kjellén, 1899–1922* (pp. 259–365). University of Helsinki.

Deniozos, N., Vlados, C., & Chatzinikolaou, D. (2019). Energy economy in the era of 'new globalization': The case of the Balkans and Greece. *International Journal of Economics and Management Studies, 6*(9), 10–19.

Dygas, R., Milewicz, W., & Napiórkowski, T. (Eds.). (2021). Wpływ wybranych krajów Azji oraz Republiki Federalnej Niemiec na budowanie nowego potencjału gospodarczego w kontekście realizacji celów zrównoważonego rozwoju Agendy 2030 ONZ, Oficyna Wydawnicza SGH. *Szkoła Główna Handlowa w Warszawie, 2021*, 1–94.

Dygas, R. (2023). The Belt and Road Initiative's impact on Poland in the period 2015-2022. International business implications. In *23rd International Joint Conference Central and Eastern Europe in the Changing Business Environment: Proceedings* (pp. 78–92). Vydavateľstvo EKONÓM. https://doi.org/10.18267/pr.2023.kre.2490.6

Frayer, L. (2022, August 19). *Why a Chinese ship's arrival in Sri Lanka has caused alarm in India and the West*. Accessed January 07, 2024, from https://www.npr.org/2022/08/19/1118113095/sri-lanka-china-ship-hambantota-port

Gasimli, V. (2015). *Geo-economics* (p. 11). Center for Strategic Studies under the President of the Republic of Azerbaijan. https://web.archive.org/web/20181024074306/http://sam.az/uploads/PDF/Geo-Economic.pdf

Gilpin, R. (1981). *War and change in world politics* (pp. 186–210). Cambridge University Press. https://doi.org/10.1017/CBO9780511664267

Grove, T. (2012, September 17). Defects delay Russian aircraft carrier delivery to India. *Reuters*. Accessed January 06, 2024, from https://www.reuters.com/article/russia-india-aircraftcarrier-idUSL5E8KHAE820120917/

Haliżak, E. (Ed.). (2012). *Geoekonomia* (pp. 1–780). Wydawnictwo Naukowe Scholar.

Karaś, D. (2020). Geopolityczne uwarunkowania rywalizacji o zasoby Arktyki. *Nierówności społeczne a wzrost gospodarczy, 64*(4), 278–290. https://doi.org/10.15584/nsawg.2020.4.19

Kugler, J., & Organski, A. F. K. (2011). Chapter 7. The power transition: A retrospective and prospective evaluation. In M. I. Midlarski (Ed.), *Handbook of war studies* (pp. 171–194). Routledge.

Lim, J. (2022, January 04). *APAC will dominate the digital economy with RCEP*. Techwire Asia. Accessed January 07, 2024, from https://techwireasia.com/2022/01/apac-will-dominate-the-digital-economy-with-rcep/

Livingstone, S. (2020). *The Chinese Communist party targets the private sector* (pp. 1–10). Center for Strategic&International Studies. https://www.csis.org/analysis/chinese-communist-party-targets-private-sector

Lorot, P. (2000). La géoéconomie, nouvelle grammaire des rivalités internationals. In S. Sur & A. Dulphy (Eds.), *Annuaire français de relations internationales 2000* (pp. 110–122). Bruylant.

Luttwak, E. N. (1999). *Theory and practice of geo-economics from Turbo-Capitalism: Winners and losers in the global economy* (pp. 1–290). HarperCollins.

MEMRI. (2024). *China's militarization of the South China Sea*. Special Dispatch No. 11243. Accessed April 11, 2024, from https://www.memri.org/reports/chinas-militarization-south-china-sea

Ministry of External Affairs. (2018, June 1). *Government of India, Prime Minister's Keynote Address at Shangri La Dialogue*. https://www.mea.gov.in/

Modelski, G. (1987). *Long cycles in world politics* (pp. 1–244). Macmillan. https://doi.org/10.1007/978-1-349-09151-5

Naval Forces. (2014). *China's maritime strategy for South Asia*, issue 04-2014. Accessed June 04, 2024, from https://www.spsnavalforces.com/story/?id=332

OECD. (2018). The belt and road initiative in the global trade, investment and finance landscape. In *OECD Business and Finance Outlook 2018*, OECD. Accessed January 07, 2024, from https://doi.org/https://doi.org/10.1787/bus_fin_out-2018-6-en

Paulson Institute. (2015, April). *Power play: China's ultra-high voltage technology and global standards*. Paulson Papers on Standards. Accessed January 07, 2024, from www.paulsoninstitute.org/wpcontent/uploads/2015/04/PPS_UHV_English.pdf

PAP, Polska Agencja Prasowa. (2021). *Prezydent Chin: jesteśmy gotowi dostarczyć Polsce szczepionki na Covid-19*. Accessed January 07, 2024, from https://forsal.pl/swiat/chiny/artykuly/8109707,chiny-dostarcza-polsce-szczepionki-na-covid-19-xi.html

Reddy, S., & Chenoy, D. (2021). Foreign Secretary's address on "New World Order Post COVID-19" to the Federation of Indian Chambers of Commerce & Industry (FICCI) (May 20, 2020). Accessed January 07, 2024, from https://www.mea.gov.in/

Saha, R. (2022). A case for Indo-Russia cooperation in the Indo-Pacific. *Journal of Indo-Pacific Affairs, July-August*, 111–124.

Shivamurthy, A. G. (Ed.). (2022, August). *India-China competition: Perspectives from the neighbourhood*. Observer Research Foundation, Special Report 197. Accessed April 11, 2024, from https://www.orfonline.org/research/india-china-competition#_edn2

Silva, S., & Tenreyro, S. (2006). The log of gravity. *The Review of Economics and Statistics 2006, 88*(4), 641–658. https://doi.org/10.1162/rest.88.4.641

Sułek, M. (2017). *O potęgonomii i potęgometrii*, Akademia Geopolityki. Accessed January 06, 2024, from https://geopolityka.net/o-potegonomii-i-potegometrii/

UN. (2017). *India. Voluntary National Review Report on the implementation of Sustainable Goals* (pp. 2–3). https://sustainabledevelopment.un.org/content/documents/15836India.pdf

Zhao, Q. (2018). The influence of Confucianism on Chinese politics and foreign policy. *Asian Education and Development Studies, 7*(4), 321–328. https://doi.org/10.1108/AEDS-03-2018-0057

Data References

FRED, Federal Reserve Bank of St. Louis. (2019). Accessed January 06, 2024, from https://fred.stlouisfed.org/series/

GFP. (2023). *Asian-Pacific military strength*. Accessed January 06, 2024, from https://www.globalfirepower.com/countrieslisting-asia-pacific.php

Ministry of Commerce and Industry. (2023). *India's overall export in November 2023*. Accessed January 06, 2024, from https://commerce.gov.in/press-releases/indias-overall-exports-in-november-2023-is-estimated-at-usd-62-58-billion-an-increase-of-1-23-percent-over-usd-61-82-billion-in-november-2022/

PwC. (2020). Regional Comprehensive Economic Partnership (RCEP) – what it means for international trade. *Customs and Trade News*. Accessed January 06, 2024, from https://customs.pwc.com/en/recent-developments/assets/trade-alert/20201124.pdf

SDG India. (2021). *SDG India, Index and DashBoard 2020-2021*. Accessed January 07, 2024, from https://sdgindiaindex.niti.gov.in/

SDIndex. (2023). Accessed Janury 06, 2023, from https://dashboards.sdgindex.org/rankings

S&P Global. (2023, August). *Look forward. India's moment* (Vol. 3). Accessed January 06, 2024, from https://www.spglobal.com/_division_assets/images/look-forward/volume-3-2023/look-forward-volume-3_2023.pdf, pp.1-67

Statista. (2022). Accessed January 06, 2024, from www.statista.com/statistics

Statista. (2021). *Countries with the highest military spending worldwide in 2020*. Accessed January 07, 2024, from https://www.statista.com/statistics/262742/countries-with-the-highest-military-spending/

The Global Economy. (2022). Accessed January 06, 2024, from https://www.theglobaleconomy.com/India/trade_openness/, https://www.theglobaleconomy.com/China/trade_openness/

Tradingeconomies. (2023). Accessed January 06, 2024, from https://tradingeconomics.com/india/foreign-exchange-reserves, https://tradingeconomics.com/china/foreign-exchange-reserves

White&Case. (2023). *Foreign direct investment reviews 2023*: *India*. Accessed January 06, 2024, from https://www.whitecase.com/insight-our-thinking/foreign-direct-investment-reviews-2023-india

World Bank. (2020). *Human Capital country brief: China*. Accessed January 06, 2024, from https://www.worldbank.org/en/publication/human-capital#Index

Three Innovative Methods for Evaluating Corporate Cash Flows: The Extended Net Present Value Criterion, the Smooth Pasting Condition, and the Markowitz Model

Contains an Application on a Sample of ICT Companies in Sardinia, Studied within the e.INS (PNRR) Project, Spoke 4

Marco Desogus and Elisa Casu

Abstract This chapter has the aim of providing a privileged perspective on cash-flow dynamics in the context of business analysis—whether evaluative or diagnostic—in general and comparatively across each business segment. In particular, the discussions presented focus on cash-flow volatility by adopting procedures that appear relevant and promising for the above purposes, whilst they are also attempting to adapt—with the auspice of contributing to scientific and technical process innovations on the topic—some models, typically applied to securities finance, more specifically to flows linked to business and the corporate finance. After an introduction to the issues addressed, three thematic sections propose an estimation method using the Extended Net Present Value (XNPV), a risk-weighting approach through the value matching criterion, and the smooth pasting condition. Finally, processes borrowed from fractal finance and an extension of the Markowitz model are applied.

Marco Desogus contribution has been developed within the framework of the project e.INS—Ecosystem of Innovation for Next Generation Sardinia (cod. ECS 00000038) funded by the Italian Ministry for Research and Education (MUR) under the National Recovery and Resilience Plan (NRRP) – MISSION 4 COMPONENT 2, "From research to business" INVESTMENT 1.5, "Creation and strengthening of Ecosystems of innovation" and construction of "Territorial R&D Leaders".

M. Desogus (✉)
Department of Law, University of Sassari, Sassari, Italy
e-mail: mdesogus@uniss.it; https://www.uniss.it/en

E. Casu
Independent Economist, Cagliari, Italy
e-mail: elisacasu84@gmail.com

E. Lau et al. (eds.), *Economics and Finance Readings*,
https://doi.org/10.1007/978-981-96-6998-1_11

Keywords Cash-flow volatility · Risk management · Corporate assessments · Extended NPV · Value matching criterion · Smooth pasting condition · Fractal analysis · Markowitz model

JEL Codes C13 · G32 · M41

1 Introduction

In corporate risk management—especially in the area of liquidity risk—it has become essential to carefully examine fluctuations in cash flows. Understanding the causes of such fluctuations and anticipating future volatility trends have become fundamental so that appropriate strategies that will ensure a company's business continuity can be selected.

This activity has taken on great importance since high volatility in cash flows can have negative impacts on financial statements by jeopardising the proper turnover of working capital, the alternation of current liability exposures, and even by slowing down the course of production—due to the discontinuity of the treasury cycle—and by generating a deteriorating loop in company performance. Thus, avoiding such value impairment has become indispensable, whilst efforts to assess and mitigate such phenomena will contribute significantly to preserving overall company value for the benefit of shareholders (Shimko, 2019).

In accordance with the assertion that large cash-flow volatility implies a need for increased focus on corporate (or business unit) performance, since there is a risk of weakening the equilibrium of finance and capital and of generating notional costs for provisions or losses. Furthermore, it has been documented that such variability has often been associated with a reduced propensity to invest (Minton & Schrand, 1999) as well as with higher costs for access to external capital. Greater cash-flow volatility clearly implies a greater likelihood that a business will encounter periods of internal liquidity shortages. However, in order to cope with this phenomenon, though there is not necessarily a change in business plans, there is often recourse to a policy of underinvestment—also due to the perceived higher cost of bank-issued leverage (Myers & Majluf, 1984)—which would not be conducive to any cash-flow realignment or stabilisation, but would instead be procyclical to further increases in volatility, forming a trap towards the onset of exacerbating liquidity crises. Even with regard to the attraction of external bond debt covenants, it has been observed that high cash-flow volatility is correlated with greater information asymmetry, the harbinger of poorer bond ratings and, consequently, higher costs to access funding (Scordis et al., 2008).

Overall, this evidence has provided a benchmark for assessing the value of assets for the purposes of risk management. Nevertheless, interventions to reduce cash-flow volatility appear to be most effective for companies in industries where that same volatility is not, strictly speaking, due to factors that are relatively unrelated to interest rates, currency exchange rates, or commodity prices, such as ICT companies or high-tech and innovative companies: the cross-sectional variability of these costs, as opposed to the potential repercussions of high cash-flow volatility, leads to interesting implications for management decisions, which will be discussed in more detail in Sects. 2 and 3 below. One crucial aspect is however the procyclical association between the historical volatility of a company's cash flows and the current costs of raising external capital (bank or private investors), which, in a broader sense, defines the (discounted) value of the company—or of the individual business unit—and affects performance maximisation or recovery strategies.

2 The Valuation of Business Units Through the Singular Volatility of Cash Flows

In order to understand corporate performance—or possibly the grounds for a crisis—whether from the viewpoint of the company's relationship with the market or from an intrinsic perspective, it is necessary to go beyond purely economic and financial analysis at an aggregate level. Although strategic decisions regarding management, planning, control, and development are not formed at a general level, they do require detailed investigation through diagnostic procedures that explore partial segmentations within the comprehensive production of the company.

This approach implies that an articulated investigation be undertaken across different dimensions of the company's economic activities, considering the most basic levels such as individual product lines and market segments. The analysis of the actualised performance at these levels provides insights into the root causes of the business' performance, from unitary to global, which represents the dashboard for crucial decisions on corporate competitiveness (Desogus & Casu, 2019).

The investigative path on potential product-market combinations starts from these basic levels. Although strategic choices regarding product range and customer positioning require systemic weighting, during critical periods it may often become appropriate to implement an analytical partition that considers how variations of individual business units are influenced with respect to the others.

In product-market analysis, it is crucial to identify the combinations, to allocate the economic-financial components proper to each and then to analyse the results. Accurate classification of combinations is decisive because an imprecise definition will limit the emergence of the strategically most important relationships.

There are multiple criteria for identifying products and markets, which should be consistent with the analytical logic of the result in terms of cash flow and which would be useful for planning and control of subsequent behaviour. The preliminary phase requires a moment to describe the principles of aggregation, which focuses on those considered most significant for the sustainability of the management plan.

Once the product-market combinations have been defined, the cash-flow values will need to be recalculated. Although complex, this preliminary process is significant since it can highlight new relationships and optimise the overall outlook.

We will now explore how the cash-flow volatility valuation method provides essential support when assessing the performance of each business sector. This method falls into the broader category of "flow models", which are designed to discount flows, whether they are financial or income in nature. From a theoretical and methodological point of view, this approach can be reflected in a general formula, expressed as:

$$Y = \sum_{i=0}^{n} y_i \bullet v_i \tag{1}$$

where:

- Y: represents the value of the product-market segment under consideration, i.e. the value of the broad business sector comprising several related and/or interconnected segments, making any further analytical separation insignificant.
- y_i: refers to the cash flow.
- v_i is the discount factor associated with each flow.

Through this method, the business' financial value is configured as the average of all flows expected $\mathbb{E}\left[\widehat{Y}\right]$ in the next N years, discounted at the time of valuation at the rate $\mathbb{R}$: $Y = \mathbb{E}\left[\widehat{Y}\right] a_{\overline{n}|\mathbb{R}}$

The next propositional emanation is to associate the calculation of the segment's flow volatility with (1), through the VaR—Value at Risk:

$$\text{Var}(y) = \frac{1}{N}\sum_{i=1}^{N}(y_i - m)^2 \tag{2}$$

With m being the mean.

Principally, this estimation model, combined with the volatility assessments in (2) is applied to:

- Composition debt and pre-insolvency valuations
- Situations wherein reliable forecasts of future flows can be constructed
- Companies in which the assets have little significance
- Contributions/disposals of business units
- Acquisitions and joint ventures

To better define the corporate complexity, matrices segmented by product/market are processed (Damodaran, 2015), which allow easy identification of the vector of cash flows $\overline{y}_i$—whether individual or partially aggregated—to then move forward with equivalent rate analyses $\tilde{\mathbb{r}}$, suitable for the comparison of the performance of the status quo with possible outcomes of (temporary) divestment strategies, i.e. with a post corporate recovery scenario (Yun, 2011). So, let us look at the Net Present Value (NPV):

$$\text{NPV} = \sum_{i=0}^{n} \overline{y}_i \bullet \left(1+\tilde{\text{r}}\right)^{-i} \tag{3}$$

With there being multiple configurations manifesting a positive NPV, the need to choose the allocation that guarantees higher values becomes evident. At this point, it would be pertinent to introduce the concept of Strategic Business Areas (SBAs), which represent individual partitions of product/market segments. These segments can also be identified or selected on the basis of their superior performance, which often show a certain degree of independence from the company as a whole, but among which specific and biunivocal relationships may nevertheless exist. In this context, the adoption of a specific comparative and competitive evaluation procedure would become especially significant.

As part of an efficiency or reorganisation strategy, the organisational model would be redefined with a specific focus on the divisional system, divesting the SBAs that are not decisive in the generation of stable cash flows, in order to create a more functional management system for the company's development. Therefore, the main objective of this type of action would then be oriented towards the enhancement of resources and assets for the recovery of corporate liquidity conditions.

This objective would be achieved through various management activities, which would include increasing cash flows (normalised by provisions and deductions from derivative products), containing and reducing cash-flow volatility, improving the discount rate through the general reduction of risks, reducing net working capital and making total invested capital more efficient.

The "XNPV—Extended Net Present Value" method has been identified as the most effective criterion for assessing the quality of the reorganisation or restructuring strategy. This method is expressed in the formula:

$$VR = \Sigma\left(y_{SBA} \bullet \text{Var}\left(y_{SBA}\right) + Po + F_j\left(y\right) + I\right) \tag{4}$$

where:

- VR: represents the value of the efficient or rehabilitated company.
- y_{SBA} is the sum of the value of the company's Strategic Business Areas, derived for each one from the Present Value of its historical cash flows.
- *Po* is the value of the strategic portfolio (higher or lower value, if negative, of the synergies among the *SBA*).
- $F_j(y)$ is the value of the options exercisable in the efficiency strategy.
- I is the value of the ancillary investments.

Application of this methodology requires in-depth knowledge of the company and the general business, as well as of each product/market segment, which is both qualitative and quantitative or *SBA*. It is then necessary to determine the flows, identify the most appropriate time horizon, and define the expressed and latent risks through appropriate equivalent rates (Quagli & Danovi, 2010).

Based on the enlarged current value and taking into account the value of the company in the cases of liquidation (*VL*) or full disposal (*VC*), reorganisation will be undertaken if it can be shown that $VR > VC \wedge VR > VL$.

3 Disposal of the Business Unit in Industrial Efficiency Plans or Reorganisation Procedures: Analysis and Estimates with Respect to Cash Flow

Following the approach of Scandizzo and Ventura (2010), now being proposed is a model to assess the appropriateness of leasing out a certain business unit on the basis of developing net cash flows and their volatility. Linking back to the previous section, this rationale can be applied during the different phases of business industrial planning steps as well as during composition or pre-insolvency proceedings. Specifically, though this model lends itself to levels of production with high technological content and specialised knowledge, such as innovative start-ups and ICT companies, it can easily be extended to companies belonging to any product sector.

The obvious premise is that the resource flows derived from a business unit's management, before being redeployed there, and being appropriately placed in movable asset investments or in interest-bearing deposits, are themselves capable of guaranteeing a certain additional active financial flow φ—which, simplifying, can be assumed to be constant—with an NPV at a risk-free rate r equal to φ/r.

Because of the characteristics of the reported companies to which the following procedure can be primarily aimed, we should consider that the segment in question will generate—over time—a net cash flow described by:

$$dy_t = \mu y_t dt + \sigma y_t dW_t \tag{5}$$

Equation (5) describes the process of evolution of the representative cash-flow variable *y*, which follows geometric Brownian motion, with drift μ and variance σ; dW_t is a Gaussian causal variable with mean $\mathrm{M}(dW) = 0$ and variance $\mathrm{Var}(dW) = dt$.

Company management—or the evaluator in charge of any future reorganisation due to partial aggregates—can make one of two (opposing) choices:

a) Dispose of the segment through a lease contract (entry strategy): option $F_0(y)$
b) Reintegrate the business unit back into the company (exit strategy): option $F_1(y)$

Assuming a cash-flow volatility risk in line with the average volatility of assets traded in the markets, we can represent the dynamics of the alternatives—by setting $j = 0, 1$—indicated above through the ODE:

$$(\mathrm{r} - \gamma) y F_j'(y) + \frac{\sigma^2}{2} y^2 F_j''(y) - \mathrm{r} F_j(y) = 0 \tag{6}$$

The convenience yield is described by $\gamma = \hat{\gamma} - \mu > 0$, with $\hat{\gamma}$ being the appropriate discount rate for the characteristics of the financial asset to be assessed as provided for by the Capital Asset Pricing Model.

The solutions of the differential equation are:

$$\begin{cases} F_0(y) = \mathrm{A}_1 y^{\psi_1} + \mathrm{A}_2 y^{\psi_2} \\ F_1(y) = \mathrm{B}_1 y^{\psi_1} + \mathrm{B}_2 y^{\psi_2} \end{cases}$$

where $\psi_{1/2} = \frac{1}{2} - \frac{(\mathbb{r} - \gamma)}{\sigma^2} \pm \sqrt{\left[\left(\frac{(\mathbb{r} - \gamma)}{\sigma^2}\right) - \frac{1}{2}\right]^2 + \frac{2\mathbb{r}}{\sigma^2}}$ and from which $\psi_1 > 1$ and $\psi_2 < 0$.

Now we will list the indifference conditions of the entry strategy (7) in $t_0 = 0$—indicating the relative cash flow with y_a—and the exit strategy (8) in $t_i \in (0; t_n)$—cash flow: y_b Respectively—to then proceed to examine their mathematical content and analytical significance:

$$\frac{\varphi}{\mathbb{r}} + F_0(y_a) = \frac{y_a}{\gamma} - \int_0^{t_n} y_a e^{-\gamma s} ds + F_1(y_a) + \mathfrak{F}_{\min} \tag{7}$$

and

$$y_b \int_{t_i}^{\infty} e^{-\gamma(s - t_i)} ds - P = y_b \int_{t_n}^{\infty} e^{-\gamma(s - t_i)} ds + F_1(y_b) \tag{8}$$

In (7), on the left, we can see the business yield, for the benefit of the current ownership prior to disposal, in terms of the discounted remuneration of the cash flows from investments and options $F_0(y_a)$. After the equals sign, we have the NPV of the cash flows coming in from the disposal discounted at the convenience yield rate, minus the discounting of the cash flows for the duration t_n of the business unit lease, plus the exit option $F_1(y_b)$ and still, plus the value $\mathfrak{F}_{\min}$, which indicates the minimum entry fee to activate the lease disposal of the business unit.

Because of the law of the balance between supply and demand, for the purpose of concluding contractual agreements, $\mathfrak{F}_{\min} \le \mathbb{F}_{\text{MAX}}$, where this latter element indicates the maximum price the transferee is willing to pay and which is in turn prescribed by the net discounted cash flows y_c expected over the lease term of the business unit, minus the maximum entry fee that one is willing to incur, the costs of further investments and normalisation of the performance of the business unit K, and an implicit function $H(y)$ (formulated on the basis of a call option) have the intention of mitigating the loss—or rather, arbitrage—on the revocation exercisable by the assignor:

$$\int_0^{t_n} y_c e^{-\gamma s} ds - \mathbb{F}_{\text{MAX}} - K - H(y_c) = 0 \tag{9}$$

Evidently, the underlying economic cost effectiveness of both strategies (entry into and exit from the disposal) increases as the cash flows generated y increase: hence, $F_0(y)$ and $F_1(y)$ must be increasing functions of y, and this is valid—taking up the solutions of (6)—when A_2 and B_2 are both equal to zero, since their exponent ψ_2 is less than zero.

The relationship expressed by (7) is therefore of the value-matching criterion: there will exist a level of y beyond which it will be advantageous to exercise the exit and reintegrate the business unit back under ownership management. Regardless, for now, we are conducting this assessment assuming low to medium cash-flow volatility. In the presence of high volatility, the cost (real or notional) of the increased risk must also be considered, which will be discussed in the following comments on Eq. (8). It would first be necessary to determine A_1 and B_1, for the optimisation of which we proceed by calculating the derivative of value matching compared to y (Smooth Pasting):

$$A_1\psi_1 y_a^{\psi_1-1} = \frac{e^{-\gamma t_n}}{\gamma} + B_1\psi_1 y_a^{\psi_1-1} \tag{10}$$

Moving on to analyse the relationship presented by Eq. (8), note a comparison between the benefits of exercising the exit option in t_i in terms of discounting the higher flows, compared to waiting for the natural maturity of the contract. On the left of the equal sign note the element P, which represents the penalty to be borne by the owner in the event of early termination of the contract, evidently bearing a negative algebraic sign.

As mentioned above, in the presence of risks of high cash-flow volatility, consideration should be given to an additional negative value, *LRC*, brought about by the costs of hedging the related liquidity risks, for example, those linked to the activation of specific credit lines, to the immediate disinvestment of securities or to the activation of insurance coverage. The smooth pasting exit condition will be (Shackleton & Sødal, 2005):

$$B_1\psi_1 y_b^{\psi_1-1} = \frac{\left(1-e^{-\gamma(t_n-t_i)}\right)}{\gamma} \tag{11}$$

On the basis of the development offered, the systematisation of the two Eqs. (7) and (8) shows that the two subsystems are independent of each other—and this is particularly significant for the indication of the possible exercise of revocation—and that the final outcomes and the related decision-making consequences are determined solely by ψ_1 during the course of the volatility of the cash flows contained therein, and in any case, by the levels of the same volatility of the flows being generated.

By the same token, from the transferee's standpoint—going back to (9)—the function $H(y)$ cannot but also be increasing with the increase in the cash flow y, since the exercise of the transferor's exit strategy increases in cost effectiveness—and therefore in probability—as seen previously, with the increase in the generation of flows. The parameter C_2 is equal to zero at the relative solutions for the same reasons for which we found $A_2 = 0$ and $B_2 = 0$, while $\mathbb{F}_{MAX}$ is determined by the same formula (9) combined with the relative smooth pasting derivative with respect to y:

$$C_1 y_c^{\psi} = \frac{y}{\gamma\psi}\left(1 - e^{-\gamma t_n}\right) \tag{12}$$

Equation (12) shows the transferee's value matching, with the maximum available entry fee being equal to:

$$\mathbb{F}_{MAX} \leq \frac{y}{\gamma}\left(1 - e^{-\gamma t_n}\right)\frac{\psi - 1}{\psi} - K \tag{13}$$

Combining (7) and (10) and solving with respect to the minimum entry fee acceptable to the assignor to trigger the disposal $\mathfrak{F}_{\min}$:

$$\mathfrak{F}_{\min} \geq \frac{\varphi}{\mathrm{r}} - \frac{y}{\gamma} e^{-\gamma t_n} \frac{\psi - 1}{\psi} \tag{14}$$

By comparing the right-hand sides of formulae (13) and (14), we can find the entry fee's balance value, for which both parties will have an inducement to enter into the business unit disposal transaction, given a risk level of cash-flow volatility that is aligned with the average volatility that can be found in commonly traded assets:

$$\frac{y}{\gamma} = \left(\frac{\varphi}{\mathrm{r}} + K\right)\frac{\psi - 1}{\psi} \tag{15}$$

Nonetheless, as cash-flow volatility increases, the entry fee that the transferee is willing to pay will also tend to decrease:

$$\frac{d\mathbb{F}_{MAX}}{d\sigma y} = \frac{\partial\mathbb{F}_{MAX}}{\partial\frac{\psi - 1}{\psi}} \frac{\partial\frac{\psi - 1}{\psi}}{\partial\psi} \frac{\partial\psi}{\partial\sigma y} < 0$$

being:

$$\lim_{\sigma y \to +\infty} \psi = 1$$

and

$$\lim_{\sigma y \to 0} \psi = \infty$$

we will have, respectively:

$$\lim_{\sigma y \to +\infty} \mathbb{F}_{\text{MAX}} = 0,$$

$$\lim_{\sigma y \to 0} \mathbb{F}_{\text{MAX}} = \frac{y}{\gamma}\left(1 - e^{-\gamma t_n}\right) - K$$

And once again:

$$\frac{d\mathfrak{F}_{\min}}{d\sigma y} = 0$$

Combining (8) with (11), with just a few further steps, we can show the exit strategy implementation threshold:

$$\frac{y}{\gamma} \geq \frac{\psi}{\psi - 1}\left(\frac{P}{1 - e^{-\gamma(t_n - t_i)}}\right) \tag{16}$$

Wanting to proceed to define the value of the temporary disposal (VC_τ) net of the investment costs K and of the entry fee $\mathfrak{F}_{\min} = \mathbb{F}_{\text{MAX}}$, going back to the above and especially (9) and (13), we can write

$$VC_\tau = \int_{t_i}^{t_n} ye^{-\gamma s} ds - C_1 y^{\psi_1} + A_1 y^{\psi_1}$$

$$= \frac{y}{\gamma}\left(e^{-\gamma t_i} - e^{-\gamma t_n}\right) - C_1 y^{\psi_1} + A_1 y^{\psi_1} \tag{17}$$

Applying $\vartheta = (-C_1 + A_1)$, then the equation will be of the type

$$VC_\tau = \vartheta_0 y + \vartheta y^{\psi_1} + \upsilon \tag{18}$$

Wherein υ is the error, and where—since the historical cash-flow values are known and the past volatility levels can be deduced—the coefficients ϑ_0 and ϑ can be estimated using the maximum likelihood method, through a procedure such as $\mathscr{L}\left(\vec{\vartheta}, y\right) = \prod f\left(\vartheta, y_i\right)$, with $y_i \sim N(\bullet)\ \forall\ i$, and therefore setting $\frac{d \log \mathscr{L}\left(\vartheta, y_0\right)}{d\vartheta} = 0$ to arrive at the maximisation of the probability $\hat{\vartheta} = \arg\max_{\vartheta \in \Theta} \mathscr{L}\left(\vartheta | y_i\right)$. Finally, the coefficients ϑ can be confirmed through the least squares method, which—given Eq. (18)—will also provide the easiest estimation of the parameter ψ.

Applying the Black–Scholes formula (2), and then rewriting (17):

$$VC_{\tau}\left(y,t_i\right)=y_{t_i}N\left(d_1\right)-\vartheta ye^{-r\left(t_n-t_i\right)}N\left(d_2\right) \tag{19}$$

Where $N(\bullet)$ is the distribution function of a normal random variable.
From which, according to the development:

$$d_1=\frac{\log\frac{y_{t_i}}{\vartheta y}+\left(r+\frac{1}{2}\sigma^2\right)}{\sigma\sqrt{t_n-t_i}}$$

and

$$d_2=d_1-\sigma\sqrt{t_n-t_i}$$

4 Fractal Finance Processes for Corporate Cash-Flow Analysis, with the Application of an Extension of the Markowitz Model

Let us now try to propose a product of fractal finance applied to the analyses of corporate cash-flow dynamics and return-on-investment dynamics.

As it is conventionally comprehended, fractal finance is a field that explores the application of fractal concepts and fractal mathematical models to financial market dynamics. Fractals are self-similar geometric patterns, i.e. they present the same type of structure at any scale of observation. In finance, this self-similarity, which can be observed in pricing patterns and market movements, highlights the presence of recurring structures at different time sequences (Drożdż et al., 2018). These models can be useful to better understand market volatility and possible price dynamics.

Concerning this, we are introducing stochastic fractal processes: geometric fractal Brownian motion in (20) and, in greater detail, its generalisation expressed by the Wiener process of fractals (Suganthi & Jayalalitha, 2019). These models have proven to be particularly appropriate for representing price movements and other financial data more accurately than traditional models.

$$dX\left(t\right)=\sigma X\left(t\right)dB_H\left(s\right) \tag{20}$$

where:

- $X(t)$ is the value of the process at time t.
- σ is the volatility.

– $B_H(s)$ represents the differential of the fractal Brownian motion, with H indicating the Hurst exponent, which determines the degree of self-similarity of the process.

Here, the key concept is that fractal Brownian motion can exhibit higher or lower volatility at different time steps, which highlights the self-similar nature of financial or accounting data in terms of cash flows (Mosteanu et al., 2019), which represent the subject of this paper.

Indeed, as far as the application to cash flows (and business investments) is concerned, the fractal model will be used here to model the variability in cash flows over time: the stochastic fractal process will be applied to the dynamic values of cash generated and variations in *ROI* (Return on Investment), considering that these variables may show complex and autocorrelated patterns.

The scientific question at the basis of this contribution is to investigate to what extent the fractal analysis presented below can assist in the identification of regularity or irregularity in cash flows and returns on investment, allowing the adoption of strategies better suited to the complex characteristics of corporate data. Although the use of fractal models in corporate finance is still under development, it is believed that fractals will offer new insights into the complexity and variability in corporate financial data.

Better affirming (20) on the Wiener fractal process (Gorev et al., 2019), its stochastic differential equation is given by:

$$X(t) = X(0) + \int_0^t \sigma X(s)\, dB_H(s) \tag{21}$$

with $X(0)$, being the initial value of the process.

Suppose we have an initial cash flow $CF(0)$ and a fractal volatility σ_{CF}; therefore, the fractal cash-flow process—from (21)—can be modelled as:

$$CF(t) = CF(0) + \sigma_{CF} \int_0^t CF(s)\, dB_H(s) \tag{22}$$

Analogously, again from (21), the return on an investment $ROI(t)$ is described by:

$$ROI(t) = ROI(0) + \sigma_{ROI} \int_0^t ROI(s)\, dB_H(s) \tag{23}$$

Fractal volatility is related to Hurst's coefficient or parameter H. The underlying theory, based on the power law, shows the long-term correlation between the changes in the variable in a certain time interval and the changes in the same time intervals that precede or follow it (Tzouras et al., 2015). The Hurst parameter assumes values that will determine whether the time series is persistent, anti-persistent, or chaotic.

Therefore, H reflects the degree of autocorrelation in the data. A value between 0 and 0.5 indicates a tendency for the process to reverse direction, whilst a value between 0.5 and 1 indicates a trend with little or no change. In greater detail:

- $H < 0.3$ indicates low fractal volatility, with a strong tendency to reverse direction over time. Cash flows show significant and unpredictable variations, with frequent reversals between positive and negative periods;
- $0.4 < H < 0.5$ shows moderate fractal volatility, still with a tendency to reverse direction, but with some persistence. Though cash flows show moderate variations over time, with some longer-term trends, there is still some unpredictability;
- $H = 0.5$ shows random volatility and no evidence of fractal structure. Cash flows are stochastic but show no autocorrelation over time.

H depends therefore on the specific nature of the company's cash flows. The Hurst parameter calculation is formulated by:

$$H = \frac{1}{2}\left(\frac{\log(R/S)}{\log(n)}\right) \tag{24}$$

where:

- R is the mean of the variation measurements of the stochastic process.
- S is the standard deviation of the measures of the change in the stochastic process.
- n is the total number of time periods in the series being analysed.

With the intention of completing a corporate diagnostic system based on what has already been illustrated in Sect. 2—in addition to the more general modelling set-up above—the fractal process for the assessment of cash-flow dynamics at a generic company e, prepared for the execution of specific investigations with empirical data input, is more clearly stated below.

Considering that each enterprise has a number of production segments within it, it seems interesting to offer further reasoning moving from the "Markowitz Model", also known as "Modern Portfolio Theory" (Safitri et al., 2020). Although the Markowitz model is not itself a fractal model, it seems that it can be linked to fractal finance through the idea of risk management and diversification, which aims to reduce risk by combining assets with different correlations (Gasser et al., 2017).

The Markowitz model's key concept is to reduce overall risk through portfolio diversification. Markowitz introduced the notion of the "efficient frontier", which represents all possible combinations of assets in a portfolio that maximises returns for a given level of risk or minimises risks for a given return.

Based on the above, let us go on to explore a broader interpretation of the theory by applying the concept of fractal self-similarity to the diversification of a company's business units: each company sub-segment being a "miniature" version of the entire company. In this context, we might consider asset allocation decisions at different time scales or market ranges as self-similar components. For example, we might imagine that the diversification of a portfolio at the macro level (investments in different asset classes) can be replicated at the micro level (diversification within each asset class). Precisely, this would invoke the principle of fractal self-similarity, wherein the general structure of the investment process would be repeated at different scales.

Integrating the Markowitz model into a fractal cash-flow valuation implies—given a certain allocation of company assets—appreciations of the fractal volatilities of the cash flows generated by each company segment.

This model will consider two types of risk:

a) Specific risk: Risk associated with each business segment.
b) General risk: Risk that is common to all segments, since it is intrinsic to the enterprise *e* as a whole.

Markowitz showed that through proper allocation, it is possible to reduce the overall risk of a portfolio (or, in our case, of the business), without sacrificing return. There is a "covariance" between the returns on the assets, which shows how the correlation between the assets of the business segments influences the overall risk of the venture.

Assuming an enterprise with evidence of two identifiable business units, *i* and *j*, a general formulation is proposed (also methodologically adaptable to any plurality of identifiable segments):

$$E(CF_e) = \sum_{i=1}^{n} w_i E(CF_i) \tag{25}$$

$$\text{Var}(CF_e) = \sum_{i=1}^{n} \sum_{j=1}^{n} w_i w_j \text{ cov}(CF_i, CF_j) \tag{26}$$

where:

- $E(CF_e)$: is the expected performance of the enterprise *e*, in terms of total cash flow. The enterprise's final performance, in terms of cash flow, would therefore be the result of the weighted combination of the flow function of the individual business units.
- $\text{Var}(CF_e)$ is the relative overall variance, which measures the dispersion of returns with respect to the mean.
- w_i and w_j are the weights of the cash flows of the two business units.
- $\text{Cov}(CF_i, CF_j)$ indicates the covariance between the cash flows of the same segments, i.e. the joint variance of the respective flows.

The integration of the Markowitz model in a fractal context implies the optimisation of the weights of the cash flows of the different business segments, in order to maximise the expected trend, set at an acceptable risk level, considering the fractal volatility of the individual cash flows. To determine the maximisation of CF_e, one must first proceed through (26): $\text{Var}(CF_e) = \sum_{i=1}^{n} \sum_{j=1}^{n} w_i w_j \text{ cov}(CF_i, CF_j) \leq$

"assumed risk level", implying $\left(\sum_{i=1}^{n} w_i + \sum_{j=1}^{n} w_j\right) = 1$ and w_i and $w_j \geq 0$, for each i and $j = 1, 2, \ldots, n$. This is a constrained quadratic programming problem, where the maximisation of the expected cash flow is subject to a restriction on the combined variance (risk) and constraints on the cash-flow weights:

$$\max_{\{Var(CF_e), w_i, w_j\}} E(CF_e) - \lambda \sigma_{CF} \tag{27}$$

with λ, being the risk aversion coefficient.

Solving this problem provides the optimal cash-flow weights in the portfolio. The steps described above represent a statement of the Markowitz model for the optimisation of corporate cash flow in a fractal estimation process.

The solution of this problem requires the use of numerical optimisation methods in order to first establish the optimal weights w_i and w_j (conjugate gradient algorithm or the Lagrange multiplier method) to minimise the standard deviation of the system, taking the covariance between the cash flows of the different company segments into account. The choice of risk aversion coefficient λ will influence the trade-off between risk and outcome in the optimisation process. The outcome describes target levels, which maximise the expected corporate return at a given (and accepted) business risk, i.e. one which would minimise the risk of investments set at a planned or desired level of return (optimal asset allocation).

5 An Application on a Sample of ICT Companies in Sardinia Within the e.INS (PNRR) Project, Spoke 4

The e.INS project is funded under Italy's National Recovery and Resilience Plan (PNRR)—Mission 4, Component 2 "from Research to Business", Investment 1.5 "Creation and Strengthening of Innovation Ecosystems and Establishment of Territorial R&D Leaders". Specifically, the e.INS ecosystem—Ecosystem of Innovation for Next Generation Sardinia—is a comprehensive programme aimed at strengthening the link between business and science, mitigating the social impacts generated by the crisis, and enhancing territorial inclusiveness. It is designed to support innovation processes and promote their dissemination, facilitate the transfer of technologies to the productive system, engage local communities in challenges related to sustainable innovation, and steer the region towards a knowledge-based economy.

The e.INS project is organised into thematic Spokes; specifically, Spoke 4—involving the University of Sassari, the University of Cagliari, the Chamber of Commerce of Sassari, and Banco di Sardegna—aims to accelerate and systematise the process of creating new innovative enterprises and supporting existing ones by providing them with a wide range of integrated services. In this context, it is critically important to define innovative credit access procedures for SMEs and an ecosystem capable of providing financial services and knowledge transfer, particularly focused on the digital transformation of SMEs.

It is within this framework that we attempted to apply the Markowitz model: considering the innovation chain in Sardinia as a unique and identity-driven entrepreneurial system, we examined which subsectors were the most performant and where it would be most appropriate to focus support policies and financial assistance in line with the PNRR provisions of Spoke 4 within the e.INS project.

The identification of the ICT (Information and Communication Technology) supply chain is a process aimed at identifying and analysing all actors and components within the ICT sector's value chain. This approach made it possible to understand how innovation and technological development are translated into ICT products, services, and solutions.

More concretely, it is necessary to map the various segments of the ICT market. This entails breaking down the supply chain into specific sectors such as hardware, software, telecommunications services, cloud services, cybersecurity, artificial intelligence, and IoT (Internet of Things). Additionally, it is essential to consider the interconnections between actors and market segments within the ICT supply chain, including identifying supply relationships, partnerships, collaborations, acquisitions, and other linkages among various entities that belong to the same category and contribute qualitative and quantitative value to the sector. This includes shared technical expertise, the creation of new knowledge and innovation, and the generation of economic wealth within the supply chain.

The extraction criterion was thus implemented concerning ATECO codes for business activities related to the (innovation) categories identified above, with further cluster sampling based on the contribution coefficient to the total production value of the Sardinian ICT system (>25th percentile). The following ATECO codes were selected (Table 1):

By advancing innovative methods of financial inclusion and contemporary creditworthiness assessment for a more effective allocation of financial resources to support the ecosystem, we—as previously mentioned—proceeded by applying the Markowitz model to the entire ICT supply chain in Sardinia, as per the ATECO sampling described above. This was done to identify which subsectors are expected to perform better in terms of cash-flow generation, and also to evaluate the sustainability and impact of potential funding lines to be granted.

The following table provides a summary of the calculation results, based on the time series data for each company and subsequent aggregations relevant to each ATECO subcategory, from the start date of business activity up to the finalised reports for the year 2021 (Table 2).

What is described and explained in paragraphs 2 and 3 of this work, as understood, are the processes that can be implemented ex post relative to assessment evaluations, and during the monitoring of assisted positions, in the event that anomalies or deteriorations emerge that require disposals, transfers, or segment refinancing.

Table 1 Results of sample extraction of ICT companies in Sardinia by ATECO categories of innovation

ATECO	Description	Number of companies
261	Manufacture of electronic components and boards	3
262	Manufacture of computers and peripheral equipment	10
263	Manufacture of communication equipment	6
264	Manufacture of consumer electronics	1
465	Wholesale of information and communication equipment	27
582	Software publishing	5
591	Motion picture, video and television programme activities	41
601	Radio broadcasting	4
602	Television programming and broadcasting activities	3
612	Wireless telecommunications activities	2
613	Satellite telecommunications activities	1
619	Other telecommunications activities	29
620	Computer programming, consultancy, and related activities	303
631	Data processing, hosting and related activities; web portals	398
951	Repair of computers and communication equipment	32
952	Repair of personal and household goods	1
Total		863

Source: Extraction based on data provided by the Chamber of Commerce of Sassari

Table 2 Results of Markowitz's model simulation on the sample of the ICT entrepreneurial system in Sardinia

ATECO	*H* di Hurst	*E(CF)*
261	<0.5	Declining on *n*+1
262	>0.5	Declining on *n*+1
263	<0.3	In oscillation and instability
264	>0.5	Declining on *n*+1
465	>0.5	Declining on *n*+1
582	<0.3	Declining on *n*+1
591	<0.5	Positive and stable trend
601	<0.3	Declining on *n*+1
602	>0.5	Declining on *n*+1
612	<0.3	In oscillation and instability
613	<0.5	In oscillation and instability
619	>0.5	Declining on *n*+1
620	>0.5	Positive and stable trend
631	>0.5	Positive and stable trend
951	<0.5	Positive and stable trend
952	<0.5	Declining on *n*+1

Source: Own calculations and elaborations

6 Discussion

In empirical observation, a generic company operating in the ICT sector exhibits irregular cash inflow cycles. Using an advanced forecasting approach can help predict future cash-flow scenarios more accurately than traditional methods, assisting managers in liquidity planning. While a limitation of the Markowitz model—at least in its conventional use for estimating stock market series—has been observed to be a slight overestimation of portfolio risks (Statman, 2013), our application simulations on corporate cash flows indicate that using this method (combined with the other criteria outlined in previous sections) offers greater advantages in identifying financial tensions and implementing processes that optimise assets with available balance sheet resources compared to, for example, the Black–Scholes model.

6.1 Generalisability of Results

Although our focus is on the ICT sector in Sardinia, the model is applicable to other industries. For example, in the energy sector, a renewable energy provider experiences variable revenues and incoming flows due to factors such as weather conditions or hourly auction dynamics. A fractal-based diagnostic approach captures these volatilities more effectively than traditional models.

6.2 Choice of Methods

We chose to propose and discuss the presented processes—particularly stochastic and fractal approaches—because cash-flow time series, especially in larger and more complex companies, often exhibit autocorrelation and fractal structure. For example, consider an ICT company investing in long-term projects: while most widely used valuation methods assume independent shocks, in reality, financial decisions depend on historical patterns. These models are sensitive to such dependencies.

6.3 Practical Implications

Companies—and their corporate advisors—could adopt these evaluation frameworks for self-diagnosis, improved investment planning, and monitoring monetary cycles. Additionally, when seeking debt capital—such as a bank loan—the application of these algorithms can be useful in assessing sustainability and the expected impact on cash-flow curves across business segments and markets.

6.4 Practical Guidelines

To implement the proposed models, historical cash-flow data must be collected for business segments and markets.

a) The first model directly generates forecasts and risk simulations concerning volatility dynamics.
b) The second model provides scenarios that may suggest corporate reorganisation and efficiency improvement plans.
c) The third model offers a deeper analysis of the first two processes, identifying fractal patterns in the data.

The combined application of all three models could provide a comprehensive decision-making framework for future management strategies, including default probability assessments for expansion projects or evaluating expected business performance.

6.5 Justification for Choosing the ICT Sector

The ICT sector in Sardinia was chosen as a practical example because it is characterised by high economic and cash-flow variability. Local and regional ICT start-ups and SMEs often experience irregular cash flows due to external factors such as public funding cycles, technological acceleration, and competition from international research developments.

7 Conclusions

Assessments and estimations of the dynamics of corporate cash flow and identifiable business units or branches are of fundamental importance in the science of business economics, as they provide essential information for financial management and corporate strategy. As indicated in this chapter, cash-flow volatility, which refers to fluctuations in a company's cash-flow generation over time, can have a significant impact on a company's valuation, its ability to finance itself, risk management, and on strategic planning for its continuity and development.

On the one hand, a company's ability to generate sufficiently stable and predictable cash flows is a key factor in business valuation and in understanding the suitability of monetary cycles to support economic phases and investments. On the other hand, having an accurate estimate of cash-flow variances aids in identifying potential financial and operational risks, and in implementing mitigation strategies, including the divestment of underperforming segments. Moreover, clear analysis can certainly support reliable financial forecasts and informed decisions regarding investments and acquisitions.

In this work, some innovative methods for addressing the procedure of cash-flow valuation that clearly complement the predictive and simulation analysis models already widely present in professional practice and scientific literature have been presented. The arguments advanced should demonstrate the expected efficacy of the proposed models.

For COI Statement Compliance with Ethical Standards.

Conflict of Interest The authors declare that they have no conflict of interest.

References

Damodaran, A. (2015). *Applied corporate finance*. Wiley.

Desogus, M., & Casu, E. (2019). A diagnostic approach to corporate sustainability based on normalized net margins and extended present value. *International Journal of Financial Management., 2*, 8–16.

Drożdż, S., Kowalski, R., Oświęcimka, P., Rak, R., & Gębarowski, R. (2018). Dynamical variety of shapes in financial multifractality. *Complexity, 2018*, 1–13.

Gasser, S. M., Rammerstorfer, M., & Weinmayer, K. (2017). Markowitz revisited: Social portfolio engineering. *European Journal of Operational Research, 258*(3), 1181–1190.

Gorev, V. N., Gusev, A. Y., & Korniienko, V. I. (2019). Polynomial solutions for the Kolmogorov-Wiener filter weight function for fractal processes. *Радіоелектроніка, інформатика, управління, 2*, 44–52.

Minton, B. A., & Schrand, C. (1999). The impact of cash flow volatility on discretionary investment and the costs of debt and equity financing. *Journal of Financial Economics, 54*(3), 423–460.

Mosteanu, N. R., Faccia, A., Torrebruno, G., & Torrebruno, F. (2019). Fractals-a smart financial tool to assess business management decisions. *Journal of Information Systems & Operations Management, 13*(1), 45–56.

Myers, S. C., & Majluf, N. S. (1984). Corporate financing and investment decisions when firms have information that investors do not have. *Journal of Financial Economics, 13*(2), 187–221.

Quagli, A., & Danovi, A. (2010). *Crisi aziendali e processi di risanamento*. Ipsoa.

Safitri, I. N. N., Sudradjat, S., & Lesmana, E. (2020). Stock portfolio analysis using Markowitz model. *International Journal of Quantitative Research and Modeling, 1*(1), 47–58.

Scandizzo, P. L., & Ventura, M. (2010). Sharing risk through concession contracts. *European Journal of Operational Research, 207*(1), 363–370.

Scordis, N. A., Barrese, J., & Wang, P. (2008). The impact of cash flow volatility on systematic risk. *Journal of Insurance Issues*, 43–71.

Shackleton, M. B., & Sødal, S. (2005). Smooth pasting as rate of return equalization. *Economics Letters, 89*(2), 200–206.

Shimko, D. C. (2019). Long-term project valuation in capital-constrained firms. *Finance, 40*(3), 121–139.

Statman, M. (2013). Is Markowitz wrong? Investment lessons from the financial crisis. *Journal of Portfolio Management, 40*(1), 8–12.

Suganthi, K., & Jayalalitha, G. (2019, November). Geometric Brownian motion in stock prices. In *Journal of Physics: Conference Series* (Vol. 1377, No. 1, p. 012016). IOP Publishing.

Tzouras, S., Anagnostopoulos, C., & McCoy, E. (2015). Financial time series modeling using the Hurst exponent. *Physica A: Statistical Mechanics and Its Applications, 425*, 50–68.

Yun, J. (2011). *A present-value approach to variable selection*. University of Chicago-Booth School of Business.

MIX
Papier aus verantwortungsvollen Quellen
Paper from responsible sources
FSC® C105338

If you have any concerns about our products,
you can contact us on
ProductSafety@springernature.com

In case Publisher is established outside the EU,
the EU authorized representative is:
Springer Nature Customer Service Center GmbH
Europaplatz 3, 69115 Heidelberg, Germany

Printed by Libri Plureos GmbH
in Hamburg, Germany